THE STUDY OF EDUCATION

The Students Library of Education

THE STUDY OF EDUCATION

Edited by

J. W. TIBBLE
Emeritus Professor of Education
University of Leicester

Contributors
PAUL H. HIRST
BEN MORRIS
RICHARD S. PETERS
BRIAN SIMON
WILLIAM TAYLOR
J. W. TIBBLE

LONDON
ROUTLEDGE AND KEGAN PAUL
NEW YORK: THE HUMANITIES PRESS

First published 1966
by Routledge & Kegan Paul Ltd
Broadway House, 68-74 Carter Lane
London, E.C.4
Reprinted 1967, 1969

Reprinted and first published
as a Routledge Paperback 1970

Printed offset in Great Britain by
Alden & Mowbray Ltd
at the Alden Press, Oxford

ISBN 0 7100 4205 1 (*c*)
ISBN 0 7100 6905 7 (*p*)

CONTENTS

INTRODUCTION

The Students Library of Education is designed to assist students in Colleges and Departments of Education with their study of what is variously called 'Education' or 'Principles of Education' or 'The Theory of Education' but which is in all cases a prescribed and major ingredient of the total course. The Library will also be of assistance to practising teachers who wish to refresh and bring up to date their study of this subject. The Library will consist of a series of basic books, each of 25,000 to 30,000 words in length, available in paper backed editions. Each book will cover a particular topic or aspect of the total field and will aim to give an up-to-date survey of thought and research on the topic in question. The topics chosen for these books fall into a number of categories. Some will illustrate the contribution to the study of education made by the different forms of thought referred to in this introductory volume: the philosophy, psychology, history and sociology of education. It is also our intention to include some books which deal with a major educational topic in an inter-disciplinary way, showing the contributions which different forms of thought can make to it. There will also be a section for curriculum studies, dealing with the nature and the methodology of the various subjects in the school curriculum or the application of general methods to a range of subjects.

This book is intended as an introduction to the Library and deals with the nature of education as a subject of study and with the nature of the contributory disciplines. The study of education has developed piecemeal from its first beginnings toward the end

Why ed. study was limited til now?

of the nineteenth century. It has developed as an ingredient in courses which, as we now see it, were too short and crowded to provide for an adequate professional education. It developed in courses with a strong practical bias and without much provision, until recently, for the continuation of the teacher's professional education after the end of the course. Too much emphasis had to be placed on short term efficiency in the classroom. In these circumstances, the study of education in the courses, as distinct from practice, or the study of other subjects in the case of the college students, was limited and cramped.

But there were other factors which limited until now the full development of education as a subject of study in its own right. Its place in the universities, for example, was peripheral. When the day training colleges were instituted, education and degree subjects were studied concurrently; but the pressures and rivalries so set up led to the relegation of education to a post-graduate year after the degree course was completed. In this position it was not easy to develop close links between the study of education and the basic disciplines which contribute to it. Furthermore, of these basic disciplines, psychology and sociology were not themselves fully accepted or developed in most universities until quite recently; and philosophers were not, in general, interested in the study of education.

The two lines of study, apart from methodology, which were most fully developed within the orbit of teacher education itself in the first half of this century were educational psychology and the history of education. The former had its origins in the changing attitudes to childhood and child development, foreshadowed by pioneers from the seventeenth century onward, and institutionalized in child study and progressive education movements towards the end of the nineteenth century. By the 1920s, educational psychology was recognized as a subject in its own right and there was already a considerable literature of theory with the delineation of lines of research. The main problems in this field were those which arise in the development of any new subject: much controversy over theorctical foundations and the need to forge new techniques for investigation and experiment. The history of education did not face the same problems, since well-established methods of historical enquiry could readily be applied to educational topics. The impetus for this study was provided by the development of national systems of compulsory education and its growing importance in terms of national politics and policy. There was no lack of trained historians, and from the last years of the nineteenth century, works which are still classics in this subject began to be published. More recently, however, new needs have arisen in this field of study, in particular through the development of local, social and economic history and the application of these to education.

The need to re-assess these older constituents in the study of education and to assess the contribution of the more recently developed disciplines raises fundamental questions about the nature and scope of the subject, education. We can see now that earlier attempts to define the nature and scope of education, its 'data and first principles' were necessarily handicapped by the embryonic state of the subject, the absence as yet of some of the necessary ingredients, and in particular of the contribution made by modern analytic philosophy: for this has led to the insistence on a critical examination of the nature and scope of the subject.

We think, therefore, that it has now become possible to see what kinds of questions should be asked about the nature of the subject and to attempt to answer them. This is what this book offers to those responsible for planning and conducting courses in education and to the more advanced students of this subject. The contributors to this volume are agreed about the questions to be asked and about the main lines of the answers to them. Within this general framework of agreement, each contributor has been given a free hand to develop his particular topic in the way that seemed most appropriate to the nature of the form of thought involved and the stage of development it has reached. The result of this will be seen in differences of emphasis in the various contributions as well as differences in the presentation of the material:

for example, selective bibliographies are appended only in respect of the aspects of study where an extensive literature exists. The differences will not, I hope, distract attention from the large area of agreement presented in this book; for it is on this that the claim of education as a proper subject for university study and research rests. Confusion about this (and the confusion is understandable enough, in view of the piecemeal development of the subject) can only retard those enhancements in the quality of teacher education which we all hope to see accompanying the large and rapid expansions in quantity.

Chapter One

THE DEVELOPMENT OF THE STUDY
OF EDUCATION

J. W. TIBBLE

This book is an exploration of the nature of the study of education as an important ingredient in the professional preparation of teachers. Discussion of this topic has been sharpened since the publication of the Robbins Report and the decisions by a number of universities to go ahead with the institution of the B.Ed. degree. The establishment of the nature and validity of the study of education as a central discipline in degree courses specifically designed for intending teachers is a matter of some urgency. The position of education as a subject in the curricula of the British universities is ambiguous and peripheral; with a few exceptions (e.g. Wales and Sheffield) it has no place as a subject in under-graduate courses: any graduate, in whatever subjects, may enter the profession of teaching without further qualifications and is eligible for the status of qualified teacher in the state system; a graduate who elects to prepare himself for teaching may enter a university education department or college of education for a year of professional training; in this year (about thirty weeks in fact) he will study education and spend about twelve weeks in practice in schools. This time limitation and the ambiguous position of the department between the universities and the schools leads to their being criticized from both sides and for opposite defects; by the universities because the study of education is superficial compared with other university courses; by the schools, for being too con-cerned with 'theory', too remote from classrooms, not giving their students enough practical preparation for all that is involved in being a schoolmaster or schoolmistress. Most of those engaged in training of graduate teachers agree that it is not possible to plan adequate courses of study and practice under present conditions. The reforms seen as essential are: that the training of graduates should be compulsory not voluntary; that the probationary year should be amalgamated with the training year giving a two year period for the study of education and its relating to practical experience; and the acceptance of education as an undergraduate study by the university. As J. W. Adamson pointed out in *Our Defective System of Training Teachers* (1904), 'Where then training is adequate, there is close association of theory and practice under conditions which permit *undivided* attention steadily maintained throughout a period of some length'.

Most universities also provide for the study of education in higher degree courses. Many of these have been research degrees though there is now a tendency to provide also for course work degrees. The situation here, too, is unsatisfactory, and mainly because of the non-existence of education as a first degree subject, thus denying a basis for higher studies. The universities have been faced with the dilemma of accepting non-graduates who are well qualified in education or graduates in other subjects with no study of education beyond the initial training stage. And since many universities do not admit non-graduates to higher degrees (or only in very exceptional cases), there is a very serious shortage of adequately qualified lecturers in education for the expanding colleges of education.

The main impetus in the present ferment of discussion about the study of education has come from the colleges of education. Since the McNair Report and the setting up of institutes of education, the colleges have had a place, though a peripheral one, within the university system. The acceptance of the three year course in the 1960s relaxed the vocational pressures and fostered the planning of courses, both in subject studies and in education, which were nearer to the university model in scope and depth of study. The recommendations of the Robbins Committee approved the aspiration of the colleges to integrate more closely with the universities, and, although the proposals for financial and administrative integration have not been accepted by the Government, the recommendations concerning closer academic links and, in particular, the development of four-year degree courses for some students in the colleges have been confirmed. Education, studied concurrently with other subjects, has long been a central subject in the college courses, originally for two years, latterly for three, and in the context of a B.Ed. course now envisaged for four years. It is the purpose of the rest of this chapter to outline briefly the historical development of this study over the 120 years since the training of teachers was inaugurated in this country.

In 1846 the minutes of the Committee of Council on Education established a system of bounties in aid of the salaries of pupil teachers, Queen's Scholarships towards maintenance in training colleges and certificate examinations for adult teachers who had gone through one form or other of professional preparation. The new system thus established owed its existence partly to the general discontent with the inadequacies of the monitorial system, partly to the specific pioneering efforts of Dr Kay (Kay-Shuttleworth); the antecedents of the new scheme were David Stow's work in Glasgow and the pupil teacher system developed in Holland. In fact the full scope of the Dutch system, which provided for the attendance of pupil teachers at centres followed by a training college course, was not achieved in this country until well into the present century.

The main defect of the pupil teacher system of training lay in the inadequacy of the academic education given to candidates for the profession. The situation in this respect was much improved after 1902 when the use of secondary schools for the training of students who were to become teachers developed into a common practice. By 1921, 85 per cent of intending teachers had passed or were passing through a secondary school, 15 per cent were pupil teachers. At the same time, one of the alleged advantages of the old system was lost—the great emphasis placed upon actual contact from the first with children in the schools and the apprenticeship

period under the guidance of an experienced master. The nature
of the recruitment to the profession was changed. As C. H. Judd
points out in *The Training of Teachers in England, Scotland and
Germany* (1914), the candidate 'is no longer a pupil teacher in
the old sense of that term, selected by the headmaster because
of his qualifications and immediately put in charge of some of
the younger children; he is rather selected for higher academic
training with a view to ultimate return to the schools after a course
of training which takes him away for the time from the classroom
and its duties'. The student teachers were 'preparing somewhat
remotely for the profession rather than actual participants. The
old conception of the pupils associated directly with a single master
has thus disappeared so far as the regular system of training urged
by the board of education and sanctioned by its authority is
concerned'. One consequence of this was that the apprenticeship
function was taken over by the training college—since its students
were expected to go out as fully fledged teachers at the end of the
course. To quote Judd again, 'the evolution of the pupil teacher
plan explains many of the characteristics of the training colleges.
Especially is this true with respect to the great emphasis which is
laid in all training colleges upon practice teaching. The apprenticeship idea has been carried over and influences the actual organization of the teaching force and the programme of teachers' colleges
in a most emphatic degree'.

It is clear from this that the main emphasis in the professional
courses was on the practical work. This was the old tradition of
course, implicit in the monitorial system, continued in the pupil
teacher stage and formalized in the training college drill of lesson
preparation and delivery from the days of the Glasgow Seminary
onward. As Dr Andrew Bell put it:[1] 'It is by attending the school,
seeing what is going on there, and taking a share in the office
of tuition, that teachers are to be formed, and not by lectures and
abstract instructions.' Judd,* writing a century later, noted:

* Judd was echoing a much earlier plaint of R. H. Quick, 'I say boldly
that what English Schoolmasters now stand in need of is *theory*; and,

In striking contrast with this emphasis on practical education is the relative neglect of education theory. One is very much impressed by the fact that in the English training colleges the whole theoretical side of pedagogy has a very meager and abstract treatment ... there is so wide a breach between pedagogical theory and actual emphasis upon practice teaching in English institutions that one is tempted to say that the teachers in English training colleges have not realized the possibility of dealing in a scientific way with the practical problems of school organization and the practical problems which come up in the conduct of recitations (p. 33).

L. G. E. Jones, writing in 1924, notes the development in recent years of a more scientific type of training, based on the study of psychology but adds:

That the effort is commendable most people will agree, but that the conditions essential to success are present in the training college is open to question. The work demands lecturers of high qualifications and long and varied experience, as well as students with mature and trained minds and leisure for sustained thought. Where these conditions are not present the result is too often merely 'potted psychology', and the assurance begotten of little knowledge, rather than that willingness to learn from experience which should be one of the fruits of a professional course. (*The Training of Teachers in England and Wales*, p. 98.)

The evidence provided by the Teachers' Certificate Examination syllabus and papers, and the text books which were written to meet the needs of those taking these examinations supports these judgments. But we can also trace in these sources the first attempts, in the last decade of the nineteenth century, to introduce some study of educational processes into the preparation of teachers. Thus in 1872 the syllabus for the Certificate Examination prescribed for the first year questions on the best methods of teaching the three Rs and other common subjects of elementary instruction as well as questions on the art of oral teaching in general. The

further, that the Universities have special advantages for meeting this need' *Proceedings International Conference on Education* (1884), Vol. IV, p. 76.

second year syllabus prescribed: (1) teaching a class in the presence
of H.M.I., (2) answering questions in writing on the following
subjects: (a) the different methods of organizing an elementary
school, (b) the form of school registers, the mode of keeping them
and making returns from them, (c) the mode of teaching geography, history and grammar and (3) questions of moral discipline.

School management and methods of teaching the basic subjects
continued to dominate the syllabus to the end of the century and
candidates had to answer in great detail questions on the keeping
of registers, drawing up of time-tables and the arrangement of
classrooms. The 1895 syllabus showed little change for the first
two years but the syllabus for the third year (for those who stayed
on) was headed 'The Art, Theory and History of Teaching' and
prescribed study of the following: The Life and Work of Dr
Arnold, Quick's *Educational Reformers*, Dr Bain's *Education as a
Science* and Sully's *The Teacher's Handbook of Psychology*.

These references indicate the two main strands, apart from
method, in the embryonic study of education that began to creep
into courses of training about the turn of the century. They had
been foreshadowed in some of the contributions made at the
International Conference on Education, 1884, already referred to.
J. M. D. Meiklejohn (Professor of the Theory, History and
Practice of Education in the University of St Andrews) noted that,
'There is, in the three kingdoms, no one man who gives the whole
of his time to observing and to thinking about the educational
processes which are going on in schools every day.'

Medicine had hundreds of professors who not only extended the
limits of different departments of their science but also taught and
trained practitioners of medicine. By contrast, 'There is, in no
University in England, a single person whose duty it is to guide a
teacher in his daily practice. So far as the English Universities are
concerned, education is still in its amateur and empiric stage.
Hence much friction, great waste of mental power, great waste of
time, and disappointing results.' He went on to define three
requirements in this much needed study of the educational

processes: examination of the growth and development of many different kinds of young minds—he referred to Galton's work in particular; the history of education, including comparative education and the study of the great educators; the study of method which he thought, should be heuristic in all subjects, not just in science. He described existing practices as routine rather than method, 'Hard steady drill, undeviating routine and the perpetual pressure of business considerations' and 'this domination of routine gives rise to mental diseases, which infect to a greater or smaller extent almost every school-room in the country'. His lively and humorous account of these mental diseases is still very relevant.

To return to the references in the 1895 syllabus, Bain and Sully were pioneers both in promoting the transition from the earlier 'mental philosophy' to the new 'scientific psychology' and in the relating of psychology to education. Professor L. S. Hearnshaw in *A Short History of British Psychology* (1964) pays eloquent tribute to Bain's pioneering work and his 'seminal ideas', foreshadowing future developments. In particular he refers to his recognition of the physiological foundations of psychology, his stress on move-ment and activity, on the importance of social influences and his awareness of the part played by emotional factors in human behaviour. These foreshadowings of future directions in psychology can be traced in Bain's book, *Education as a Science* (1897). Bain did not discard the general framework of concepts provided by the dominant faculty psychology and its corollary of formal training. But within this framework he brought a powerful and critical mind to bear on what he calls the 'ambiguous import' of fashionable terms and phrases like 'memory', 'judgment' and 'imagination' or 'training', 'cultures' and 'discipline'.

Most definitions of training are obscured through the mode of describing mind by faculties. We have seen that to train 'memory' is a very vague way of speaking.

Equally vague is it to talk of training Reason, Conception, Imagina-tion and so forth. Moral training is much more intelligible; there is here

a habit of suppressing certain active tendencies of the mind, and fostering others: and this is done by a special discipline—like training horses
or making soldiers. The analogy is not very close between these exercises
and the improvement of the intellectual powers ... (Bain, p. 139.)

This semantic questioning is refreshing at a time when the text
books for students were full of statements like the following.
'The objects of education are: to strengthen the faculties that are
too weak, to restrain those that are too vigorous, to store the intellect with moral, religious, scientific and general knowledge and to
direct all to their proper objects'.[2] Equally refreshing is Bain's description in Chapter Six of the peculiarities of the infant mind
leading to a discussion on learning readiness. 'Nothing but observation of cases will avail us here.'

The further development of this theme was the main contribution of James Sully who, in Sir Cyril Burt's words:

'Appears to have been the first to introduce systematic instruction
on child psychology into the courses for teachers and students proposing
to enter the teaching profession. As his syllabus explained, it treated
"the science of the human mind with its various branches as a department of natural science". It started with the general theory of paedology
or child study ... Sully always laid great stress on practical work with
children. "Students", he wrote, "should be encouraged, if not required,
to make a careful methodical observation of at least one individual
child"'. *The Year Book of Education* (1955), pp. 84–5.

In the first edition of his *Teachers' Handbook of Psychology* (1886)
Sully dealt with mental development mainly in terms of the
growth of the faculties of the mind. 'One of the most valuable
doctrines of modern psychology is that there is a uniform order
of development of the faculties', and he spoke of memory training,
for example, as designed to produce 'a good type of the acquisitive
or learning faculty in general'. The change in his position by the
time of the fifth edition in 1909 is marked. 'In these days there is
no excuse for forgetting that the child is a living organism which
grows by the exercise of its own functional activity; and that the
work of the educator is to excite and to direct this activity in a way

most favourable to a sound and complete development of mind.' His statement about memory training is much more cautious and new material dealing with recent work in child study, social psychology, emotions and sentiments and the development of individuality indicate the new trends affecting 'educational psychology'.

In the period 1890 to 1910, as W. S. Monroe has pointed out, 'the psychological background relating to learning consisted of a mixture of the modified faculty psychology, Herbartian apperception, associationism (structural and functional) and physiological psychology'.[3] The Herbartian theory of learning with its 'scientific' prescription for the organization of the lesson was a dominant influence during this period, and is still to be traced in the form of the lesson notes which many students meticulously prepare. William James in his *Talks to Teachers* had a chapter on 'apperception' and Bagley's popular *The Educative Process* (1905) dealt with learning largely in terms of apperception—though by this time the term was falling into disrepute among psychologists. In fact the first decade of the century saw the founding of most of the major schools of modern psychology—psycho-analysis, hormic psychology, behaviourism, Gestalt psychology—but there was a considerable time lag before these new and exciting lines of investigation began to affect courses of study in training colleges and university departments of education. By the 1920s, however, important changes had begun to take place in the organization of the professional work. The term 'Master of Method' was falling into disuse and 'Lecturer in Education' took its place. Some of these, as L. G. E. Jones noted began 'to develop a more systematic type of training, based on the study of psychology and developed as far as possible experimentally . . .' and he notes also that, 'discussions, demonstrations, experiments by lecturers or by selected students, essays read before groups of students and discussed by them, all figure prominently even in the more theoretical part of professional training'. (*The Training of Teachers in England and Wales* (1924), pp. 92 and 98.) In 1924 the Board of Education ceased to examine for the Teachers' Certificate and regional examining boards were set up consisting of representatives of the colleges and U.D.E.'s.

In the 1920s then 'educational psychology' became established as a subject of study. The term appears in the British Museum Subject Catalogue in 1921 as the title of a sub-division of psychology. The basic concepts and terminology used in reference to educative processes were quite different from those in use in 1900. 'Training' had been replaced by 'development'; 'faculties', 'mental powers', 'apperceptive masses' had fallen into disuse; in their place we find 'instinctive tendencies', 'innate propensities', 'sentiments' and in other contexts 'factors', 'gestalts', 'S-R bonds'. The controversies raging among the different 'schools' of psychologists were a feature of the years between the two world wars.

Among the men who contributed to and directly fostered the development of educational psychology were Cyril Burt, appointed in 1913 to the London County Council as the first educational psychologist, Charles Spearman, who began work at University College in 1907 and was Professor there till 1931 (the chair was called *Mind and Logic* till 1928, after that *Psychology*), and Godfrey Thomson who became principal of Moray House Training College, Edinburgh in 1925. The contribution of these men in the field of the testing and assessment of abilities and factorial analysis, coinciding with the need for more effective selection procedures in the developing secondary school system, not only stimulated much controversy and research but founded a new minor industry. It is noteworthy that there were contributions from London County Council inspectors: C. W. Kimmins, P. B. Ballard, W. H. Winch and A. G. Hughes. Ballard's books *Mental Tests* (1920) and *Group Tests of Intelligence* (1922) were widely used as prescribed textbooks, while *Learning and Teaching* by A. G. and E. H. Hughes became in the years following its appearance in 1937 the most popular general textbook used in training college education courses.

Notable also were the contributions to the development of

educational psychology made by the staff of the London Day Training College (later, University of London Institute of Education) from its foundation in 1902: John Adams, its first Principal; Percy Nunn, Vice-Principal from 1905 and Principal from 1922 to 1936; Cyril Burt, who held the chair of Educational Psychology from 1926 to 1931; Susan Isaacs, appointed to run the new department of Child Development in 1933; H. R. Hamley in charge of the Special Department of Higher Degrees and Research and Professor from 1932; P. E. Vernon, who held the chair of Educational Psychology from 1947. Of Adams' *The Herbartian Psychology Applied to Education* (1897) R. R. Rusk has written, 'The work burst like a new star into the educational firmament, and everything thereafter was different. Educational Science, instead of being a dead language, became a modern living tongue.' He adds, 'There was really more of Adams than of Herbart in the work, and it was this that accounted for its appeal to students of education.'[4] 'By placing "interest" in the centre of the educational picture, and by questioning the generally accepted notions of formal training, it had a stimulating effect on educational thought. It did not shock educational feelings by disparaging the intelligence, and it made teachers realize the importance of a clearly worked out psychology as the basis of educational theory.'[5]

A similar comment might be made on Nunn's *Education, its Data and First Principles* which appeared in 1920 with a new impression almost yearly up to 1930 when a second edition with some expansion and revision appeared. There was a third edition in 1945 with further revision and a new chapter on Mental Measurement. The success of Nunn's book can be attributed in part to the timing of its appearance, in part to the challenge of the title and the vigour and clarity of the exposition. The 'principles' of Nunn's title were those deriving from the basic assumption 'that nothing good enters into the human world except in and through the free activities of individual men and women'. The view 're-affirms the infinite value of the individual person; it reasserts his ultimate responsibility for his own destiny; and it accepts all the practical corollaries that assertion implies'.[6] The 'data' which Nunn educed to support his central position were drawn mainly from the fields of biology and psychology, in particular the 'hormic' psychology developed by William McDougall in his very popular *Introduction to Social Psychology* (1908). The appearance of Nunn's book coincided both with the peak of this doctrine's popularity and also with the rapid spread after the war of 'new' or 'progressive' ideas and practices in education. These had a long history in the European Utopist tradition, Rousseau's writings and the educational work of Basedow, Pestalozzi, Fellenberg and Froebel. The first kindergarten in England based on Froebel's ideas goes back to 1854.

The Froebel Society was founded in 1874 and *Child Life* began publication in 1899. Ten years before this Cecil Reddie founded Abbotsholme School and this was followed by Bedales in 1893 and other schools dedicated to 'progressive' principles in England, Germany, France, Belgium and Italy. An international conference in Calais in 1921 founded the New Education Fellowship, which linked the pioneers of progressive education throughout the world. The work of Maria Montessori for basic training in sensory discrimination and motor activity and her condemnation of classroom teaching based on the 'simultaneous' method attracted much attention in this country and led to the founding of a Montessori Society and the opening of Montessori Schools. The pioneer work of Margaret Macmillan in her open air nursery school at Deptford and her book *Education Through the Imagination* (1913) had a profound effect on the development of nursery and infant education. Societies for the promotion of child study date from the 1890s; a journal *The Paidologist* was founded in 1899 and was renamed *Child Study* in 1908. The movement stimulated much amateurish collecting of records as well as more weighty contributions by James Sully, Cyril Burt, W. Boyd and W. H. Winch. In the years between the two world wars psychological study of children of a more methodical and vigorous kind was developed in the department of child development at the London Institute under Susan Isaacs[7] and at the University of Birmingham under C. W. Valentine.[8] A major stimulus to this work was provided after 1926 by the translation of J. Piaget's early works into English and the influence of his later research in concept formation has been equally marked. Special contributions by British child psychologists were made in the fields of speech[9] and play.[10] Melanie Klein lectured in London in 1925 on her work as a child analyst and settled there permanently in the following year. In *The Psychoanalysis of Children* (1932) she described the play techniques which extended the process of analysis to the early years of infancy and disclosed basic destructive and aggressive tendencies as 'an integral part of mental life, even in favourable circumstances'.

These various strands and applications of the 'progressive' movement, rooted historically in the study of education of young children, gradually spread to the education of older age groups. After the First World War, the Dalton Plan, providing for individual learning based on assignments, was imported from the U.S.A. and was adopted by some elementary schools. John Dewey's name was added to the list of 'great educators' (in most cases the only contemporary one) read about if not read by training college students; his emphasis on a closer relating of education and life and on the social aspects of the educative process, on the importance of motivation and active experience influenced both the theory and practice of education, the latter by stimulating the use of 'projects' and 'activity programmes'. Students in this period would also hear about Homer Lane's 'Little Commonwealth' where progressive ideas were applied to the education of delinquents and they would almost certainly read A. S. Neill's *The Problem Child* (1928) and Bertrand Russell's *On Education* (1926) and hear about Summerhill and Beacon Hill and the Malting House School and Dartington Hall.

The importance of Nunn's *Education* in the thirty years following its first appearance lay in that a man of his academic and pedagogical eminence (he was President of the Mathematical Association and of the Aristotelian Society and made important contributions both in the fields of philosophy and the teaching of mathematics) came out wholeheartedly in favour of progressive education. His book gave the movement an academic underpinning and justification and lifted the 'principles of education' (the term was first adopted in the Board of Education Certificate Syllabus in 1907 and is still commonly used as a title for the main Education course in the Colleges and Departments) out of its dreary preoccupation with school management and methods.

Unfortunately, Nunn's book embodied the mistaken notion, as we now see it, that educational principles can be derived from the study of some scientific field of enquiry outside education and then 'applied' in educational practices and institutions. In Nunn's case the 'principles' were derived from biology and while it is indeed, as he said, 'profitable to seek help from the "biological view" of human life', he not only derives help from but allows himself to be dominated by biological conceptions, not recognizing any change of gear in passing from animal to conscious life and regarding cultural facts and values as belonging to the same order as the biological.[11]

Nunn's treatment of social factors illustrates the dilemma he is in. It certainly cannot be said that Nunn undervalued social influences and the claims of society on the individual. He gives these full weight at many points and with illuminating examples from his experience as a teacher. But he sees them either as outside the scope of his basic theory, as providing the necessary limiting conditions within which man's assertion of his individuality must operate or else he sees them as applications of the herd-instinct or gregarious tendency as when he says, 'The social instinct . . . begins its finer work as adolescence approaches'. In either case he has no just grounds, within his theory, for judgments about the 'necessity' of the 'limiting conditions' or indeed about the validity of his central thesis. It is our contention in this book that an adequate discussion of such questions requires contributions from the fields of sociology, philosophy and history, as well as from biology and psychology.

The study of children and their development, first introduced as a topic into the Board of Education Certificate syllabus in 1914 was established as a central theme in the college of education courses in the period between the two world wars, and it affected practice as well as theory. The change from teacher-centred to child-centred education has taken place most fully in the education of young children and in the colleges: in the latter it meant not only a focusing of attention on the study of children and the use of methods deriving from this, 'the play way', 'activity programmes', 'centres of interest', but also that the college of education as a whole became in varying degrees student-centred. In the students' own courses there was a growing emphasis on individual work, tutorial and group discussion, the choice of special topics for study and, after the Second World War and the establishment of institutes of education, the replacement of formal examination assessment in some institute areas by assessment based on course work. The changed content of educational psychology in training courses was described by Professor Hamley in 1936 in his article 'The Place of Psychology in the Training of Teachers'[12] and its pervading influence on practice is mentioned by H. S. N. McFarland: 'From it stems all the classroom methods, all the apparatus and text books associated with child centred education . . . Some of the pedagogic practices stemming from child study are: the more careful grading of education materials to match differing degrees of ability; the emphasis on activities, concrete objects and pictures as valuable precursors or companions of the spoken and written word: and the greater attention paid to physical, emotional and social education as being the complements of intellectual education.'[13] And the effect on the lecturers' attitudes to their students is referred to by M. Phillips: 'We could no longer avoid recognizing our students—theoretically as well as in practice—as persons as well as teachers. . . . We had simultaneously to educate our students as persons and train them as teachers. But in the conflict, as we now see, was implicit the reconciliation. Students by learning to understand children could come to know themselves.'[14] More recently the emphasis of this child and self study has come to be placed on the individual in a social context: 'Attention turned from social setting to social relationship, from membership of society to membership of group . . . to an awareness of the potency of social pressures . . . and an awareness of conflicting tensions in social situations. . . . The study of child personality was recognized as a study not of the child as he is, but as the study of the child in relation to his teachers, to his parents, to his contemporaries.'[15] Stimulus for this change of emphasis has come from the development of new ideas and techniques in the field of social psychology, in particular the work of Moreno and Kurt Lewin.

The report of a joint working party of the British Psychological Society and the Association of Teachers in Colleges and Departments of Education gives us a picture of the place of educational psychology in the training college courses in 1959. The average time spent on teaching psychology in the seventy colleges which were able to give a definite estimate was 40 per cent out of the total time spent on education as a whole. The colleges found this question difficult to answer because of the predominant practice (in seventy-six out of the ninety-eight replying) of not separating the psychological aspects of education from the study of aims, values, history, philosophy, etc. As to the topics included in the psychology course, about a quarter of the time was spent on child development and rather more than a third on attainments, abilities and non-statistical aspects of psychometrics. The psychology of learning and adjustment accounted for about a quarter of the time. An analysis of the examination questions for 1959 showed a similar total proportion of psychological topics, 41.8 per cent: but the breakdown revealed some major differences between time allocated to teaching and the number of questions asked.

There were, for example, relatively few questions on educational attainment of normal children but many on educational failure and remedial treatment. There were very few questions on motivation, and over three-quarters of the questions on adjustment were on the causes, diagnosis and treatment of maladjusted children though the teaching would appear to cover a much wider field. It is possible, however, that the large number of questions on Play should be included as part of adjustment. If this is done, there is much less discrepancy.

The general coverage of topics was similar in most colleges and there was considerable similarity between questions even from different Institutes. On the whole the approach appeared to be empirical rather than theoretical. The questions on learning, for example, seemed to be based on a knowledge of established classroom practice together with some of the more important experimental findings. Very few asked for general underlying theoretical principles about learning. Similarly with child psychology and developmental psychology, there were few questions on general principles most of the questions being essentially descriptive. It is noteworthy that in 1959 there were very few questions indeed which appeared to assume a knowledge of Piaget's contributions to the understanding of child development. Again the questions on intelligence were almost wholly on the practical application of tests in school.

There were some areas in which there were very few questions. There was, for example, only one question on transfer of training, very few on any aspect of thinking or problem solving or on group relations and social factors in classroom motivation and reinforcement. There was only one question which implied a knowledge of statistics although mental testing, examinations, selection and record cards accounted for about one-seventh of the questions on psychological topics. (*Teaching Educational Psychology in Training Colleges*, August, 1962, p. 21.)

A further comment on the place of the psychology of learning seems called for; in view of its importance for both the study and practice of education, one would expect it to be given more attention than is indicated by the analysis of the syllabuses and questions (13 per cent). This is partly a reflection of the relative neglect of this branch of psychology by British psychologists in the inter-war period. Professor Hearnshaw notes, 'In general, however, there was a conspicuous absence among British psychologists during the inter-war period of a sustained attack on the question of learning, either animal or human, or on the problems of skills'.[16] He also refers to Bain's work as 'one of the main foundation stones of contemporary learning theories' and says that while he was largely forgotten in this country after the turn of the century, his true successors were Thorndike and the American learning theorists. E. L. Thorndike's *Educational Psychology* (1913) had as sub-title *The Psychology of Learning* and was a landmark in the development of modern learning theory. The period 1910–40, in America and on the continent, was marked by a ferment of experiment and theorizing and sharp controversies among the rival 'schools'—Thorndike's stimulus-response theory of learning, Watson's behaviourism, the reflexology of Pavlov and Bekterev, and, contrasting with the analytical approach implicit in all these schools, the Gestalt psychology inaugurated in Frankfurt by Wertheimer and developed by Kohler and Koffka. If this ferment was largely ignored by British pyschologists, or discounted on the grounds that 'the fundamental subject matter of psychology is conscious experience, not conduct',[17] it is not surprising that very few questions on the nature of learning are to be found in the 'principles' papers set for college students during this period, or indeed in the 1940s and 1950s. It may be added that in so far as lecturers in education were aware of the American and continental work, its highly controversial nature and the difficulty of applying findings derived from experimental situations to the learning of children in classrooms made this a somewhat intractable topic.

What *is* surprising is that the joint working party found only one question on transfer of training; for this is a topic of central importance to all teachers. Surely the justification for most of the learning that goes on in schools is that it can be applied in contexts other than that in which it is learned. It is true, as G. P. Meredith has pointed out, this is a 'difficult and elusive' problem and 'at least seven different problems have been investigated under the heading "transfer of training",'[18] but if educators were fully seized of its central importance for their work they would create a demand for systematic research in this field. Can it be that the assumptions implicit in the earlier theories of formal discipline, deriving from faculty psychology, are still very much alive, embedded in educational practices?

The second main strand in the study of education was defined by Meiklejohn at the International Conference of 1884 as 'the history of education', including comparative education and the study of the great educators. The 1895 syllabus prescribed the study of Quick's *Educational Reformers* and the life and work of Dr Arnold. R. H. Quick's *Essays on Educational Reformers* appeared in 1868. In the preface to the second edition of 1890 he mentions his difficulties in getting it published and that when the 500 copies of the first edition had sold off (at a reduced price) it had remained for twenty years out of print. It had been reprinted in the U.S.A. several times, without his consent. In the 1890s the educational climate was more propitious. Professor H. C. Barnard has recently[19] called attention to the remarkable spate of studies in educational history published by the Cambridge University Press between 1897 and 1920. The Cambridge Syndicate to provide for the training of secondary teachers was set up in 1879 and the history of education had a prominent place in the courses of lectures—Quick and Oscar Browning were lecturers in the early days. Later on J. W. Adamson was a visiting lecturer and advised the C.U.P. The Cambridge examinations were for many years taken by students at university colleges and when other universities instituted certificate courses they followed the Cambridge lead.

The Cross Commission minority report had advocated not only the training of teachers in universities but also the formation of educational faculties to foster the academic study of education and research in this subject. One of the first of the 'university day training colleges' set up to implement this recommendation was that of King's College, London, and J. W. Adamson was appointed head of the training department in 1890; he became professor in 1930. In 1905 the Cambridge University Press published his *Pioneers of Modern Education* 1600–1700, his first contribution in what was to become his special field of scholarship,

the history of education. It dealt not only with the educational
theories and controversies of the seventeenth century but related
these to the schoolroom practices of the time. In 1919 appeared
Adamson's *Short History of Education*, which gave a comprehensive
and coherent outline of education in England but with some
reference to those foreign ideas and activities which had influenced
it. His *English Education 1789–1902* was published in 1930 after
his retirement from the chair at King's College. By this date study
of the history of education was a well established tradition in most
of the university departments of education as is evidenced by the
names of Michael Sadler, F. A. Cavenagh, W. H. Woodward,
R. L. Archer, Foster Watson, and Frank Smith. The *Syllabus
of a course on the History of Education in England, 1800–1911* by
Michael Sadler which the Manchester University Press published
in 1911 is one of the earliest attempts to work out a detailed course
with booklists for each lecture. Foster Watson, who succeeded
to the chair of education at Aberystwyth in 1894 was another
of the early pioneers with his study of *Vives* and his books on the
English grammar schools. He contributed some 150 articles to the
American *Cyclopedia of Education* (1911) and his collaboration with
Paul Monroe on that project led to his planning of a *Dictionary
of Education*, to give to British education the self revelation and
critical stimulus that Dr Monroe gave to American education.

The history of education in the courses provided by the
university departments normally includes both a study of English
educational institutions and of the work of the great educators.
Many departments have compulsory papers in this subject; others
provide for it as an optional study. As a compulsory study it is
usually limited to the more recent history of English education.
Some departments specialize also in comparative education (e.g.
the London Institute, where there is a chair in this subject,
King's College, London and Reading). The departments also
actively promote research and higher degree studies in this field.
Of the four disciplines with which we are concerned in this book,
history provides the largest number of intending teachers who

have a first degree qualification in the field of study. There is therefore no lack of historians who are prepared to apply their skills to the study of the history of education. As evidence of this we may note that in *The British Journal of Educational Studies*, begun in 1951 under the sponsorship of the heads of university departments and institutes of education to promote the publication of studies of education in all fields except educational psychology, the majority of the articles are historical. This is not due to editorial policy but to the difficulty in getting enough articles on other aspects.

In the colleges, after the setting up of Regional Examining Boards in the 1920s, references to historical studies, both of the great educators and of the English educational system, begin to appear in the syllabuses. In the examination papers on principles of education, there was very commonly a question on the former, often leaving the choice of educator to the student. The latter was usually represented by questions on one of the Education Acts or one of the reports of consultative committees. It is understandable that, under the intense pressures of the two year course, and with the main emphasis on educational psychology outlined earlier in this chapter, historical studies were relatively meagre. The three year course, and the development of four year B.Ed. courses offer much more scope for these studies. But given the time, what of the motivation? Some recent surveys of student attitudes to the courses have brought out very clearly that college students in general prefer educational studies where the short term application from theory to practice is most evident. Many of them do not readily 'see the point' of historical studies.

The sociology and philosophy of education, as they are envisaged in this book, barely come within the scope of a historical survey. Their history is too recent and can better be dealt with in the relevant chapters which follow. But they do have antecedents. The growing emphasis on social factors in the psychological studies has been mentioned and this at any rate prepared the way for the emergence in the last few years of the sociology of education as a study in its own right. Questions on social mobility and the effects of class structure have begun to appear in recent years. The syllabuses vary widely in their references to this field. General headings like 'The Philosophy and Sociology of Education' are common, but the last named is most commonly represented by sub-sections headed 'The Individual in Family and Society' or 'School and Society'. 'Sociology of Education' does however appear as a sub-heading in some syllabuses and this example gives some idea of the scope of the course. 'The structure of society in its relationship to education. The effects of various sub-cultures on human development. Contrasting culture patterns in this and other countries. Education and social changes. Contemporary educational problems.' Another example has the following sub-headings '(a) The School as a Social Unit. (b) The Role of the Teacher. (c) Social Class and Educational Opportunity. (d) Education and Cultural Change. (e) School and Society'.

The treatment of 'Philosophy' where it appears in the main headings is equally diverse. It may appear in a sub-heading as 'Aims and Ideals in Education' or as 'Principles of Education' or as 'Educational Thought'. In one example where it is called 'The Philosophy of Education' it includes '(a) Brief history of educational thought chiefly through the study of the contributions of great educators and of their influence both past and present; (b) the nature of education. Educational aims and ideals and their relevance to contemporary issues'. This briefly indicates the amorphous and ambiguous nature of this subject in its historical development in the courses. When the word 'philosophy' is used, it is usually in the context of 'The need for a philosophy of education'.

Traditionally, the 'Principles of Education' was a term used for the whole field of study as distant from the 'Practice of Education'. It is still commonly used as the heading of the examination paper which is concerned with general theory (there may be other papers dealing with methods of teaching various subjects or with health education). As we have seen much of the paper will be concerned with educational psychology but there will usually be a question or two on aims or values or freedom and authority, and these represent the 'philosophical' element in the course.

In the early years of the century the syllabus for the Teachers Certificate Examination changed its heading from 'School Management' to 'Theory of Teaching', and in 1907 to 'The Principles of Education'. This was also the title of a book by T. Raymont, published in 1904, often reprinted. Raymont was Warden of Goldsmith's College, and later Professor of Education at the University College of South Wales. Part I deals with the meaning of education and theory and practice, Part II with the school and education and the State, Part III with the study of children, Part VI has ten chapters on curriculum and methods and Part V four chapters on the training of teachers.

In his first chapter Raymont makes a useful distinction between the wider and narrower meaning of the term education. In the wider sense 'education means that process of development in which consists the passage of a human being from infancy to maturity, the process whereby he gradually adapts himself in various ways to his physical, social and spiritual environment', whereas the narrower meaning 'includes only the operation of measures expressly intended to modify the child's development and devised in accordance with a more or less clearly conceived purpose'. In his definition of the wider meaning, Raymont uses two terms which represented the two main views of the educative process held by most educational theorists in the first half of this century—development and adaptation or adjustment. As we have seen, Sir Percy Nunn was a notable exponent of the first: 'the primary aims of all educational effort should be to help boys and girls to achieve the highest degree of individual development of which they are capable'. *Education as Adjustment* was the title of a book by M. V. O'Shea, published in 1903.[20] Professor Peters comments on the nature of such concepts in Chapter Three and makes the point that all educational practices, of necessity, have embedded in them underlying assumptions about the nature of the

C

educative process, whether the teachers responsible for the practices are aware of it or not. What we can say is that in the period
covered in this chapter, educators used these terms without feeling
the necessity for any critical analysis of their meaning. C. D.
Hardie's *Truth and Fallacy in Educational Theory* (1942) broke
new ground in this respect.

There were, it is true, during this period philosophers who
wrote about education and educationists who attempted to classify
educational theories in terms of the traditional philosophic 'schools
of thought'. Sir John Adams' *The Evolution of Educational Theory*
(1909) was a pioneer work in this second category and as R. R.
Rusk has pointed out, 'it served as a prototype for a library on this
aspect of education, both in Britain and in America and it added a
new examinable subject in the Faculties of Education'.[21] In the
former category, to mention names which commonly appear in
the booklists of department and college courses, were John Dewey,
A. N. Whitehead, Bertrand Russell, E. T. Campagnac and T. P.
Nunn.

Nunn and Dewey have been mentioned earlier in this chapter
and they form an interesting contrast. The many students of
education who are familiar with Nunn's *Education: its Data and
First Principles* and with his contributions to the teaching of science
and mathematics will probably be unaware that he was also a
philosopher, 'the first, in England, to formulate the characteristic
doctrines of the New Realism. . . . Best known as an educationalist,
Nunn wrote little on philosophy, but that little had an influence out
of all proportion to its modest dimensions'.[22] His writings on
philosophy were published in the *Proceedings of the Aristotelian
Society*, of which he was President in 1925. His discussion of the
relationship between sense objects, physical or commonsense
objects, and scientific objects led him to develop a theory of
epistemological levels which is similar to the description of the
three phases of learning in Whitehead's *Aims of Education*. His
discussion of the influence of conative and affective processes on
cognitive processes,[23] foreshadows a central theme in his *Education*

though one would wish that more of Nunn's capacity for vigorous analysis and original thinking shown in the articles had gone into the book on education. It is as if Nunn the philosopher and Nunn the educationist were two different persons.

Dewey, in his writings on education is unmistakably a philosopher; his discussion of the educative process as 'reconstruction or reorganization of experience which adds to the meaning of experience and which increases ability to direct the course of subsequent experience' is clearly related to his general pragmatic theory. He rejected all theories of education which viewed it as a process directed toward preconceived goals; it was an end in itself not a means or a preparation.

Whitehead's *The Aims of Education* published in 1932, with a number of impressions and new editions in subsequent years, is lucid, seminal and as Lord Lindsay said, 'full of practical wisdom.' It is eminently quotable, alas until recently more quoted from than applied. 'Except at rare intervals of intellectual ferment, education in the past has been radically infected with inert ideas.' 'Let the main ideas which are introduced into a child's education be few and important, and let them be thrown into every combination possible.' 'Education is the acquisition of the art of the utilization of knowledge.' 'The problem of education is to make the pupil see the wood by means of the trees.' His description of the rhythmic process of education provides a blueprint for the planning of lessons and syllabuses, though students' lesson notes even today provide little evidence that this has been realized. There are, however, signs in the current ferment of curriculum revision, in the studies of concept formation in young children, and in the introduction of fundamental mathematic and scientific ideas at the primary stage, that some of Whitehead's seminal ideas are beginning to germinate.

Bertrand Russell's *On Education* (1926) also appears frequently in the course booklists; it was a clear and lively exposition of the aims of progressive educators and parents. E. T. Campagnac, Professor of Education at Liverpool, wrote about education from

the standpoint of traditional idealist philosophy, considering how
the claims of the individual and of society might be reconciled.[24]
Study of the philosophy of education entered a new period after
the Second World War with the application of modern analytical
techniques to educational ideas and processes. A landmark in this
development was the institution of a Chair in the Philosophy of
Education at the London Institute of Education of which the first
occupant was Louis Arnand Reid. (The practice of having desig-
nated Chairs or Readerships in the different aspects of the study
of education has been followed for some years in the London
Institute. Elsewhere 'Professor of Education' indicates the administrative responsibilities of the head of a department or institute
of Education rather than the nature of the study he professes.)

   It remains to comment on the third ingredient mentioned by
Meiklejohn in his delineation of the study of education—method.
This has certainly not been neglected; the emphasis on practical
training, noted by C. H. Judd, has remained strong in both
departments and colleges of education: and this meant provision
for practical experience in schools and the provision of courses in
both general methods of class teaching and special methods applic-
able to different subjects. The original heading of the Certificate
syllabus was 'School Management and Methods'. The syllabus
from 1914 to the mid-twenties was headed 'Principles of Teaching'
and had three main sub-divisions. The first included child development, physical conditions and discipline: the second covered the
curriculum at different stages and general methods of teaching;
the third covered the methods of teaching the specific subjects
in the elementary curriculum. In present day courses the method
ingredient is still there but it does not usually appear as a section
heading; it is distributed in ways which vary greatly from one
Institute to another, and sometimes from one college to another
within an institute. The usual main divisions of a modern course
are (1), education; (2), subject courses of which a student usually
specializes in one or two; (3), professional or curriculum courses.
The method ingredient may appear in all three sections in some

cases; or it may be concentrated in (1) or (3) or divided between (1) and (3). Since education usually includes practice as well as theory and since it is customary for a student to study education with special reference to a particular age group (infant, junior, secondary or combinations of these), some attention to methods of teaching is most usually included in (1). But whether the special subject courses and the curriculum or professional courses are mainly concerned with content or include some reference to methods of teaching and learning is a matter on which there is much variation. Some of the problems arising from the relating of the studies in these different sections will be discussed in the last chapter.

NOTES

1. R. and C. C. Southey, *Life of the Rev. Andrew Bell*, 1844.
2. George Combe, quoted George Collins, *Notes on School Management*, 1884, p. 2.
3. *Teaching-Learning Theory and Teacher Education*, 1952, p. 33.
4. *British Journal of Educational Studies*, Nov. 1961.
5. L. S. Hearnshaw, *A Short History of British Psychology*, pp. 257–8.
6. *Education: its Data and First Principles*, 3rd ed. 1945, pp. 12–13.
7. *Intellectual Growth of Young Children*, 1930; *Social Development in Young Children*, 1933.
8. *Psychology of Early Childhood*, 1942.
9. G. Seth and D. Guthrie, *Speech in Childhood*, 1935; M. M. Lewis, *Infant Speech*, 1936.
10. Margaret Lowenfelt, *Play in Childhood*, 1935; Ruth Griffiths, *Imagination in Early Childhood*, 1935.
11. See R. R. Rusk, *Philosophical Basis of Education*, 1956; also J. W. Tibble, 'Sir Percy Nunn', *British Journal of Educational Studies*, Nov. 1961.
12. *British Journal of Educational Psychology*, Vol. vi, Feb. 1936.
13. *Psychology and Teaching*, 1958, p. 212.
14. 'The Place of Psychology in Colleges and Departments of Education', *The Bulletin of Education*, No. 26, Nov. 1951, p. 9.
15. C. M. Fleming, 'The Basic Discipline', *The Bulletin of Education*, No. 29, Nov. 1952, p. 10.
16. Op. cit., p. 222.
17. C. S. Myers, The Nature of Mind, in *In the Realm of Mind*, 1937.
18. G. P. Meredith, *Occupational Psychology*, Vol. xv, 1941.

19. Review, *British Journal of Educational Studies*, May, 1965.
20. See also J. E. Adamson, *The Individual and the Environment*, 1921.
21. 'Sir John Adams', *British Journal of Educational Studies*, Nov. 1961.
22. John Passmore, *A Hundred Years of Philosophy*, 1957.
23. 'On the Concept of Epistemological Levels', *Proceedings of the Aristotelian Society*, Vol. 8.
24. *Studies Introductory to a Theory of Education*, 1915; *Society and Solitude*, 1922; *Education in its Relation to the Common Purposes of Humanity*, 1925.

Chapter Two

EDUCATIONAL THEORY

PAUL H. HIRST

In the somewhat chaotic historical development of the study and teaching of education outlined in the previous chapter, it is possible to see two distinct emphases. On the one hand there has been a serious concern for the fundamental aims and values of education and on the other a marked desire to base educational practice fairly and squarely on the results of scientific investigation. Although the first emphasis has only too often resulted in the production of educational sermons intended to commend certain specific aims and to exhort students and teachers to the ardent pursuit of them, it has also led at times to a critical examination of aims and values in an attempt to find a rationally defensible basis for educational practice. Maybe there is a place for educational preaching, but to exhort or commend is not to rationally justify. The second emphasis, though it has suffered at times from the prevailing fashions in psychology and sociology, has likewise resulted in most valuable efforts to get rid of purely personal opinion and prejudice in settling educational questions. Wherever soundly based empirical knowledge is available about learning, child development, the influences of social factors on educational attainment and so on, it is by these that we now wish to be guided.

But to recognize both these elements in the development and teaching of educational theory is one thing, to characterize accurately the nature and function of that theory as a whole and as a distinctive pursuit, is quite another matter. From the historical analysis of the previous chapter it is surely plain that though educational theory has in many ways made great strides in recent years it still lacks a clear and precise concept of what the whole enterprise is about. Such questions as: What is educational theory, as a theoretical pursuit, trying to achieve? How does this theory relate to educational practice? What kind of theoretical structure has it got and how in fact do the various elements that are obviously part of it fit in? These questions have received far too little sustained attention. As a result educational studies have tended to become either a series of unrelated or even competing theoretical pursuits, or a confused discussion of educational problems where philosophical, psychological, sociological or historical and other issues jostle against one another, none being adequately dealt with. This chapter is therefore concerned with examining the concept of educational theory in the hope that we can move towards a more adequate framework within which research and teaching in this area can develop.

[I]

The particular concern of some educationists for the aims and values involved in the enterprise has not infrequently led them to a belief that educational theory is in the last analysis philosophical in character. They have taken it as obviously true that from a system of philosophical beliefs there must follow directly and necessarily certain clear explicit implications for educational practice.[1] For after all, if people differ about the nature of ultimate reality, surely they must for instance differ in judging what is important in the school curriculum. Must not a religious person think religious education absolutely essential and an atheist think it thoroughly undesirable? Must not a western liberal democrat, because he holds different ethical doctrines, necessarily disagree with a communist on at least some issues in moral education? And must it not therefore be true that philosophical beliefs do determine clear educational principles which must be put into practice if obvious inconsistencies are to be avoided?

Certainly few people would wish to deny that a system of metaphysical, epistemological and ethical beliefs that provides a theory of what is ultimately real and ultimately important in life must have some significant contribution to make to educational ideas and practice. But whilst it is perhaps obvious that there is here some connection between philosophy and education, the view being discussed takes this to be one of direct implication, assuming that thoroughly valid principles for determining educational practice can be readily inferred straight from philosophical beliefs. Even if the view that philosophy is a body of beliefs of this kind is accepted, what is here said about its connection with education is surely not only far from obvious but in fact quite unacceptable in two important respects.

Firstly, the account is far too simple and as a result gives a seriously misleading picture of what is involved in making judgments on educational issues. It is too simple because it implies that on philosophical grounds alone we can satisfactorily answer the central questions of educational practice. This, however, is not so. By their very nature all such questions are necessarily complex and any answers based on philosophical beliefs only, must therefore be regarded as ill-considered. No matter what one's ethical views may be, to ignore in issues of moral education what is known of the psychological development of moral understanding is bound to result in irresponsible judgments. Similarly, to decide matters of curriculum content without due regard to social and psychological, as well as philosophical considerations, is quite indefensible. Whether we are thinking about particular practical decisions made whilst teaching or, as here, about the formation of general principles that state what ought to be done in practice, there are many diverse aspects to the issues that must be taken into account. The philosophical alone can never be sufficient for the task. This is not to deny that on the basis of certain philosophical beliefs alone some valuable general statements about education can be made and that these have an important place in educational discussion. But it is to deny that such statements are adequately formed principles that ought to be allowed to determine our educational practice.

An attempt might be made to avoid this criticism by trying to draw a sharp distinction between the aims of education and the methods or means, arguing that the former are philosophically determined whereas only the latter depend on other considerations. This distinction, however, simply will not do, for, in judging what we are to aim at in education, psychological and social factors for instance are clearly of central importance. If the term 'aims' is to be used of what we practically wish to achieve in the conduct of education, then we cannot judge this purely philosophically. What kind of curriculum is appropriate at the sixth form level, or whether an educational system should be co-educational or comprehensive in pattern, are not in any sense simply philosophical issues. However much one may think that 'the aims of life' or 'what is good' can be known or justified philosophically, it is a confusion to think that the aims of education as a practical enterprise can be set up in the same way. And surely the function of educational theory is the determination of these practical aims, not the determination of the aims and values of life in general.

The distinction between aims and methods or means can be further criticized as a quite false dichotomy when we are concerned with many educational matters. In developing mathematical understanding, say, what is achieved depends crucially on the methods used. Methods are not simply different routes or different modes of transport that will get us to the same destination. For, while sharing certain goals, they involve developing quite distinct elements of understanding (or misunderstanding) and may convey also quite different notions of what mathematics is. In education the journey is as important as the destination reached —indeed no two methods can in fact take us to precisely the same place in the development of understanding. Aims and methods are inextricably intertwined and neither presents us with problems that are essentially either philosophical or empirical in character.

If this is so, it means that responsible educational principles need to be formed by a serious attempt to build together whatever knowledge, values and beliefs are relevant to the practical issues.

And further, it means that, between philosophical beliefs in general and educational practice, we must clearly recognize a domain of theoretical discussion and investigation concerned with forming these principles. To this domain of educational theory, philosophical beliefs make their own distinctive contribution alongside history, social theory, psychological theory and so on. The view that there is a direct connection between philosophy and educational practice either totally ignores, or heavily underestimates, the real significance of educational theory in this sense. It fails to recognize the important truth that, unless philosophical beliefs are to influence educational practice in a distorting manner, they must influence it indirectly through the medium of educational theory, where they are considered conjointly with many other elements before any particular principles for educational practice are explicitly formulated.

In reply to this it might be argued that, if the term philosophical beliefs is interpreted broadly enough, it will embrace all the considerations that could possibly be relevant to judgments of educational principle. In that case, it would be true to say, after all, that educational principles do follow directly from philosophical beliefs. But this reply simply covers up the problem by a blanketing use of the term 'philosophy'. If the term is to be used so as to include psychology, sociology, and all else that is significant for education, then by definition the theory is 'philosophical'. One can then only protest at the refusal to recognize important distinctions and point out that without them we must give up all hope of distinguishing the role of philosophy in educational affairs from that of psychology, sociology, etc. For a purely verbal victory one must pay a very high price. And even if the application of the term 'philosophical beliefs' is restricted so as not to cover those psychological, sociological and other elements that are of immediate importance when it comes to formulating educational principles, there are still serious difficulties about the genuinely philosophical character of the remaining domain. For if philosophy is still thought to be supplying to educational theory a whole area of general beliefs about the nature of man, of reality, of the good life, etc., then one must protest that these general beliefs are the result of no distinctively philosophical enterprise, being derived from much knowledge of diverse kinds about human nature, society, the physical world, etc.

One can only conclude that conceiving educational theory as essentially philosophical in character involves failing to do justice to the complex nature of the problems it has to deal with, seriously underestimating the importance of other forms of knowledge in dealing with these, and conceiving philosophy in so ambiguous a way as to make it the label of no clearly distinctive form of understanding.

In some of its forms this concept of educational theory has associated with it a second feature which is open to serious criticisms of a different kind. Not infrequently it seems to be held that educational principles can be, and ought to be, formally deduced from philosophical beliefs. And even when it is granted that philosophical beliefs are not of themselves adequate to the task, it might still be maintained that, given all the necessary understanding whatever its nature, educational principles ought then to be derived in much the same way as we can derive the theorems in Euclidean geometry from the axioms.

The process of deduction depends entirely on the formal manipulation of statements and the conclusions to which it leads are therefore based solely on what is actually and literally expressed in the premisses. The process must begin with statements that cover quite explicitly all the considerations that are involved in the issues. What is more, all the concepts and terms that are used must be fully related to each other so that no gaps appear in the chains of argument. Deduction can never be used unless we can start with premisses equal to the task, covering all the necessary facts and beliefs and relating these so that the conclusions are reached in a purely formal manner.

Can we then set out our beliefs and knowledge in series of statements so that from them we can work out deductively what our educational principles must be? There are several reasons why in general this is impossible. Sometimes when an issue is clear cut and the factors on which it depends are limited, deduction may be used, and small pieces of deduction may well occur too as part of some larger argument. But in general the complexity of practical issues is so great that it is quite impossible to set out explicitly all the facts and beliefs which must be taken into account. Nor is this difficulty simply one of time and space for the job. Many of the terms in which we express the knowledge and beliefs that are vital for educational issues are not exact and precise but vague and ill-defined. Terms expressing personal relations and moral values are notoriously lacking in the quite clear constant meaning that the deductive use of statements assumes. Again much of our relevant understanding is not expressible in literal terms but depends on metaphor, analogy, and even paradox. Deductive arguments using, or rather misusing, such statements are quite valueless even when they make sense. In addition, to evolve educational principles by deduction certainly means using, amongst other statements, a set of moral principles; and whilst these can be used formally in this way, if they are it means that, morally speaking, educational judgments are being produced by rule. Yet moral principles are never once-for-all rules whose formal implications should be invariably accepted. If they are used formally to produce educational principles, they are likely to be as destructive of what is good in educational practice as mechanical living is in everyday affairs. Finally, it is difficult to see how conclusions that depend on the putting together of considerations from practical experience, from psychology, social theory and philosophy, weighing them up, estimating their relative importance, could possibly be reached in an uninterrupted chain of deduction. The process that is employed generally is far removed from the formal manipulation of accepted statements, being rather a form of judgment based on as comprehensive a view of the issues as it is possible to get.

Again this is not to deny that from statements of our knowledge and beliefs we can by a process of deduction come to make some valuable statements for education. It is the adequacy of these as principles for practice that is in question. For the reasons given above deduction seems to be far too limited, and in some respects far too dangerously perverting, a method for us to work by it uncritically in this field. It follows from the nature of adequate educational principles that in general they cannot and ought not to be formed in this way. We need to think in terms of a much looser and much more open process of judgment to which philosophical beliefs, psychological and social theory, historical knowledge, etc., contribute in their appropriate ways. Beliefs, knowledge of facts and general values provide the grounds on which judgments of educational principle are made and it is by reference to these that we give the reasons for what we advocate. But this does not mean that there is some logically necessary connection between the knowledge, beliefs and values on the one hand and the educational principles on the other. It is not that we work out formally our conclusions from explicit statements which are the complete and necessary grounds for the resulting principles. It is rather that in the midst of a complex network of understanding which cannot be adequately and formally expressed, we form reasons, draw attention to the major considerations which have influenced us. This being so, it is not at all surprising that people who agree to certain statements of their beliefs do often in fact advocate quite different educational principles. It is not at all uncommon, for instance, to find Christians who favour a secular school system, and not a few atheists judge there to be good reasons for having universal religious instruction. Contrary to the crude assumption mentioned earlier, it appears on closer inspection that educational principles that are adequate for directing practice do not follow by simple deduction from philosophical beliefs. This is borne out by the fact that philosophical agreement is no guarantee of educational agreement and fortunately many educational principles are acceptable to the holders of very diverse philosophical views. This does not mean that philosophical beliefs are unimportant for educational theory, it means simply that the part they play is not that of axioms in a deductive system. Their role is highly influential but much more subtle than what some envisage, being part of a broad over-all understanding that lies behind all educational judgments. A philosophical system of considerable generality may of course greatly determine a set of educational principles even when other factors have been taken into account. It is then tempting to speak loosely of the principles as derived or even deduced from the system. This is, however, most misleading and it would be better to describe the principles as constructed so as to be consistent with the system. Consistency between beliefs and principles denotes nothing more than the absence of any contradiction between the two. This there must be, but it by no means follows that there must also be an explicit deductive chain that leads from the one to the other.

[II]

In criticizing too philosophical a view of the nature of educational theory, it has nevertheless been taken for granted thus far that philosophy is indeed concerned with establishing certain beliefs and values and that these beliefs and values do have a legitimate and important place in the theory. In his book *An Introduction to the Philosophy of Education*, Professor D. J. O'Connor goes much further and questions even these concessions to philosophical imperialism. Early in this volume, the author makes it clear that in his view, 'philosophy is not in the ordinary sense of the phrase a body of knowledge, but rather an activity of criticism or clarification'. It is not 'a kind of superior science' which can 'be expected to answer difficult and important questions about human life, and man's place and prospects in the universe' by using special techniques. Rather it is 'an activity of criticism or clarification',[2] an attempt to answer questions where the meaning of terms and their relations to each other have produced complex and far reaching difficulties in our understanding. Clearly this analytical activity, which can be exercised on any subject matter, can be used to deal with questions in educational theory. Certainly when trying to formulate educational principles difficulties of this sort arise. On this view, philosophy still has some place in educational debate, but now it no longer seems to contribute significantly to the substance of the theory, it is but an aid, clearing up confusions of meaning wherever these appear. This is not the place for a general discussion of the nature of philosophy. It must, however, be said that, whilst most contemporary British philosophers would be in considerable agreement with O'Connor's emphasis on the analytical function of philosophy, many would find his treatment of metaphysical beliefs and moral values far too dismissive. And when it comes to characterizing educational theory, the significance of these elements in it is crucial. From accepting a markedly analytical view of philosophy therefore, it does not necessarily follow that it has quite the insubstantial function for education that O'Connor seems to think.

But whatever the rights and wrongs in this matter, the specific account of educational theory that O'Connor gives raises quite different issues. Professing to look for the 'job an educational theory is supposed to do',[3] O'Connor first distinguishes four main senses of the word 'theory', two of which seem to be important in educational contexts. In one of these, theory is contrasted with practice and here the word refers to 'a set or system of rules or a collection of precepts which guide or control actions of various kinds. . . . Educational theory would then consist of those parts of psychology concerned with perception, learning, concept formation, motivation and so on which directly concern the work of the teacher'.[4] In the other, the word 'theory' is used as it occurs in the natural sciences where it refers to a single hypothesis or a logically interconnected set of hypotheses that have been confirmed by observation. It is this sense of the word that is said to provide us with 'standards by which we can assess the value and use of any claimant to the title of "theory". In particular this sense of the word will enable us to judge the value of the various (and often conflicting) theories that are put forward by writers on education'.[5]

Judged by these standards, a great deal of educational theory certainly comes off rather badly. For as O'Connor himself states, educational discussions are not usually entirely empirical in character but include as well value judgments and appeals to metaphysical beliefs. These other two elements differ quite radically from the first, as his earlier analysis of them has shown. The importance of value judgments in this field is not questioned and O'Connor's chief concern is that we should recognize them for what they are so that we do not get into muddles by confusing them with assertions of fact. Of metaphysical statements however, it is said that we have no way of confirming what they assert and that we cannot even be sure that they have any cognitive meaning at all. Their contribution to educational theory is therefore of very doubtful value. He thus concludes:

'We can summarize this discussion by saying that the word "theory" as it is used in educational contexts is generally a courtesy title. It is justified only where we are applying well established experimental findings in psychology or sociology to the practice of education. And even here we should be aware that the conjectural gap between our theories and the facts on which they rest is sufficiently wide to make our logical consciences uneasy. We can hope that the future development of the social sciences will narrow this gap and this hope gives an incentive for developing these sciences.'[6]

The first thing that must be said about this account is that O'Connor has singularly failed to do what he set out to do—to discover the job educational theory performs. If in fact he had begun to discover this a very different picture of the theory would certainly have emerged. In addition, because of his obsession with scientific theory as a paradigm for all theories, he totally misjudges the importance of the non-scientific elements that he himself diagnoses in educational discussions. In the last analysis metaphysical statements and value judgments are dismissed as not being elements that fundamentally characterize this field of discourse.

D

If we accept O'Connor's classification of the two main senses of the word 'theory' that are important for education, it is surely the first of these that gives the primary meaning here, not the second as he suggests. Educational theory is in the first place to be understood as the essential background to rational educational practice, not as a limited would-be scientific pursuit. Even when O'Connor momentarily recognizes this, he nevertheless fails to realize the complex kind of theory that is necessary to determine a whole range of practical activities. He therefore falls back on his scientific paradigm maintaining that the theory must be simply a collection of pieces of psychology.[7]

Yet the theories of science and the theories of practical activities are radically different in character because they perform quite different functions, they are constructed to do different jobs. In the case of the empirical sciences, a theory is a body of statements that have been subjected to empirical tests and which express our understanding of certain aspects of the physical world. Such tested theories are the objects, the end products, of scientific investigation, they are the conclusions of the pursuit of knowledge. Where, however, a practical activity like education is concerned, the place of the theory is totally different. It is not the end product of the pursuit, but rather it is constructed to determine and guide the activity. The function of the theory is to determine precisely what shall and what shall not be done, say in education. The distinction I am drawing between scientific theory and say educational theory is the traditional distinction between knowledge that is organized for the pursuit of knowledge and the understanding of our experience, and knowledge that is organized for determining some practical activity. To try to understand the nature and pattern of some practical discourse in terms of the nature and pattern of some purely theoretical discourse can only result in its being radically misconceived.

O'Connor's important distinctions between different uses of the term 'theory' draw attention to the fact that the phrase 'educational theory' can have two quite different meanings. It can be used as

O'Connor wishes for the body of scientific knowledge on which rational educational judgments rest. It is, however, also used for the whole enterprise of building a body of rational principles for educational practice. In this second sense it is the label for a domain of theory that not only draws on educational theory in the first, scientific sense, but draws on much else besides by way of other forms of knowledge and belief, and results in the formation of practical principles. Neither of these uses can be said to be the correct one and what matters is not a fight over the right to a label but the recognition that the two types of theory concerned are radically different in kind. If we are not to run into serious confusions, therefore, it is vital to keep track of the meaning of the term in any discussion. In this volume it is with educational theory in the second, larger sense that we are concerned, certain chapters, for instance those on psychology and sociology, discussing the place of educational theory in the narrower scientific sense within the larger whole.

O'Connor's account of the matter is misleading not so much because he wishes to restrict the use of a term but because of his tendency to reduce the whole concept of educational theory in the larger sense to the narrower scientific concept. It is on the development of the theory in its larger sense that rational educational practice depends, not simply on the development of scientific study. Reductionism of this kind, which conceives all educational theory as essentially scientific in character, is as unacceptable as the philosophical reductionism discussed in the first section of this chapter. And that because it again mis-characterizes the theory in two major respects, first as to its content and second as to its logical form. As to its content, the wider theory is necessarily drawing on knowledge other than science; it must, for instance, draw on historical, philosophical and moral understanding as well. In particular whatever one may think of the truth claims of metaphysical beliefs and the form of justification of moral values, both these enter into the formation of educational principles and judgments. They cannot be ignored or wished out of the way. As to its form, the wider theory is not concerned simply with producing explanations on the scientific model but with forming rationally justified principles for what ought to be done in an area of practical activity. In the last analysis, therefore, scientific theory and educational theory are as different logically as judgments of what is the case are different from judgments of what ought to be the case.

[III]

From the discussion thus far it would seem clear that an adequate account of educational theory must do justice both to its connection with educational practice and its connection with a vast range of different forms of purely theoretical understanding. Its further characterization, therefore, turns on showing precisely how knowledge of such different kinds is organized into a theoretical structure which culminates in rationally justified principles for educational practice. In order to bring out the features of this logical structure it is necessary to distinguish it as one of three quite different structures or organizations that knowledge has or can have. In the first place all knowledge can be seen as necessarily structured into what will be referred to as distinct 'forms'. Secondly, knowledge can be organized into what will be called different 'fields'. And thirdly, it can be organized into a variety of 'practical theories'.

(i) Forms of knowledge

All knowledge that man has achieved can be seen to be differentiated into a number of logically distinct domains or forms. That this is so comes from the fact that knowledge is possible only because of the use of patterns of related concepts in terms of which our experience is intelligible. Our understanding, be it in the affairs of everyday or in matters of advanced research, in science or history or morals, is achieved through the development and use of conceptual schemes by means of which we make sense of things.

Successive generations acquire these conceptual schemes by learning to use meaningfully the symbolic systems in which they are expressed and in their turn these generations can develop further both the schemes and their use. But knowledge depends on more than the existence of such schemes. For unless in their use we are able to distinguish truth from error, fact from fable, what is valid from what is invalid, what is right from what is wrong, then we are not in a position to claim anything by way of genuine understanding and knowledge as distinct from conjecture and fantasy. Our knowledge is thus dependent on the use both of conceptual schemes and criteria for validity or truth. In public terms, this means that our knowledge is expressed in symbolic statements which have been judged for their validity according to recognized criteria that are appropriate to them.

That there are distinct forms within knowledge can be seen by the logical analysis of the whole domain. These forms can be distinguished from each other in three interrelated ways. First, within the domain there are distinct types of concepts that characterize different types of knowledge. Mathematical concepts such as number, integral, matrix, generate a different form of understanding because they have a different function in relation to experience from say the scientific concepts hydrogen, atom, magnetic field, or the religious concepts, God, sin, heaven, or the moral concepts, good, ought, virtue. Secondly, these concepts occur within different networks, whose relationships determine what meaningful propositions can be made. Moral terms can only be used meaningfully in certain relations to other concepts that occur in moral discourse. Scientific terms like 'atom' can be related to other terms only by strict adherence to a whole network of logical rules for them. One can no more make meaningful statements about the colour of atoms than one can about the goodness of right-angled triangles. Thirdly, the domains can be distinguished by the different types of test they involve for the truth or validity of propositions. In science the tests of observation and experiment are final. In mathematics the criteria are those of deduction from axioms. Likewise moral and aesthetic judgments are each unique in their forms of justification. In recent philosophical work, even where no really adequate positive account of the logical features of the domains has been achieved, there would seem to be growing agreement that we must recognize as distinct those forms of understanding we have in science, mathematics, history, morals, aesthetics, philosophy and religion. Whether or not the domain of religion can be regarded as one of knowledge rather than belief is a matter of dispute, and some might question the autonomous character of history. Maybe there are good grounds for thinking that the human sciences are logically distinguishable from the physical sciences. What would certainly seem to be beyond dispute is that the history of the development of knowledge is the story of its progressive differentiation into a number of logically distinct forms, each providing unique understanding because of the uniqueness of its concepts, its conceptual structure and its criteria for validity. If this is so, then the growth of an individual's knowledge involves the progressive mastery and use of the appropriate conceptual schemes and their criteria. Understanding or knowledge if it is to be anything other than superficial, cannot be acquired in random fashion, for to understand is in part to appreciate a whole network of ordered conceptual relations and to be aware of the appropriate bases for truth and validity that are involved. Here there is an implicit structuring of knowledge into distinct forms, an organization in no sense optional to understanding, conventional or convenient in its divisions. It is an ordering that is essentially part of knowledge as we have it. These conceptual structures may become further differentiated, they may be extended, they may be applied in new ways, but it would seem logically impossible to conceive of the growth of knowledge, either as a public deposit or as a personal development, outside this framework.

If what is being said here is not to be seriously misunderstood two further points must be made. First, within the forms which have been logically distinguished by their formal structural features, further distinctions can be drawn in terms of their content. The domain of science, for instance, can be subdivided into physics, chemistry, zoology, biochemistry and so on. These divisions, made according to an interest in a particular selection of empirical phenomena, or the use of particular methods, do not, however, result in domains that are logically distinguishable, for in logical respects the sciences are all strictly similar. All the sciences have the same type of structure and test. These sub-divisions are in fact convenient or conventional, being logically coherent selections from the larger domain, sub-sections which can be developed and taught in relative independence. To a greater or less degree, therefore, each of a multitude of existing and possible sciences is an expression of the same logical form but is different in content.

Secondly, to say that the forms are each unique in their essential logical features is not to say that they are totally divorced from each other. That would be manifestly false when, for instance, the sciences make such great use of mathematics, history uses the results of scientific investigation and moral judgments equally depend on much empirical understanding. But in these inter-relations one form is making use of some other. In each case one form A accepts the relevant contribution of some other form B entirely as it is, without any right to question, and it employs this knowledge as an instrument to its own ends. As far as form A is concerned, it is simply the achievements or results of form B that matter, and these it takes in, formulating its own theories or state-ments of principles to be tested according to criteria uniquely appropriate for form A. A theory in physics may use the results of some vast mathematical system. It is then taking over mathemati-cal knowledge which for the purpose of the theory is assumed to be valid according to mathematical criteria. But the theory itself then stands or falls not by any mathematical tests but by those of empirical experiment and observation appropriate to a science. A theory in physics is not even a starter as a scientific theory if it is based on faulty mathematics. But the mathematical validity of a theory in no way guarantees its scientific truth. One form may indeed employ the findings of one, or several others, but this in no way invalidates the general truth that the forms are unique in kind having their own structures and tests for validity.

(ii) Fields of knowledge

Apart from the forms of knowledge and the sub-divisions within them, we do also organize knowledge into artificial units. Round some kind of object, phenomenon, abstract entity or other interest, knowledge from many different forms can be collected. Such 'fields of knowledge' are frequently formed as a basis for use in education under such titles as, for instance, 'the neighbourhood', 'power', 'the modern European mind'. These fields may, of course, be of considerable value in promoting the growth of knowledge in certain areas and they are not necessarily organizations developed simply for teaching purposes. Though the nature of geography is hotly disputed by professionals, the subject as commonly found would seem to have all the features of a field. Centring round an interest in 'place' or 'man and his environment' historical knowledge, for instance, rubs shoulders with the results of work in the human as well as the physical sciences. What is more crucial, however, is that all the questions with which geographers deal seem to be intelligible and answerable only within the canons of one of the several forms. Certainly geography has concepts which other areas of knowledge do not use, but that does not make them unique in kind. From a logical point of view they would all appear to be either, say, scientific or historical in character and geographical solely by virtue of their use for those particular empirical and historical matters which geographers wish to consider. If there are geographical truths which are unique in logical kind, where the tests for truth are not simply of a type used elsewhere in say scientific or historical pursuits, it is not clear what these are. Geography may be marked out as a distinctive area because of the subjects with which it deals, but that is not sufficient to distinguish it as a form. There must also be a conceptual structure that leads to propositions with their own unique criteria of validity, and that geography has not been shown to possess.

What is meant by a field here is in fact simply a collection of knowledge from various forms which has unity solely because this knowledge all relates to some object or interest. There is no inherent logical structure which gives unity to the domain. There are no concepts of a kind peculiar to the field. And the field is not concerned with the validation of distinctive statements according to unique criteria. It follows from this that whereas the advancement of a form of knowledge depends on the development of the relevant conceptual scheme and its wider application according to its own canons, the advancement of a field is a far more complex affair. It consists in the development and application of whatever forms of knowledge are considered valuable and relevant in coming to understand the selected topic. Whereas a professional historian must have mastered the canons and methods of historical thought, being primarily engaged in extending these and their use, the geographer is necessarily involved in employing the canons and methods of several different forms, those of the historian, the economist, the physicist and so on. And this not because the canons of geography presuppose these other forms in any sense, as the historian may need to draw on scientific knowledge. It is rather that there are no distinctive canons and methods of geography, for all those it employs are in fact those of the relevant forms it uses. To master a field of knowledge is therefore necessarily a complex and difficult matter. To understand 'the modern European mind', for instance, involves at least a grasp of the conceptual schemes and criteria of history, science, philosophy and the arts as applied to the selected cultural phenomena.

(iii) Practical theories

Both the patternings of knowledge considered so far are important if we are to understand the growth of knowledge both publicly and personally. Forms like history or science and fields like geography or the modern European mind are all organizations of knowledge significant primarily because of their importance for the development of cognition, of understanding in itself. We do, however, also have organizations of knowledge which will be called 'practical theories', whose whole *raison d'être* is their practical function. In these it is not a patterning of understanding that is of first importance but the determination of what ought to be done in some range of practical activities. This distinction between practical theories and forms and fields of knowledge is exactly that discussed in Section II as a distinction between the theories of practical knowledge and those of theoretical knowledge. It is now, however, possible to pursue further the question of the differences in logical structure that are involved.

In practical theories knowledge is collected from several different forms because of a particular interest, just as in the various fields mentioned above. The interest now, however, is a particular range of practical activities as, for example, in engineering, medicine or education. But whereas fields of knowledge are simply collections of knowledge from the forms, practical theories are collections of knowledge used in the formulation of principles for practice. Educational theory, like political theory or engineering, is not concerned simply with collecting knowledge about certain practical affairs. The whole point is the use of this knowledge to determine what should be done in educational practice. In the process the theory draws on all the knowledge within the various forms that is relevant to educational pursuits but proceeds from there to grappling with practical problems. The educationist is not simply interested in, for instance, the nature of historical explanation, the place in it of moral judgments and the psychological aspects of acquiring historical concepts. He is concerned with using these kinds of knowledge to form rationally defensible principles about the place of history teaching in education, what history should be taught in schools and how it ought to be done. Thus educational theory, like all other practical theories has a logical unity that a mere field of knowledge centred on education would not have. The unity of the theory goes beyond that of a collection of knowledge centred on some interest to that of a rational structure where knowledge from the forms provides the basis of justification for a series of educational principles.

From this it might be supposed that a practical theory is in structure more like a form of knowledge than a field. For could it not be argued that just as physics uses mathematics but results in distinctive, validated scientific statements, so educational theory uses philosophy, psychology, sociology, etc., and issues in distinctive, validated educational principles? Just this has been argued by those who have wanted to maintain that education is in some sense an autonomous discipline.[8] On closer examination, however, the parallel cannot be maintained. Whatever the relationship between mathematics and physics, any scientific theory involves distinctive empirical concepts unique in character so that the theory's validity turns on related empirical tests. In educational theory no such concepts exist any more than they do in say geography or any other field. There is nothing logically unique about such educational concepts as, for example, classroom, teacher, subject, comprehensive school. These simply serve to pick out those particular empirical, moral, philosophical and other elements with which education is concerned. These concepts are used to mark out the area of education and its interests but do not pick out any unique form of awareness or knowledge for, indeed, educational theory has no such function. Because this is so, it follows that there can be no unique form of test for educational principles. However they are validated, it is in no way that is logically parallel to the experiment and observation of the sciences. In spite of the claim to some unique type of test within educational theory and one by which the contributions of philosophers, psychologists and others can be assessed, no such tests have in fact been produced. And if the analysis here given is correct, by the nature of the case they cannot be.

What is happening in this parallel between educational theory and a form of knowledge is a total mis-characterization of educational principles. This can be seen if the place of mathematics in physics is at all carefully compared with that of philosophy, psychology, etc., in educational theory. For, granted the validity of any mathematics involved, the truth of statements in physics turns on empirical evidence. But granted the validity of the historical, psychological, moral or other elements involved, the validity of the educational principle rests on nothing further. Granted the mathematics, statements in physics must survive crucial scientific tests. For these, however, educational theory has no parallel and its principles stand or fall entirely on the validity of the knowledge contributed by the many forms. Of course a statement or theory in physics can be invalidated by faulty mathematics, yet to establish any mathematics used does not begin to validate the theory as a scientific theory. An educational principle, however, whilst it can likewise be invalidated because it rests on say faulty psychology, can only be justified by virtue of the psychological and other knowledge on which the principle rests. In the pattern of justification in science, some statement or theory A is validated because granted the truth of $x, y, z, . .$, the items of mathematics and other forms of knowledge that may be used, there are crucial scientific reasons $a, b, c, d, . . .$ for its truth that stem from the appropriate empirical observations. In educational theory some practical principle A is validated simply in terms of $x, y, z,$ .. , where these are items of empirical, philosophical, moral or other knowledge which are relevant to the educational issue. There are no strictly educational reasons $a, b, c, d, . . .$ which are not empirical, philosophical, moral, etc., in form. A principle that all secondary education ought to be given in comprehensive schools must be justified by appealing to all the sound empirical evidence that is available on the effects of selection and non-selection both psychologically and sociologically, on the administrative possibilities and difficulties for institutions of this kind, etc.; the case must be argued in the light of the historical context in which appropriate changes would have to be made; it must rest on certain general value judgments which in their turn can be given justification and so on. In the light of all this, but only this, can the specifically educational judgment be rationally made. Similarly, a principle for compulsory religious instruction in maintained schools must be defended in terms of the philosophical status of claims to religious knowledge, what is known of the psychological development of religious concepts and beliefs, the relationship between morals and religion logically, psychologically and sociologically, the historical significance of religious beliefs, the guarding of the principle of complete religious liberty, etc.

Educational principles are, therefore, justified simply by producing reasons for them of an empirical, philosophical, moral or other logical kind. Once it is understood that the validity of the principles turns on nothing 'educational' beyond these, it is clear that the only way to attack or defend them is by a critical examination of these reasons. The psychological reasons must be shown to stand according to the strictest canons of that science. Equally the historical, philosophical or other truths that are appealed to must be judged according to the criteria of the relevant discipline in each case. Any significant debate about educational principles must be about reasons for them and this immediately turns into the discussion of a series of questions radically different in kind, questions answerable only within the terms of highly developed distinct forms of knowledge and their sub-divisions. Far from being an autonomous discipline, educational theory would seem to be rather as complex as any field of knowledge can be, and different from those fields not because some unique form of understanding is involved, but because the elements are used in the making of practical principles. It is but a confusion to regard the formation of practical principles as parallel to the development of an autonomous form of knowledge or thought when those principles stand or fall on nothing but knowledge contributed by other forms.

If educational theory is not, then, in any sense, autonomous, it might well be argued that it or any other practical theory for that matter is a sub-division of what has been referred to as the form of moral knowledge. Though to prevent serious misunderstanding a quite separate classification for practical theories has been argued thus far, there is in fact a great deal to be said for characterizing these theories under moral knowledge. What is distinctive about them is that they issue in practical principles for a particular range of activities. Just as within science the different sciences are distinguishable according to the different topics considered, so practical theories are distinguishable from each other by the range of activities for which they formulate principles. Engineering, medicine, political theory and educational theory clearly differ from each other because of the activities with which they are concerned. What is perhaps most important in this is that the activities differ widely in kind and that they therefore call for practical principles of varying types. By and large the central problems involved in engineering and medicine can be marked out with little difficulty. With this goes the fact that in large measure the aims of engineering and medicine are commonly agreed. In political and educational theory, however, the area of activities being discussed is not so clear and the precise aims of those activities are often matters of serious dispute. Professor R. S. Peters in his papers 'Education as Initiation'[9] and 'What is an Educational Process'?[10] has sought to outline the criteria for those activities we label 'educational' and therefore to demarcate the territory of educational theory. One thing that is abundantly plain from his analyses is that, certainly in this case, it is a fundamental task of the theory to determine the ends and goals to be pursued as much as the means to be employed. Thus whereas engineering consists almost entirely of the use of scientific knowledge in determining efficient means to agreed ends, educational theory in large measure depends on the making of value judgments about what exactly is to be aimed at in education.

Whatever the character of engineering may be it is certainly characteristic of educational theory that it formulates principles of a distinctly moral kind. In doing this it, of course, relies on the logic of moral reasoning and therefore rightly falls within the domain of moral knowledge. At the same time, however, the principles formulated are not high level statements about what is good or what ought to be done in general. They are principles specifically concerned with education and it is the function of the theory in moral reasoning to use general moral principles and all other relevant knowledge to this end. In so far, then, as practical theories of this kind are regarded as sub-divisions of moral understanding it must be remembered that the problems they deal with directly are practical. Educational theory as such is not concerned with the justification of such fundamental and basic principles as those of freedom, respect for persons, truth telling, that other things being equal a man has a right to worship as he pleases and a responsibility to provide for his family. It is concerned with establishing what ought to be done in educational activities. The justification needed for the most fundamental moral principles may well be quite different in form from that needed for those at lower levels. The pattern of reasoning for practical principles outlined earlier is that in which knowledge of many kinds, including fundamental and high level moral principles is brought to bear on restricted and specific practical issues. This can be considered as a form of moral reasoning but it is not the only form. It is simply that form appropriate to dealing with practical problems of a moral kind.

From this discussion it emerges that even when a practical theory centrally involves moral questions, its restricted focus limits the level and character of these moral considerations and introduces the need for much specialized knowledge of empirical and other kinds. In these theories too by no means all the questions are essentially moral. Educational theory has to deal with many questions about, for instance, teaching techniques and administrative organization, which are purely technical. As has been pointed out previously there are also practical theories like engineering which are almost entirely of this character. There are thus good reasons for thinking of practical theories as organizations of knowledge distinct in kind. They are the product of interests in groups of related practical activities, they are concerned with forming principles saying what ought to be done, and to varying degrees they are not only technical but also moral in character.

Earlier in this section great emphasis was placed on the fact that educational principles stand or fall entirely on the validity of the relevant knowledge contributed from the various forms. Judgments stating what ought to be done morally or technically are based on nothing beyond the empirical facts, more general value judgments, etc. From this it might be thought that educational principles must somehow follow from a theoretical synthesis of all the contributory elements, that unless some harmony is brought to the relevant philosophy, psychology, history, etc., the principles will lack adequate justification. Not only would this be a task for educational theory that is quite impossible practically, for no one could have mastered all the relevant specialist knowledge, it would be asking for something that might well be logically impossible. It is not at all clear what is meant by synthesizing knowledge achieved through the use of logically quite different conceptual schemes. But such a synthesis is in fact quite unnecessary for the formation of practical principles. The diverse character of the contributions of psychology, philosophy or history, to a discussion of the comprehensive school and equality of opportunity is immaterial. That many of the considerations may pull in different directions, and that they have not been technically harmonized, is not germane. Indeed it is precisely the function of the theory to form practical principles in the light of diverse and conflicting evidence. Educational theory is not to be thought of as starting with a purely theoretical structure, integrating elements of science with some history and philosophy, etc. It is a theory which formulates principles the reasons for which are radically diverse in kind, a theory which by these principles alone unites knowledge from many different forms.

In this analysis of the nature of educational theory the following important characteristics have emerged:

(i) It is the theory in which principles, stating what ought to be done in a range of practical activities, are formulated and justified;

(ii) The theory is not itself an autonomous 'form' of knowledge or an autonomous discipline. It involves no conceptual structure unique in its logical features and no unique tests for validity. Many of its central questions are in fact moral questions of a particular level of generality, questions focused on educational practice.

(iii) Educational theory is not a purely theoretical field of knowledge because of the formulation of principles for practice in which it issues. It is, however, composite in character in a way similar to such fields.

(vi) Educational principles are justified entirely by direct appeal to knowledge from a variety of forms, scientific, philosophical, historical, etc. Beyond these forms of knowledge it requires no theoretical synthesis.

It is a necessary consequence of this characterization of the theory that its development depends crucially on the progress of scientific knowledge, philosophical work, etc., which is relevant to questions of educational practice. It is only by rigorous work within these forms, according to their own critical canons, that valid reasons can be brought to the formation of educational principles. If work or study in the theory is to be anything but superficial it must readily become differentiated out into the serious and systematic treatment of the relevant philosophical, sociological or historical questions that are raised. Given a particular educational problem, recognizing the philosophical or psychological issues it involves is by no means a simple matter. Nor given a great deal of philosophical or psychological understanding is it easy to see its bearing on educational questions. To discern where, and precisely how, a given discipline contributes to the

E

theory demands first a highly specialized knowledge of the discipline and the kind of problems with which it deals. It demands too the ability to see beneath the practical problems of education those underlying questions which this discipline alone can hope to answer. Philosophy of education must indeed be philosophy. Educational psychology must indeed be psychology. But as contributing to educational theory these and other specialisms aim at determining educational practice by providing the basic understanding on which rationally justified principles can be built. In the chapters which follow the authors seek to bring out what is distinctive in the approach of several different disciplines to educational questions. They are concerned, too, to indicate which areas and methods within the wider disciplines are most intimately related to fundamental issues in education and which are, therefore, the most appropriate for students to study. Yet although these are necessarily essays in the differentiation of knowledge and thought, as areas of understanding in general and as areas lying within educational theory there are certain relationships between these various domains which cannot, and must not, be overlooked. There can thus be found in some of the papers not only the particular characteristics of, say, philosophy of education and educational psychology, but some indication of how vitally interrelated these areas are.

Throughout this chapter educational theory has been regarded as a body of theory which issues in principles for practice. But principles are one thing, practice is another, and nothing whatever has been said of the relationship between them. The link has in fact to be forged by the making of particular judgments in individual cases according to the relevant principles and the facts of the situations. If it is the job of educational theorists to formulate the principles, it is certainly vital for educational practice that teachers and others who both take and implement individual decisions fully understand the principles and their bases. But they must in addition be equipped to adequately distinguish the features of the particular situations in which judgments have to be made. Granted all this, there remains the formation of the judgments themselves in a process which, for all its importance, is still little understood either logically or psychologically. It is not the function of this chapter to discuss the place of theory in the education and training of teachers. Comments on this occur in other parts of this volume, particularly in the last chapter, where the problems of teaching educational theory are discussed. This much, however, must be said, that whilst a serious study of the theory at the level of general principles is absolutely basic to enlightened practices, of itself this is a quite inadequate treatment for the intending teacher. The theory must be understood as stemming from practical problems and it must be continually brought to bear on particular complex issues. To divorce the theory from the particulars of practice, and to fail to develop the appropriate art of judgment, is to mislead students about the whole *raison d'être* of the theory and to fail to equip them to cope with the very questions they have to face. The analysis here undertaken has been concerned with the nature of theory and not with the making of particular judgments. It has, however, been specifically directed at clarifying the whole question in the light of the theory's practical function, and thus at providing a more adequate framework within which the particular questions of educational practice might be approached. If we can begin to understand more accurately than in the past the way in which such fundamental disciplines as history, psychology, sociology and philosophy can in fact contribute to the rational determination of educational practice, then there is serious hope that the study of education by intending teachers will in future bear much greater practical fruit. Just that has been the aim behind this chapter and indeed is the aim behind the whole of this volume.

NOTES

1. For a further statement and criticism of this view see H. W. Burns, The Logic of the 'Educational Implication', *Educational Theory*, Vol. XII, No. 1, 1962.

2. D. J. O'Connor, *An Introduction to the Philosophy of Education*, 1957, p. 4.
3. Ibid. p. 74.
4. Ibid. p. 75.
5. Ibid. p. 76.
6. Ibid. p. 110.
7. See the passage quoted earlier, ibid. p. 75.
8. See F. McMurray, 'Preface to an Autonomous Discipline of Education', *Educational Theory*, Vol. V, No. 3, 1955.
   This, and many other questions mentioned here, are discussed in: J. Walton and J. L. Kuethe (eds.), *The Discipline of Education*, 1963.
9. R. S. Peters, *Education as Initiation*, 1964; and included in R. D. Archambault, *Philosophical Analysis and Education*, 1965.
10. R. S. Peters, 'What is an Educational Process?' in R. S. Peters, *The Concept of Education*, 1966.

Chapter Three

THE PHILOSOPHY OF EDUCATION

R. S. PETERS

1. *What is philosophy?*

The limited role which Professor Hirst ascribes to philosophy in
his preceding chapter on the nature of educational theory is due
in part to the revolution in philosophy which has taken place
during this century. There was a time when the philosopher was
thought of in Platonic terms as 'the spectator of all time and all
existence'. It was not surprising, therefore, that he felt competent,
qua philosopher, to pronounce on matters to do with education and
politics as well as on God, freedom, and immortality. Nowadays
the philosopher feels competent, *qua* philosopher, only to tackle
limited questions about such topics, not to give voice to omnibus
pronouncements; for the main characteristic of the 'revolution in
philosophy' has been an increasing awareness of what philosophy is.

It is not that philosophers have suddenly begun to do something
startlingly different from what was done in former times by Plato,
Aristotle, Hume, and Kant; rather they have become more increasingly aware of what is distinctive of philosophical inquiries and
more cautious about making pronouncements on matters which
are not strictly philosophical in character. Nevertheless there is a
sense in which they are still spectators of all time and all existence,
in that they can have something to say, *qua* philosophers, about
almost any form of human activity. It is significant, for instance,
that Professor Hirst has conducted a philosophical inquiry to
show both the limits of philosophy and the place of other inquiries
such as psychology, sociology, and history in relation to the complex enterprise of education. What then is common both to the

old and new conception of philosophy which entitles philosophers to range about so widely as spectators?

The distinctive feature of philosophical inquiries, which accounts for the spectatorial role of the philosopher, is their second-order character, their concern with forms of thought and argument expressed in Socrates' questions, 'What do you mean?' and 'How do you know?', and Kant's questions about what is presupposed by our forms of thought and awareness. In asking such questions about concepts and about the grounds of knowledge, philosophers ponder upon and probe into manifold activities and forms of thought in which they and others already engage. There is thus a philosophy of law, politics, art, science, morals, and religion as well as logic, epistemology, and metaphysics which are concerned with questions of meaning, truth, and categories of thought at the most general level. This is what gives philosophical inquiries their second-order character, which is often caricatured by saying that they are concerned with talk about talk.

Philosophers are rightly compared to spectators in so far as they are concerned with questions which have a second-order character, but the comparison is not apt if it is taken to imply a passive or inert role. Hegel, for instance, thought that philosophers could only make explicit the principles and presuppositions of an age that was passing. But this is misleading in three respects. Firstly it ignores the very active role that philosophers have played in the development of differentiated forms of thought. In the seventeenth century, for instance, considerable progress was made in the differentiation of law from morals, and of morals from religion; in the eighteenth century science began to be clearly separated from mathematics and from metaphysics. Thus there developed the philosophy of law, morals, science, and religion; but philosophers were most active in demarcating these different forms of inquiry. They were the spearheads in this process of differentiation.

Secondly in doing this sort of work philosophers were not merely the prisoners of the presuppositions of their age. For by that time philosophy, though it was mixed up with other things, had achieved a fair degree of autonomy as a form of inquiry. Philosophers relied on distinctions and forms of argument which had a history going back to Plato and Aristotle. They were the inheritors of a tradition which had achieved an autonomous status in relation to the particular presuppositions of evolving societies. Nowadays philosophers can return to the work of Aristotle, Descartes, and Kant and learn much in the way of distinctions and forms of argument; they can refresh themselves from the sources of the tradition which they have inherited, as well as challenge some of the assumptions made by previous thinkers and the arguments which they deployed.

Thirdly philosophy is not inert in the sense that it involves merely making explicit what is implicit in forms of thought that have developed. Neither is it merely critical in the sense that it involves merely challenging such systems of thought. It can pass over into attempts to reconstruct conceptual schemes and think out anew the basic categories necessary for describing the world. For instance recent work done on concepts such as that of 'person' and 'action' is very positive in its endeavour to get clear about the family of concepts which we must have if we are to give an adequate account of human behaviour. Arguments and distinctions first formulated by Aristotle and Kant jostle with more recent ones developed by Wittgenstein. In brief, philosophy is both critical and constructive and, like science, represents an autonomous type of inquiry that is not imprisoned completely within the presuppositions of a particular period.

The main feature, then, of the recent 'revolution in philosophy' has been the explicit recognition of this second-order character of philosophical inquiries. For a time philosophers who formed the vanguard of this revolution concerned themselves both with attacking representatives of the old order and with re-examining central questions in logic, epistemology, metaphysics, and ethics in the light of reformulated theories of meaning and truth. They were, perhaps, somewhat cavalier in their attitude towards some of the more speculative and constructive thinkers of the past such as Whitehead, Hegel, and Bradley and they paid little attention to peripheral fields such as those of politics and art which are more deeply 'immersed in matter'. The climate of opinion has now changed. On the one hand philosophers are prepared to admit that there is much to be learnt from the old metaphysicians if what they were trying to do is distinguished from the somewhat slap-happy and obscure way in which they set about doing it; on the other hand many philosophers who have been brought up in 'the revolution' are now turning with sharper tools and a more precise understanding of what they are doing to problems in the philosophy of law, politics, psychology, social science, and art. They are also, at last, beginning to interest themselves again in problems of education.

When, however, philosophers turn their attention to the philosophy of education as a form of inquiry which is institutionalized in Colleges of Education and University Departments of Education, they are usually appalled at what they find. For it seems to them as if fossilized deposits have been left there of a bygone era, of a time when philosophy, as they understand it, had not been distinguished from general wisdom about life or from a record of the thoughts of great thinkers of the past. Before passing to a more positive account of what the philosophy of education ought to be, it will be as well, therefore, to give a brief description of what passes for it at the moment in most Colleges and Departments of Education.

2. Current conceptions of philosophy of education

There are, roughly speaking, three conceptions of philosophy of education which permeate such institutions, in addition to the conception of philosophy of education which will be later developed in this article.

(i) Principles of education
The first conception parallels the everyday notion of a 'philosophy

of life', which suggests deep probings into and ponderings on the meaning of life issuing in high-level directives for living. One often hears the question 'What is his philosophy of education?'. This type of question makes any professional philosopher wince; it is like asking him 'What is your logic of politics?' Nevertheless it is understandable, for the philosopher is both traditionally and etymologically the lover of wisdom. It is not surprising, there-fore, that reasonably sophisticated lecturers in institutions con-cerned with the education of teachers regard it as their function to dispense wisdom about education, usually called 'principles of education'. In most institutions of this sort it is usually recognized that there are distinct questions of an empirical sort falling under the differentiated disciplines of psychology, history, and sociology. Specialists are often appointed to deal with them. That leaves over residual questions of value which are thought to be the peculiar concern of the lecturer in 'principles of education'. His task is to enunciate values, not simply to ask limited questions of a philosophical sort about the meaning and justification of value judgments. Classics in this tradition are A. N. Whitehead's *The Aims of Education* (1929) and Sir Percy Nunn's *Education: Its Data and First Principles* (1920).

No one who knows anything about the training of teachers would dispute the need for wisdom about teaching which must be handed on by those who have practical experience. The best way of passing it on is, of course, in relation to the practical problems which teachers actually encounter during their teaching practice. There is also a place for the enunciation and discussion of general principles of teaching in a more abstract formalized way. But it is important to realize that the philosopher, *qua* philosopher, cannot formulate such principles, as Professor Hirst has already shown, any more than he can formulate principles of medicine or politics. Such principles are logical hybrids. They are distilla-tions of complex empirical generalizations and of value-judgments. So their validity will depend partly upon matters about which the philosopher is not an authority *qua* philosopher. Of course, because of his spectatorial standpoint, the philosopher is in a very good position to sift out the different strands of empirical fact and moral judgment which contribute to a principle such as 'Corporal punishment should not be used in schools' or 'Streaming is undesirable'. But he is not in a position, *qua* philosopher, to pronounce on the truth of such principles.

This does not mean, or course, that there is no place for principles of education in educational research or in the training of teachers. Quite the reverse; for teachers are trained, in the main, by being initiated into a tradition in which such principles are implicit and educational research should be concerned with providing the evidence and arguments which will enable such principles to be clarified, improved, and modified in the light of advancing knowledge and changing conditions. All it means is that the formulation, discussion, and passing on of such principles cannot be the peculiar function of the philosopher of education. This omnibus conception of his task is partly a relic of the old conception of the philosopher as a kind of oracle and partly due to an undifferentiated conception of educational studies which dies hard in some educational circles.

(ii) History of educational ideas

A second and more specific conception of the philosophy of education is to back up this dispensation of wisdom about education with snippets from what the great educators of the past have said about it. Most Colleges of Education have courses on what is more aptly described as the history of educational ideas, which take the student on a Cook's tour of thinkers from Plato to Dewey. Valiant attempts are made to relate these works to modern problems and to extract guidance from them. Plato's thought, for instance, is used as a launching pad for discussions about élites, indoctrination, and the use of fables; Rousseau's for animadversions about child-centred education and learning by experience.

Again no one would want to dispute the desirability of such courses. A teacher can scarcely be described as 'educated' if he has no awareness of the history of ideas about education and if he is unfamiliar with how the great thinkers of the past have thought about it. Such knowledge should be part of the heritage into which every teacher should be initiated. But such initiation should be regarded as supplementary to and not a substitute for the philosophy of education. The objections to regarding such courses as courses in the philosophy of education are twofold. In the first place the works dealt with are, strictly speaking, works in general theory of education which includes a mass of moralizing, and empirical generalizations as well as strictly philosophical inquiries. Plato's views on education, for instance, include all sorts of empirical generalizations about learning and child development, and it is usually these aspects of his thought rather than his theory of ideas, his conception of dialectic, and his analysis of knowledge which are singled out for attention. Similarly no one who knows any philosophy would rate Rousseau's *Émile* very highly as a piece of philosophical analysis or argument. But it is assuredly a classic in the history of educational ideas. Recently Kingsley Price has compiled and edited a book of Readings called *Education and Philosophical Thought* (1962) in which he has attempted to disentangle the different strands in the somewhat undifferentiated thought of these classical theorists and to single out the genuinely philosophical questions about education.

The second defect of this approach is that the ideas of the great thinkers are extracted from the text and applied to modern conditions without giving students any training in the form of thought which is necessary for the criticism of these ideas. Even historically speaking such an enterprise has its limitations; for most lecturers, who really understand something of the conditions under which Plato wrote his *Republic*, feel pretty uneasy about discussions which proceed under the aegis of Plato To-Day. But, philosophically speaking, such discussions are usually nugatory. The lecturers are usually historians by training and neither they nor their students have the training to discuss with much rigour the fundamental issues in ethics and epistemology which the thinkers of the past have raised. The question is whether, from the point of view of the philosophy of education, the best starting point for the discussion of such issues is in relation to works of the past or to contemporary educational issues. Could it be argued nowadays that courses in educational psychology should be based on the works of Locke, Mill, Herbart, Wundt, and Thorndike? If not why should it be assumed that courses in the philosophy of education should be based on the writings of the great educators such as Comenius, Locke, and Rousseau?

(iii) Philosophy and education

A third conception of the philosophy of education is one that derives from the determination to make such discussions philosophical in a strict sense. The traditional problems of pure philosophy are therefore presented to students and attempts are made to draw out their relevance to education. This conception has been prevalent mainly in American Colleges of Education where professors have been on the defensive and have attempted to demonstrate that they are as competent in the 'pure disciplines' as their rather supercilious critics in universities and liberal arts colleges. Realists, idealists, pragmatists, and existentialists have emerged and have attempted to examine the implications for education of their different philosophical positions, as in the N.S.S.E. 41st and 54th Yearbooks and in A. V. Judges Education and the Philosophic Mind (1957). An example of this approach by one trained in the 'revolution in philosophy' was D. J. O'Connor's lucid and provocative Introduction to the Philosophy of Education (1957). Surveys of such approaches can be found in H. Burns and C. Brauner, Philosophy of Education (1962). Needless to say this approach has led to a plethora of articles puzzling about what the relationship between philosophy and education might be. A similar phenomenon in the psychological field has been the attempt to approach educational psychology through the 'pure' gateway of classical theories of learning. In both cases the question of relevance has been a most pertinent one.

The defect of this third conception of the philosophy of education is the obverse of the former two conceptions. Whereas they are open to the criticism that they are both concerned, in different ways, with many matters that are not strictly philosophical, the third conception is open to the criticism that it is not concerned specifically enough with what is educational. It might be argued that in philosophy one cannot go very far without tackling fundamental issues in logic, epistemology, and metaphysics; so one might as well begin with the most general and most fundamental issues. This is dubious as a teaching method; for learning is more effective when it is related to the actual problems and interests of the learner. In matters of learning, as in many other spheres of life, everything has its proper time. If students are worried about problems to do with education, they are more likely to acquire the form of thought necessary to clarify their ideas if they are initiated into it in relation to their interests and worries rather than in a more abstract way. A parallel is the learning of statistics in psychology which presents itself as a great problem to students without mathematical training. Experience shows that they acquire the necessary techniques and form of thought much more readily if instruction goes hand in hand with the design of actual experiments rather than if they are introduced to it in a more abstract way. The same holds good for philosophy. The rudiments of ethics and of epistemology are much more readily acquired in relation to actual problems, such as those connected with punishment, equality, liberty and the nature of school subjects than in more abstract courses on ethics and theory of knowledge.

It is dubious also in relation to the actual structure of philosophical inquiries if its organization is looked at in terms of degrees of relevance to educational problems. Questions about the nature of space and time, about the reality of the external world, and about substance and personal identity are not so glaringly relevant to educational problems as are questions in ethics and theory of knowledge. A good parallel is that of political philosophy, in which there is a concentration on issues in ethics, epistemology, and the philosophy of mind, that are of particular relevance to political questions. The issues discussed, for instance, by Locke in his *Second Treatise* or by J. S. Mill in *On Liberty* are of more obvious relevance to politics than those discussed by Berkeley in his *Three Dialogues*. Of course, as philosophical probing proceeds, there may come a stage when the issues discussed by Berkeley may have to be faced. But they are reached by a route leading out from the centre provided by political problems, as can be seen in Plato's *Republic*. It is the same with education which provides a similar focus for philosophical problems. The philosophy of education is a family of philosophical inquiries linked together both by their philosophical character and by their relevance to educational issues. This relevance to education provides the point of entry which determines their selection from the general corpus of philosophical inquiry. The inquirer may be led, of course, by the logic of his probing into the most general problems of metaphysics and logic. But if he is, his route will be marked by a thread leading back to the centre. He may, of course, get lost in the delights of such abstract issues and become almost oblivious, like Theseus in Ariadne's arms, of the bull-ring from which he was lured. But he will never be beset by misgivings about the relevance of philosophy to education.

Perhaps Dewey is the best historical example of a philosopher of education who set about his task in the right sort of way. He was a philosopher of distinction who wrote voluminously about the general problems of philosophy. When, however, he turned his attention to the philosophy of education he started from educational issues and plunged into analyses and arguments in ethics and the philosophy of mind which were of obvious and immediate relevance. His thought was often obscure and when understandable, it may often seem mistaken. But most of the crucial issues in education were discussed in terms of his own more general theories. He set up the subject in the right sort of way. In Dewey's 'philosophy of education' there was no occasion

my approach.

for puzzlement about the relevance of philosophy to education. In this respect he exemplified his own theory of thinking as problem-solving.

3. *A new approach to the philosophy of education*

The pioneer in approaching educational issues from the standpoint of 'the revolution in philosophy' was undoubtedly C. D. Hardie in his *Truth and Fallacy in Educational Theory* which was first published in 1942, and later republished by the Bureau of Publications at Teachers' College, Columbia, in 1962, with a preface and bibliography by J. E. McClellan and P. Komisar. In this he employed tools of analysis fashioned mainly by G. E. Moore and C. D. Broad at Cambridge to criticize forms of argument used by educational theorists such as Pestalozzi, Herbart, and Dewey.

A surprising feature of Hardie's analysis was the limited consideration given to the concept of 'education' itself. This I attempted to rectify in my Inaugural Lecture at the University of London Institute of Education in 1963.[1] Whatever the merits of this analysis it does at least provide signposts to the central issues with which the philosophy of education must be concerned. Some of the paths indicated have already been trodden by philosophers who have dealt with the problems raised in a more general way and without any explicit concern for their relevance for education; others are as yet almost unexplored. In the rest of this article these signposts will be used to indicate what these main paths are. They can be conveniently related to more general subdivisions of philosophy which are already well established, namely philosophy of mind, ethics and social philosophy, and epistemology.

(*i*) *Education and the philosophy of mind*
In asking the basic philosophical question about 'education', the question 'What do we mean?', we plunge straight away into that branch of philosophy known as philosophical psychology or the

philosophy of mind. What has to be made explicit is not only what is implicit in the use of the general term 'education' but also the similarities and differences between the types of processes which belong to this family such as training, learning by experience, imitation, instruction, and teaching. A great deal of detailed work has been done by psychologists in testing empirical hypotheses about these matters, but, as yet, philosophers have done little on what Ryle calls the 'logical geography' of these concepts. The exception is Israel Scheffler's work on the concept of 'teaching' in his *The Language of Education* (1960) and one or two articles in the collection by B. O. Smith and R. Ennis called *Language and Concepts in Education* (1961). This was followed up at the University of London Institute of Education, with a series of public lectures on 'Processes in Education' an expanded form of which will soon be published under the title of *The Concept of Education*.

Behind all such analyses lies the crucial distinction between the logical and the psychological aspects of learning. The need for such a distinction is felt strongly by anyone who studies the work of psychologists such as J. Piaget and J. Bruner which are very relevant to education. For when one is talking about the development of thought and the learning of concepts, what are conceptual issues which can be decided by reflection on concepts such as 'learning', 'development', and 'thinking', and what are psychological issues which have to be settled by empirical investigation? A beginning towards clarifying such problems has been made by D. W. Hamlyn and P. H. Hirst in their articles in the forthcoming collection called *The Concept of Education* to which reference has been made above.

The same type of query arises when one considers the use by educational theorists of motivational concepts such as 'interest', 'need', and 'drive', which have been taken over from psychology. These concepts are cloudy ones in psychology and have become even cloudier when transplanted to educational theory. Philosophers have done quite a lot of work on such concepts,[2] but educational theorists have remained largely oblivious of their labours. They have gone their way in a state of mild euphoria, undisturbed by such radical probings. Educational theory abounds, too, in more unitary concepts such as those of 'character', 'personality', 'the whole person', and 'self-realization', which are also very much the concern of the philosophy of mind. Philosophers, dating back to John Locke, have done a lot of work on the concept of 'the person',[3] but have rather neglected more specific concepts such as those of 'character' and 'personality'.[4]

Returning to the analysis of the concept of 'education', the first point to make about it is that it is a highly general concept. Many misleading things have been said about it because of the failure to grasp what sort of concept it is. 'Education' is a concept like 'reform'; it picks out no particular process but rather it encapsulates criteria to which a family of processes must conform. The first is that something valuable should be transmitted in a morally unobjectionable manner. It is the task of the philosophy of mind to make explicit how this transmission of what is valuable is to be conceived. Traditionally it has been thought of after the model of production or of taking means to ends. These models have haunted and distorted thinking about education. A more adequate way of conceiving of it is in terms of a family of tasks relative to achievements. Failure to realize that 'ends' or standards are built into the notion of 'being educated' as an achievement has led people to search mistakenly for 'aims of education' which are extrinsic to it.[5] The question 'What is an aim?' and what could be meant by 'aims of education' is therefore a crucial one in this area of the philosophy of education.

In relation to the task aspect of education certain ways of proceeding would be ruled out on moral grounds. But what processes can be ruled out on conceptual grounds? Obviously conditioning in a strict sense is excluded on both grounds; not only is it morally objectionable, it is also inappropriate to regard it as a task on the part of the learner. It is not a process of learning in any strict sense. There are, too, other ways of picking things up, especially in transactions between persons, which cannot be represented as

F

tasks either on the part of teacher or learner, e.g. ways in which enthusiasm for a subject or style are acquired. Are these to be called processes of education? If not what criteria built into 'education' rule them out? Such issues are dealt with in many of the articles in the forthcoming *The Concept of Education*.

The task of philosophy in the sense of conceptual analysis is to make explicit criteria built into 'education'. But the obvious one that something of value must be passed on in a morally unobjectionable manner straightaway raises further questions; for this is but a formal requirement. The question is what is morally desirable and how do we know that it is? At this point the philosophy of mind, which is concerned basically with the question 'What do we mean?', must give way to the question 'How do we know?' as it arises in relation to moral judgments. We must therefore pass to ethics and social philosophy and sketch their relevance to educational issues.

(ii) Ethics and education

Questions of justification can arise in relation either to the achievement or in relation to the task aspect of education, to its matter as well as to its manner. Education consists largely of passing on activities and forms of thought and awareness that approximate to poetry rather than to push-pin, or to use a more modern contrast, to science rather than to shovehalfpenny. How can such preferences be justified? Surely this emphasis must rest on firmer grounds than on those of tradition, individual whim, or technological pressure? If so, what are they? Are Mill's arguments in his *Utilitarianism* for the justification of qualitatively superior types of activity any good? Are Moore's arguments for them in his *Principia Ethica* any better? If they cannot be justified by such naturalistic or intuitionist types of argument, how can they be justified? The school curriculum consists largely in such activities. A teacher is surely in an anomalous position if convincing reasons cannot be produced for them; for otherwise he would be the arch-priest of an irrational cult.

Questions of ethics are equally important in relation to its tasks or manner. One of the main contributions of the child-centred movement in education has been to emphasize procedural principles such as autonomy, liberty, and respect for persons as norms prescribing the manner of education. There is then the question of equality in education which is such a controversial issue in English education at the moment. How are these principles to be interpreted when they are applied to education and how are they to be justified? What about the ethics of punishment when dealing with children? What is the basis of the distinction between punishment and discipline? What is the proper role of authority in the educational situation?

The philosophical issues underlying these problems are, of course, dealt with in general works on ethics and social philosophy. Little, however, has been done by philosophers of education since John Dewey in his *Democracy and Education* (1916) and W. H. Kilpatrick in his *The Philosophy of Education* (1951) to apply such principles systematically to the school situation—and their works, though powerful and perceptive, owed little to the 'revolution in philosophy'. L. A. Reid's *Philosophy and Education* (1963) represents a welcome step in this direction. I myself, in my *Ethics and Education* (1966), have tried at least to provide signposts for more rigorous discussion in this sadly neglected area of the philosophy of education.

(iii) Epistemology and education

Built into the concept of 'education' as an achievement are also criteria to do with knowledge and understanding. We do not call a person educated who has simply mastered a skill, even though the skill be very worthwhile like that of moulding clay. For a man to be educated it is insufficient that he should possess merely a 'know-how' or knack. He must also know that certain things are the case. He must have developed some sort of conceptual scheme at least in the area in which he is skilled and must have organized a fair amount of knowledge by means of it. But this is not enough, for we would be disinclined to call a man who was merely well-informed an educated man. To be educated requires also some understanding of principles, of the 'reason why' of things.

But is even this enough? Could a man be educated whose knowledge and understanding is confined to one sphere—mathematics, for instance? There is a strong inclination to deny that we would call a man 'educated' who had only developed his awareness and understanding in such a limited way; for 'educated' suggests a more all round type of development. 'Education is of the whole man' might well be a conceptual truth in the sense that 'educated' rules out merely specialist training. People are trained *for* jobs, *as* mechanics, and *in* science. No one can be trained in a general sort of way. But this lack of specificity is just what is suggested by 'education'. It is not altogether clear, however, whether this is due to the concept of 'education' itself or to our refusal to grant that what is worthwhile could be confined to one form of awareness. 'Education is of the whole man' might therefore be an expression of our moral valuations about what is worthwhile rather than a purely conceptual truth.

Matters to do with this close-knit family of criteria built into 'education' as an achievement have received much more attention by modern philosophers of education than those to which ethics and the philosophy of mind are relevant; for they have been much more concerned with the application of epistemology to education than with the application of other branches of philosophy. There is first of all the general problem of the relation of a school or university curriculum to the development of mind. If the development of mind is marked by increasing differentiation into distinct forms of knowledge (e.g. scientific, mathematical, historical, moral) how is a curriculum to be conceived which will not end in the fragmentation of knowledge and specialization so deplored by advocates of 'liberal education'? What is 'liberal education' anyway? Is it a unitary concept? Does it demarcate a distinct form of education or is it mainly a concept whose function is to recommend the removal of typical restrictions on education which vary from age to age—e.g. confinement to specialisms, the harnessing of knowledge to utilitarian and vocational purposes and authoritarian methods of teaching? In the 1930s and 1940s in the U.S.A. a concept of 'liberal education' was promulgated at the University of Chicago by Robert Hutchins and Mortimer Adler (e.g. by Hutchins in *The Higher Learning in America* (1936) and by Adler in *How To Read A Book* (1940)). Their Aristotelian approach and point of view were bitterly and acutely attacked by Sidney Hook in his pungent *Education for Modern Man* (1948). A much abler and more sophisticated defence of classical realism and its implications for 'liberal education' was however put forward by H. S. Broudy in his *Building a Philosophy of Education* (1954).

Contributors to this debate in England have been C. P. Snow in his Rede Lecture entitled *The Two Cultures and the Scientific Revolution* (1959), F. R. Leavis in his *Two-Cultures? The Significance of C. P. Snow* (1961) and G. H. Bantock in his *Education in an Industrial Society* (1963). These issues have also been discussed by J. Maritain in his *Education at the Cross-Roads* (1943), by M. Oakeshott in his 'The Voice of Poetry in the Conversation of Mankind' in *Rationalism in Politics* (1962) and by P. H. Hirst in his 'Liberal Education and the Nature of Knowledge' printed in R. Archambault's collection of articles entitled *Philosophical Analysis and Education* (1965), which is shortly to appear expanded into a book in this series called *Philosophical Foundations of the Curriculum*. There have also appeared recently two important books on the general philosophical basis of the curriculum. There is one by H. S. Broudy, B. O. Smith and J. R. Burnett entitled *Democracy and Excellence in American Secondary Education* (1964) which examines the curriculum from the point of view of the American conviction that it must be of some 'use'. The other is P. H. Phenix's *Realms of Meaning* (1964), which raises wider questions in epistemology.

The problem of curriculum construction also raises questions about the nature of school subjects. Is there any logical basis for the organization of the curriculum or is it the product of historical accident? The relationship of school subjects to forms of knowledge opens up again the distinction between the logical and psychological aspects of learning referred to above in the context of the philosophy of mind.

In addition to general problems about the curriculum there are also, of course, even more general problems about 'knowledge' as distinct from 'belief' and more specific problems relating to the particular forms of knowledge into which students are to be initiated in schools and universities. These problems have been discussed exhaustively ever since philosophy began; indeed, as was indicated above, philosophy has been one of the most potent catalysts in the differentiation of forms of knowledge.

Not a great deal of work, however, has been done in exploring the implications for education of these philosophical distinctions. For instance no one has worked out in any detail the implications for scientific education of K. R. Popper's brilliant account of scientific method in his *The Logic of Scientific Discovery* (English Ed. 1959). An exception is W. H. Burston's *Principles of History Teaching* (1963) which bases recommendations for the teaching of history on an examination of current views of historical explanation developed by philosophers such as Walsh, Dray, and Popper. There has also been a certain amount of work done on moral education based on an examination of the characteristics of moral knowledge. Examples are W. Frankena's article called 'Towards a Philosophy of Moral Education' in the *Harvard Educational Review* of 1958, my own article on 'The Paradox of Moral Education' in W. R. Niblett's collection of articles entitled *Moral Education in a Changing Society* (1963), and Oakeshott's famous Inaugural Lecture on 'Political Education' reprinted in his *Rationalism in Politics* (1962). Other pieces of work in this field have been collected together by Israel Scheffler in his book of modern readings called *Philosophy and Education* (1958). In the field of epistemology and logic generally Israel Scheffler's work has had a wide influence amongst the younger generation of philosophers of education in the U.S.A. It is to be hoped that his *Conditions of Knowledge* (1965) will prove a definitive starting point for those who wish to explore in a more rigorous way the relevance for education of recent work done on more general problems of logic and epistemology.

The one form of knowledge about whose relationship to education philosophers of education have not been at all reticent in recent times is that of philosophy itself. It is a normal preoccupation amongst philosophers, especially since the 'revolution in philosophy', to brood upon the nature of philosophy, though it can degenerate into almost an occupational disease. It is not surprising, therefore, that philosophers of education should be susceptible to it. The first part of H. Burns' and C. Brauner's *Philosophy of Education* (1962) is devoted to this topic. This includes an outstanding article by Kingsley Price, written from the analytical point of view, on 'What Is a Philosophy of Education?'

'Educational theory' is notoriously as cloudy a concept as 'political theory'. When, therefore, the question is asked what part philosophy of education can play in educational theory vast vistas are opened up for discussion. The issues involved are often raised by the question 'Is education a discipline?' which was discussed exhaustively at a conference at Johns Hopkins University in 1961, issuing in a collection of papers edited by John Walton and James Kuethe entitled *The Discipline of Education* (1963). A more or less definitive article on 'Philosophy and Educational Theory' by P. H. Hirst is to be found in the November 1963 issue of the *British Journal of Educational Studies*, in which a lucid analysis is given both of the nature of educational theory and of the part played by the philosophy of education in it. Professor Hirst's preceding article in this book includes his further reflections on this topic and is a clear-cut and concise statement of the view of educational theory which permeates both this book and the series of monographs which it introduces. It represents very well the spectatorial stance of the philosopher in commenting not only about the nature of educational theory but also about the nature of philosophy itself and the role which it plays as part of educational theory. And so we return to the point from which this article started.

4. *The 'use' of philosophy of education*

The question is often asked 'What is the use of philosophy?' The most fundamental way of dealing with this question is to challenge the unarticulated presuppositions about 'use' which underlie it. Such a challenge might proceed in the following way:

QUESTIONER: So you are a budding philosopher are you! Please tell me what use there is in studying philosophy.

PHILOSOPHER: I am not quite sure what sense of 'use' you are employing. Are you asking me whether philosophy has a use in the sense in which, shall we say, engineering has a use?

QUESTIONER: Yes; that is the sort of thing that I mean. Engineering enables us to build roads, houses, and hospitals. Surely philosophy is pretty useless when compared with something like that.

PHILOSOPHER: Perhaps. But let us pursue this matter a bit further. Engineering, you say, is useful because it enables us to build houses, to warm them properly, to provide drains for them and so on. But what use is that? What are houses for?

QUESTIONER: To live in, of course, with some kind of comfort. Surely even philosophers do that nowadays!

PHILOSOPHER: And by 'live' you don't mean just keeping your heart beating, or taking in nutriment and getting rid of it as waste-products?

QUESTIONER: Of course I don't. I mean enjoying life as well.

PHILOSOPHER: By doing what? Playing Bingo? Making love to your wife? Discussing Plato's views about love with her. . . ?

QUESTIONER: Oh don't be ridiculous! You know what I mean! Doing what everyone else does in their houses. . . .

PHILOSOPHER: But people do different things and perhaps some things are more worth doing than others. All really worth-while things are absolutely useless in your sense of 'use'. For things which are useful in your sense are only so because they make possible things like philosophy, art, and literature, which also have the function of transforming how things which are 'useful' in your sense are conceived.

QUESTIONER: Tell that to Lord Bowden!!

The point of constructing this little Socratic dialogue is to exhibit the logical incompleteness of questions about 'use'. As they raise questions of instrumentality, of means to ends, anyone asking them must make explicit the end he has in view in relation to which something is useful. Once this form of questioning begins it cannot end until something is arrived at which is to be regarded as valuable in itself and not just as a means to something else that is thought valuable. Philosophy, art, and science are forms of activity which are worthwhile in themselves; they are part and parcel of a form of life which we think desirable. It is absurd, therefore, to expect the same sort of justification of them as is to be given for activities like boarding buses or building banks.

This then is the most radical way of dealing with the question 'What is the use?' when asked about philosophy—or about psychology, sociology, history, or any other form of inquiry. It should not be thought, however, that studying such 'subjects' is a means to the good life; it is more aptly described as an initiation into it. Such forms of thought involve the explanation, evaluation, and imaginative exploration of forms of life. As a result of them what is called 'life' develops different dimensions. In schools and universities there is concentration on the development of these determinants of our form of life. The problem of the educator is to initiate others into these forms of thought and awareness so that they take root in the minds of others and gradually transform the world and hence how they feel about it. The process is a long one which can only be set in motion in such special institutions. Those, for instance, who begin to think in these ways if they study philosophy, literature, history, psychology, and sociology in Colleges of Education will gradually have their view of children, schools, and subjects transformed. They ~~will come to think more~~ clearly and sensitively about what they are doing and will be clearer about what the justification is for their activities; they will understand children and themselves a little better and the social and historical conditions which provide the backcloth to their lives.

It might be said that this shows that the philosophy of education has an obvious 'use'; for it enables people to go about their business in a more clear-headed way and to expend less energy and time on muddling around with their minds clogged by cotton wool. It will make them critical of clichés and insistent on reasons being produced for policies which they are required to implement in schools. Furthermore it might be said that this clear-headed and critical outlook is essential for citizenship in a democratic community.

All this is true—but only in a limited sense and for two reasons. Firstly philosophy is not useful in any straightforward instrumental sense. It cannot be, as it were, fed in for the production of any particular end or the implementation of any particular policy. It is doubtful, as a matter of fact, whether even an empirical science such as psychology has much widespread use in schools in this limited sense of 'use'. For education is not a technology like medicine or engineering. Secondly it is not the case that the qualities of mind such as clear-headedness and a critical attitude, which are developed by philosophy, are just means to the democratic way of life; they are constitutive of it. It is not so much that philosophy is 'useful' in the development of democracy as a way of life; it is rather that this way of life cannot be characterized without reference to the qualities of mind which are immanent in philosophical thinking.

Philosophy, as has been argued by Professor Hirst, is an integral part of educational theory. To explicate the sense in which it is 'useful' to educators is therefore really to explicate the way in which theory is related to practice in the field of education. To question its 'use' is really to question the 'use' of educational theory as a whole of which philosophy forms an essential part.

prenticeship system

Under the conditions in which the modern teacher has to operate this is not a real issue. There was a time, I suppose, when the view was defensible that teachers could pick up their art entirely on an apprenticeship system from experienced practitioners on the job. Education had relatively agreed aims; procedures were more or less standardized; few fundamental questions were raised about principles underlying school organization, class management and the curriculum; the general standards of the community, which they were meant to pass on in training the character of children, were relatively stable; and little was known about the psychology of children and the social conditions under which they lived which transcended common sense and common-room conversation. Teachers were gradually initiated into the tradition of teaching. And what happened, of course, was that teachers handed on the matter which they had acquired from their teachers in the manner in which they had acquired it. There is an astonishing similarity, for instance, between how the classics were taught right up to the nineteenth century and how they were taught in ancient Rome. Teaching methods perpetuated themselves in the same sort of way as child-rearing practices in the family.

The importance of this learning on the job under skilled direction must not be minimized. Indeed I think all would agree that it must be the lynch-pin of any system of training, but there is no need to expatiate on its limitations as a sufficient type of training under modern conditions. The point is that nowadays just about none of the conditions obtain which provided the milieu in which the old apprenticeship system was viable. Education no longer has agreed aims; procedures are constantly under discussion and vary according to different people's conceptions of the subjects which they are teaching; fundamental questions concerned with principles underlying school organization, class management and the curriculum are constantly being raised; and in the area of moral education the task is made more perplexing by the variations of standards which characterize a highly differentiated society. The question therefore is not whether a modern teacher indulges in philosophical reflection about what he is doing; it is rather whether he does it in a sloppy or in a rigorous manner.

Similarly our knowledge about the psychology of children and about the historical and social conditions which affect their behaviour and the organization of schools has vastly increased. There may be two—or more than two—opinions about how much has been definitely established in these areas. But there can be no two opinions about the extent to which work in these areas has developed and percolated through to people at all levels in society. The teacher can no longer rely on experience, common sense, and common-room conversation about such matters if he is going to hold his own against vociferous and intelligent parents and against every type of 'expert' who is advising him what should be done with children. A working knowledge of these sciences of man is becoming as essential to a teacher as a knowledge of anatomy and physiology is to a doctor. Education is becoming increasingly a matter of public concern and public scrutiny. Unless teachers are well versed in these sciences which are ancillary to their task there is little hope of their establishing for themselves a profession which can retain some kind of authority in the community. Again the question is not whether the teacher has opinions on psychological, sociological, or historical matters; for any educated person has these. It is rather whether he can defend his opinions in an informed and intelligent way so that he can hold his own in the welter of public discussion. The simple truth, in other words, is that the teacher has to learn to think for himself about what he is doing. He can no longer rely on an established tradition.

Many would admit the necessity for such knowledge but would equate it with the product of 'educational research' conceived of narrowly as the building up of a body of empirical knowledge in the spheres of psychology, sociology, and economics. This, of course, must be done; but it is not sufficient, for reasons which anyone can supply who has understood this article and Professor Hirst's paper. In the first place educational judgments necessarily involve judgments of value and these cannot be settled by answering empirical questions alone. We may be able to find out empirically, for instance, why some children steal or what are the probable consequences to an individual of punishing him in a certain way. But the justification of punishment does not depend solely on its effects on offenders. Such questions of justification cannot be settled either by simple appeals to feeling, 'intuition', or 'decision'. Complex and difficult questions in ethical theory are raised as soon as anyone asks this type of question in a determined way. They cannot be satisfactorily answered without a good deal of hard, clear thinking of a philosophical kind.

In the second place research cannot begin until the conceptual issues involved have been sorted out. In the sphere of moral education, for instance, research is likely to be pretty unilluminating until the different meanings of 'moral' have been distinguished clearly together with the different elements involved in the moral life—e.g. knowledge of rules, grasp of underlying principles, ability to apply rules intelligently, strength of character in sticking to rules, and so on. This preliminary clarification is philosophical in character.

Thirdly controversies about policy, which still float in regions where research has not yet penetrated, often continue at this level for lack of conceptual clarity. How, for instance, can issues to do with religious education in schools be tackled unless a sustained attempt has been made to tackle difficult issues concerning the status of religious awareness and its relation to morality? Did not the Snow–Leavis debate rest on fundamental confusions about the status of moral knowledge in relation to science and literary appreciation? And is not the thinking of government reports—e.g. Hadow, Crowther, Robbins, and Newsom—vitiated by the most appalling confusions and cloudiness about educational aims? Clarity, like patriotism, may not be enough; but it is certainly a necessary preliminary for tackling any problem in educational theory. Philosophy is not, as was once thought, sufficient for determining questions of educational policy; but it certainly is necessary. This article has attempted to sketch what the philosophy of education is and to demonstrate both that and how it is a necessary part of educational theory.

5. *The teaching of philosophy of education*

It is one thing to sketch in outline what the philosophy of education is; it is quite another to decide how it should be taught in colleges and departments of education. There is little problem about teaching it as part of an advanced course; for students will by that time be more mature. They will have had plenty of experience to which theory can be related and they will need little convincing of the necessity for a good theoretical foundation to educational practice; for presumably that is one of their reasons for embarking on an advanced course. With prospective teachers undergoing a course of initial training the situation is very different. For philosophy has to be taught in such a way that it gradually transforms their outlook and manner of approach to educational problems. It would be most unfortunate if, in a genuine attempt to get rid of clichés and woolliness of thought, formalized courses were introduced which dealt with matters beyond the interest and experience of students who simply swotted up a 'subject' in order to pass an examination.

In order to avoid the danger of philosophy becoming a corpus of inert ideas it must arise naturally from the student's developing experience in training. Philosophical questions must gradually be differentiated out from the practical and personal problems encountered in schools. These problems—e.g., those of discipline, teaching methods, and the organization of the school—have psychological and social aspects as well. It would be desirable, therefore, if the different forms of thinking which contribute to educational theory could be differentiated out gradually in relation to a common corpus of practical problems. Gradually, as the student develops in maturity and begins to get accustomed to the different ways of thinking about these problems, he or she will be able to go deeper into the contributing disciplines and will be ready for more formal courses in them. For there comes a time when what Whitehead calls 'the stage of precision' is reached. It is one thing to develop an interest in problems and to begin to grasp what the problems are; but it is quite another thing to develop the mental apparatus necessary for tackling them with clarity and precision. This takes a very long time and only a beginning can be made with it in Initial Training. It is hoped that with the coming of the B.Ed. students will be able, in their fourth year, to develop some precision of thought in at least one of the disciplines which contribute to educational theory.

There are thus at least three principles underlying the teaching of philosophy or any other branch of educational theory at the level of initial training:

(i) relevance to practical problems and interests of teachers in training;
(ii) possibility of linking with other disciplines;
(iii) desirability of leading on to fundamental problems in philosophy itself.

(i) Let us start with the first principle. There are bound to be differences here according to the age range of the children whom the teacher is being trained to teach. Discipline and problems to do with the nature of school subjects, for instance, tend to much more live issues for secondary than for primary teachers, whereas an emphasis on the needs and interests of children and the collection of philosophical issues to do with 'child-centred' education is much more apposite at the primary level. With all classes of teachers in initial training, the following topics usually get a lively response:

(a) What is 'education'? What should be its aims? What is the teacher meant to be doing *qua* teacher? How is education different from training? How can civilized activities such as science and poetry be justified?

(*b*) Problems to do with the authority of the teacher.

(*c*) The ethics of punishment and discipline.

(*d*) The content of 'child-centred' education, together with notions such as learning from experience, and gearing the curriculum to the needs and interests of children.

(*e*) Freedom—of the child and of the teacher.

(*f*) Equality in education.

(*g*) Moral education.

(ii) In relation to the second principle—all the topics mentioned above are excellent ones for linking with psychology and sociology. In dealing with equality, for instance, the analysis and justification of 'equality' as a principle can be excellently illuminated by sociological facts about social class and social mobility and by psychological investigations of the determinants of intelligence and aptitude, streaming, and linguistic ability.

I would like to insert a special plea here for the importance of philosophy in this co-ordinated approach. Students are often brought up on too one-sided a diet purveyed by those with predominantly psychological interests. The result is that they can come to feel guilty about using their common sense. A director of an Institute of Education once initiated a discussion with some third years at a Training College by asking them the following question: 'If you were taking a class which was beginning to get out of hand because of the disruptive influence of a rebellious boy, which thoughts would come into your minds: "How can I restore the rule of law in this class?" or "I wonder what that boy's home background is".' They answered: 'The first sorts of thoughts, but we would feel *guilty* about it; for all we learn at college is to do with the second sorts of thoughts!' One need not delve very deeply into the complexities of 'authority' and 'punishment' to realize that these teachers had been brought up on a one-sided diet! They lacked an adequate rationale for what they were doing. Similarly one often comes across disillusioned primary teachers who have been nurtured rather delicately by psychologically oriented lecturers in the ideology of activity methods, who have found themselves in tough situations where they simply could not apply them. They were at a loss what to do and developed a hard-bitten contempt for those who trained them. What they lacked was the rationale underlying such methods which would permit intelligent adaptation to diverse circumstances. They lacked what Aristotle called an understanding of 'the reasons why' of things. Perhaps, too, they were brought up on a widely prevalent but quite unrealistic model of an educational situation which envisages one teacher dealing with one child!

(iii) From the point of view of the third criterion some topics are far better than others. The ethics of punishment, for instance, or 'equality' provide excellent avenues into the fundamental issues of moral philosophy; the analysis of 'education' itself is an excellent introduction to conceptual analysis and leads readily into ethical issues to do with the justification of what is worth handing on. But it may well be that other topics satisfy the other two principles better. At this level of teaching the philosophy of education there is a constant tension between attempting to illuminate and clarify concrete issues so that teachers can go about their business in a more clear-headed way, and drawing them deeper into the discipline so that they can begin to develop a distinctive form of thought which will entail a more rigorous overhaul of their fundamental beliefs and ideals. The effectiveness of teaching philosophy at this level will be revealed both in the autonomy and critical experimental attitude which teachers begin to show in the later stages of teaching practice, as well as in their desire to return to the philosophy of education in a more rigorous way when they are established as teachers.

For such a concept of philosophy of education to be implemented, there must be much more cross-fertilization between philosophy and educational studies. On the one hand some of those who have been trained in 'the revolution in philosophy' must apply themselves seriously to the concepts and arguments

G

which are bandied about in educational theory. A step in this direction has been taken by getting five professors of philosophy to contribute to the series of public lectures at the University of London Institute of Education already referred to, which will be published shortly under the title of *The Concept of Education*. On the other hand some lecturers or potential lecturers in education must spend a few years acquiring a philosophical training so that they can tackle problems with which they are only too familiar with more rigour than has been exhibited in the past. A welcome move in this direction has been the recent decision of the Department of Education and Science to second lecturers from Colleges of Education to do a special one-year course in philosophy of education at the University of London Institute. It is hoped also that the series of monographs in philosophy of education which is to succeed this present volume will provide some help in cementing the marriage from which this volume has sprung.

Plato once argued that society could only be saved if either philosophers became kings or kings became philosophers. This was somewhat dangerous and pretentious advice at the political level; but it has point if it is applied to the kind of co-operation which is necessary between educationalists and philosophers in ploughing the uncultivated field of the philosophy of education. A concrete beginning towards such co-operation has been made recently with the founding of the Philosophy of Education Society of Great Britain in December 1964, which already includes amongst its members many professional philosophers as well as educationalists. Such co-operation, of course, will not unearth the philosopher's stone; but it may help to clear away some of the rubble which has prevented many clear-cut furrows being driven through this field in the past.

NOTES

1. R. S. Peters, *Education as Initiation*, 1964.
2. Examples: G. Ryle, *The Concept of Mind*, 1949; R. S. Peters,

The Concept of Motivation, 1958; A. Kenny, *Action, Emotion and Will*, 1963.

3. For recent works see P. Strawson, *Individuals*, 1951 and S. Shoemaker, *Self-knowledge and Self-Identity*, 1964.

4. See, however, R. S. Peters, 'Moral Education and the Psychology of Character' in *Philosophy*, Vol. xxxvii, January 1962.

5. See R. S. Peters, *Education as Initiation*, op. cit., and 'What is an Educational Process?' in *The Concept of Education* (ed. Peters), 1966, or 1967.

Chapter Four

THE HISTORY OF EDUCATION

BRIAN SIMON

[1]

There is no need to make out a case for the study of the history of education as an essential aspect of the course offered to intending teachers. It has long been accepted as such in most colleges and universities and is almost universally taught, in its own right, as part of the education course. There is, however, considerable room for discussion about what is taught. It may well be that this subject could be better treated if it were more closely related to other educational studies and that in this way the real objective of historical study could be more fully realized.

It is the present tendency to review the past development of the English educational system, and of particular institutions within it, as if this took place by its own momentum rather than in relation to changing social pressures and needs. As a result, what is likely to emerge is a somewhat indigestible mass of dates and facts, orders and Acts. This is all the more likely in that educational ideas are usually treated separately as if they belonged to a separate world. To approach the matter in this way, it may be argued, is to miss the whole point of historical study.

Education is a social function, and one of primary importance in every society. It should be one of the main tasks of historical study to trace the development of education in this sense, to try to assess the function it has fulfilled at different stages of social development and so to reach a deeper understanding of the function it fulfils today. Not only have educational institutions been socially conditioned, but also the body of educational theory which lies behind the practical day to day business of teaching and school organization. This too has developed, not in isolation, but in dependence upon the practical possibilities for education, the demand for it at different times from various sections of the community for various ends. It is necessary and important, therefore, to consider educational development as a whole, and not to relegate institutions and ideas to separate categories.

The historical approach should bring educational developments into perspective, and in so doing open the teacher's eyes to the real nature of his work. It is the most difficult thing in the world to view *objectively* a system in which one is immediately involved. Historical study can be a powerful means to this end. It enables the student to understand that educational 'principles' contain historical components, some of which may no longer be relevant—or, in the light of advancing knowledge, viable—and which are, therefore, open to reconsideration. The same applies to institutions which have often been changed in the past and will certainly be changed in the future. There is, perhaps, no more liberating influence than the knowledge that things have not always been as they are and need not remain so.

It is with the study of education as a social function, then, that historical study should be primarily concerned. But while it is clear that education has changed as society itself has changed—many examples from the nineteenth century spring to mind—it is also clear that these changes have often been slow, or only very partially accomplished. To recognize this, and inquire further into the matter, is to come up against the fact that society has not always been united in its educational demands, that the impulse for reform often comes from only one section while it is in the interests of another to maintain the *status quo*. It is often a great deal easier to keep things as they are than to change them, and here tradition makes its weight felt.

The older established schools and colleges tend to lay great emphasis on their traditions and these may have some very positive aspects. But the appeal to tradition can also be suspect, a matter of unexamined assumptions rather than based on solid historical fact. For instance, it has been argued that English grammar schools have traditionally been concerned with the clever child and have, in this sense, made a valuable contribution to English life through the centuries. But the briefest acquaintance with educational history is sufficient to question both these claims. No institutions stagnated more painfully in the late eighteenth and nineteenth centuries than the endowed grammar schools up to the time when they were rescued and set on a new footing by the Endowed School (and later the Charity) Commissioners. It is only since the Education Act of 1944, which provided for the abolition of fees, that entrance to many of these schools has been solely by selective examination. This is not to pass any judgment on their present effectiveness.

Mention of the selection examination at eleven-plus, and its relatively recent origin, brings to notice another major advantage of historical study, that it encourages a sceptical approach to ideas which may simply rationalise existing practice. It is a tendency among educationists, psychologists and philosophers of all ages, to advance theories as if these represented not the *present* level of social development, or of knowledge deriving from inquiries of various kinds, but ultimate, proven truths. The trend continues even in a scientific age. No theory was advanced with more certainty, for example, than that 'intelligence' is a fixed quality of the mind which can be measured accurately by means of intelligence tests. Psychologists no longer adhere to this theory; as knowledge has increased it has been replaced by others much less sweeping and more tentative. But the idea still lingers on in the schools, in the minds of many teachers, with immediate effect on their attitudes to children and methods of teaching. To study the history of education attentively, to discover just how and why the division between primary and secondary education became fixed at the age of eleven, to trace the course of development from the 'scholarship' examination first introduced in the 1890s to the eleven-plus of the post-1944 years, is to become aware that the main factors at work were often political and economic rather than educational and psychological. Awareness of this

necessarily implies a critical approach to educational and psychological arguments advanced in support of this procedure long
after it became established. There is the less tendency to accept
such theories unquestioningly, only to face the painful process of
growing out of them with all that this implies in terms of entering
on an educational *cul-de-sac*.

One of the most enlightened educationists of recent times, the
late Sir Fred Clarke, one-time director of the University of London
Institute of Education, laid great stress on the need for 'critical
self-awareness' in teachers and the place of historical study in
promoting this kind of outlook. In *Education and Social Change*
(1940) he argued that to live unquestioningly in the immediate
present is to run the danger of developing a conditioned response
to current practice: a set of attitudes unconsciously determined
rather than consciously formed. The teacher in a particular type
of school which goes about the business of education in a particular
way, comes to believe that this procedure—and only this—is
education. Faced with the suggestion that other methods might be
possible and desirable he reacts not with interest and inquiries
but impatience and annoyance. A recent example (1962) is the
response by teachers in junior schools, in which children are
streamed into A, B, C classes, to an inquiry as to whether it might
not be better educationally to abolish streaming.[1] Many answers
were given with an absolute assurance, as if it were ridiculous
(or, as one teacher said, 'the height of professional irresponsibility')
to entertain the idea of such a change. At the same time it seems
clear that these teachers were unaware that streaming in junior
schools was only generally introduced some thirty years ago, when
a change to this practice took place. Nor did they know that this
procedure is almost unique to England. Knowledge of either of
these facts could have made the difference between an open or a
closed mind.

Here it may be noted that comparative study of the educational
systems of different countries is an important adjunct to historical
study in the sense that has been outlined. The intrinsic interest

of learning about other practices apart, this brings home the fact that educational development is not a preordained process which must follow particular lines, as in England, but that there is a great variety of possible lines of development. There are, indeed, examples on our doorstep in the school systems of Wales, and particularly Scotland, though all too little use has been made of them. Even more illuminating, perhaps, is study of the part played by education in societies of different levels of social development, particularly primitive societies of various kinds but also those more advanced. Such anthropological study brings out most strikingly differences in the role of education—of the family, peer groups, institutions—and can, therefore, fulfil the same educative or liberating function as comparative or historical studies.

Clarke looked at English education—in particular, social and educational distinctions between different kinds of school which have so often been taken for granted—with the sceptical eye of one who had spent twenty-five years in the Dominions. He noted that writers on the subject 'show little explicit awareness of the social presuppositions of their thought', pointing out that while 'highly generalized principles' of education figure largely in the textbooks, as the supposed determinants of educational practice, in fact both thought and practice 'are much more closely conditioned by social realities which are themselves the result of historical and economic forces'. This led him to insist on a new function for the educational historian, that of unravelling the social and historical influences which have played so potent a part in shaping both the schools and what is taught inside them; and, most important, of distinguishing the genuine educational theory from the rationalization which seeks to explain away rather than elucidate.

Seen in this light, the history of education takes on a new aspect, as a vital contribution to social history—rather than a flat record of acts and ordinances, punctuated by accounts of the theories of great educators who entertained ideas 'in advance of their time'. Consideration of the social origins of these ideas brings to light the elements in society ready for change at different times, and leads on to inquiry into why changes of a particular kind were needed, what assisted or prevented their realization, what compromises were made, break-throughs achieved, and with what effect. In the same way, to study legislation in its origin and development is to understand much more fully what this represented or failed to achieve. The 1870 Education Act, the Act of 1902, did not spring readymade from the mind of a Forster or a Balfour but were the products of much controversy, the balancing of forces representing sectional interests, general political considerations and the like. If these acts have had a powerful effect in shaping the educational system, it cannot be accepted that the shaping has been solely in accordance with educational considerations; to see this is also to get a clearer view of what remains to be done and how to go about it.

The educational system is not, of course, merely an institution to be studied for its own sake—so many nursery, elementary, secondary schools, so many special services, colleges of various kinds which have come into being in a variety of ways. Education is, by its very nature, concerned with the formation of men. 'He who undertakes the education of a child undertakes the most important duty of society', wrote Thomas Day, author of the famous eighteenth-century treatise *Sandford and Merton*. He was writing at a time when the family took a far greater part in education than it now does and outlined a course of upbringing designed to develop the qualities he esteemed most highly, both in terms of the kind of knowledge to be acquired and traits of character. Many past reformers have epitomized their educational aims in this way, and the procession of models through the centuries tells us much about changing social and educational values—the medieval scholar, the Renaissance gentleman combining classical learning with active skills, the seventeeth-century virtuoso and amateur of science, through Locke, Chesterfield and others to the modern age. If the models come predominantly from the upper classes, there are interesting contradictions and variations even within this range. Just as, in the early seventeenth century,

Peacham's *Complete Gentleman* was more polished and less puritan than Braithwaite's *English Gentleman*, so in the nineteenth century Thomas Arnold's ideal of the Christian gentleman combining 'godliness and good learning' gives place to the Kingsley-Maurice ideal of 'manliness'. This brings a spotlight to bear on differences between the 'public' school ethos of 1830 and that of 1880, for if ever schools set out to form their pupils, it was the public schools of this age.

This raises yet another point of great importance, the relation between educational aims and educational achievement. The body of theory with which the educationist operates is often anything but clearly organized and adequately validated, in the sense that other disciplines represent an ordered body of knowledge. But he has got a means of testing the viability of his ideas in terms of the end product of teaching. To return to the example of the late Victorian public school is to find that this did, to a noteworthy extent, successfully form its pupils according to the model desired. Whether or not the model was desirable, in social terms, is another matter, irrelevant in this connection. The point to be made is that education, as a social function, can be judged by its fruits, and often has been down the years. Today education draws much more than in the past on psychology and sociology for methods and theories and gains very much in the process. Not, perhaps, until psychology becomes a fully fledged science can education have a sound scientific basis—a goal towards which educational reformers of the modern age have looked, as history shows. But if this goal is to be reached there must be insistence, despite the debt to other disciplines, that education itself is a viable field of study going beyond all these, and so having its own points of reference. In other words, the present position of educational studies in this country must be seen as only a stage in the historical process.

These are some general examples of ways in which the historical approach can assist the study of education. If the emphasis has been on the practical applications of this study it is because the teacher in training is not a student of history but of the history of *education*. 'Truth as founded upon knowledge is like a mountain peak accessible from many sides', wrote Foster Watson, one of the pioneers of the historical study of education, 'and he knows the mountain best who has ascended it from many starting points'.[2] As is argued elsewhere in this volume, education now makes use of many disciplines, of philosophy, as well as psychology, and sociology. History introduces an extra dimension which helps to bring all these into focus. It has, therefore, a vital coordinating role, the more necessary now that philosophy has abandoned its former generalizing function to concentrate on logical and conceptual analysis. At the same time it is one of the main functions of historical study to foster objectivity of mind, that 'critical self-awareness' which is the mark of the teacher who is both knowledgeable and ready to extend his knowledge and develop his practice. This is the educational justification for its place in the intending teacher's course.

[11]

In criticizing English social blindness and outlining a fresh approach to the historical study of education, Clarke provided some apt practical examples and suggestions. In the Report of the Consultative Committee to the Board of Education on secondary education published in 1938 (the Spens Report) there is no mention whatsoever of the public schools. This in itself is surprising enough, once thought is given to the matter. Still more astonishing to Clarke was the fact that no one remarked on the omission; it was regarded as entirely natural that an official committee investigating secondary education should leave out of account the only schools which, on their own estimation, are peculiarly national in character, the best fruits of British genius in education. This example is cited to illustrate how far it is taken for granted that there should be two systems of education—a fact so curious as to impress any outsider.

A closely allied question is that of different types of school within the public system of education; the underlying reasons for these divisions, Clarke was one of the first to note, 'are much less educational than they ought to be. They are rather social, historical and administrative.'[3] In fact, to examine secondary education in its origin and development is also to bring to light the changing nature of generalized statements about children's abilities over a comparatively brief period. If the Taunton Commission (1868) estimated that boys of 'exceptional talent' from the working classes, intellectually worthy of a secondary education, constituted well under 1 per cent of the child population, the Bryce Commission, nearly thirty years later conceded that the proportion was slightly larger. Forty years on the Spens Committee (1938) estimated 30 per cent as worthy of a selective education and, in 1959, the Crowther Committee raised this to 50 per cent—though here the idea is expressed in more modern terms, as the proportion capable of learning through grasping abstractions. This is but another way of indicating that the educational principles enunciated at different times may be less worthy of attention than the social and administrative considerations which remain unvoiced and must be sought out.

Once preconceptions are set aside, a host of questions arise for investigation. The age of transition from primary to secondary education has already been referred to, and is now under active discussion, but what concrete historical reasons determined that this age should be fixed at eleven and how far were the psychological and educational justifications advanced rationalizations covering existing practice? The raising of the school leaving age also brings forward some fundamental questions on which historical inquiry can throw considerable light, in particular the relation of this matter to the use of adolescent labour by industry—still a very actual question as it concerns, for instance, the system of day release. This kind of inquiry, which links educational measures to the really determining factors in social life, has been singularly lacking.

There has been little effective historical study of the evolution of the curriculum, the changing content of education. Here again it is worth directing attention to Clarke's argument which relates this closely to the changing demands of different social classes. The British conception of education for culture, he says, is 'shot through with compromise', the uneasy resultant of two conflicting traditions—that of the aristocracy, clergy and gentry embodied in the classical tradition in the grammar schools and ancient universities, and that of puritanism and dissent, with its insistence on science and the 'relief of man's estate'. The latter outlook, that of modern studies, the teaching of science, found a home in the dissenting academies and later in those schools and colleges founded by the radical middle class in the nineteenth century. This is the background to problems which still weigh on the schools for when science was generally introduced in the nineteenth century it was simply tacked on to a traditional core, while the organization of 'sides', or later, of specialist studies merely reflected the two conceptions of culture which Clarke defined as the literary (or classical) and the scientific (or modern). J. D. Bernal has aptly described the kind of syllabus we present to pupils today as 'a kind of geological record of the education of the past in which stratum after stratum is laid down one after the other'—the classical, the mediaeval scholastic, the renaissance humanist, the eighteenth century enlightenment, the factual Gradgrind, with, 'rather unconsolidated at the top', various efforts at a child-centred project education.[4] Similarly, as new sciences develop, or as science itself advances, the tendency is simply to add to the existing syllabus without any attempt at a fundamental readjustment.

Steps are now being taken towards recasting courses as a whole, particularly in science and mathematics, but much remains to be done. Detailed inquiry into the way the subject matter of different disciplines has accumulated, the balance sought and achieved at different periods, the relation between special and general education and varying arguments in support of different proportions for each—all this leads to a deeper understanding. The student who has studied these developments will be in a better position to plan his own courses, recognize their relation to others, and perceive the educational programme as a whole, its sense and direction. He will also be forewarned against the tendency to justify existing practice on the grounds that it corresponds to certain innate qualities of the child's mind—such, for instance, as the Crowther Committee's claim that grammar schools rightly provide a highly specialized form of education in their sixth forms because children are essentially 'subject-minded'.*

In the field of methodology and school organization, one of the major questions at issue is the role of class teaching (which bears on the question of streaming and setting), the place of individual work and the value of group projects. At the university and college level there is the lecture, a mediaeval survival, which may well not be the best method of imparting knowledge (or stimulating thought) in the 1960s. To study the evolution of teaching method is to find that it has closely depended on general pedagogic ideas, the availability of teachers and their standard of training, the kind of technical aids to be drawn upon, the nature of school buildings provided and so on. Class teaching (the 'Prussian' system, as it used to be known) appears as the product of a specific set of circumstances, particularly during the past century. All this is both full of interest and a material help to getting present problems and possibilities into perspective. Do we want schools with separate classrooms in the future, as in the past, or do the new technical aids now coming into use, the methods of teaching at our disposal, and indeed our whole approach to the educational process, suggest considerable changes in the arrangement and organization of the school? It is only if such questions are well thought out, and teachers press for the facilities necessary to engage in new methods of education, that it is possible to short-circuit, as it were, the tendency of educational institutions to be rooted in yesterday's needs. How great an influence on the progress

* 'On the whole, the better the intellectual quality, the more "subject-minded" a boy is likely to be'. 15 to 18, Vol. I (1959), p. 223.

of education has been exerted by the all too solid barracks erected
by the Victorians who built to last!

This raises the question of what may be called educational
archaeology. History is on the ground, particularly in the great
cities of the industrial age, and more may be learned by a day's
tour of school buildings of different periods than from a dozen
lectures or books. The reactions of students when they first go
into the schools to teach, their comments and criticisms, are
sometimes a revelation to an older generation which has learned to
accept things as they are. An integral understanding of the
educational system in its origin and development can help to
preserve this freshness of outlook.

Examinations are another matter which tends to be taken
for granted and these, again, have often been justified by appeal
to the intrinsic nature of the child; competition is the best, if
not the only, motivation to learning, hence the constant use of
mark sheets and form orders in certain types of school. Here it is
instructive to compare, for instance, the attitude to competition
of Wordsworth (*The Prelude*) and Bentham (*Chrestomathia*) at
the outset of the period when competitive examinations began
to enter on the educational scene. To what extent was the increasing use of competition as a motivational technique the product
of growing individualism, what were the corresponding educational
arguments and the relevant factors outside the schools in terms of a
new development of the professions and the setting of minimum
standards of entry? Or, to approach the matter from the opposite
angle, there is a movement of opposition to be traced in some
circles and some schools up to the progressive schools of today.

All this is, of course, closely linked with ideas about the learning
process. As has already been noted it has been a prevailing
tendency of recent years to interpret children's abilities in terms of
available educational facilities, in particular the overall proportion
of places in selective schools. But new light can be thrown on this
matter by taking a long view of educational history. To do so is to
find that at certain periods the emphasis has been on educability,

on the potentialities of human beings and on educational policies and methods framed to realize these potentialities. In other words, failure to learn was not ascribed to some form of innate incapacity —rather to inadequacies in the methods of teaching used. The predominant attitude was one of optimism, a belief in human powers and in the possibility of developing them by education. One might cite the educational ideas and projects of the humanists in the fifteenth and early sixteenth centuries, the age of the Commonwealth in England, the late eighteenth century in France (and among some circles in England), as times when the formative role of education was particularly stressed; a corollary was the attempt to develop a scientific approach to the psychology of learning, of education. This raises a key question, the extent to which educational ideas and aims are themselves socially conditioned, however unaware of the fact their authors may be. How far, for instance, has the tendency to stress the limitation of children's abilities in England been a product of the economic and social circumstances of the decades between 1900 and 1940? How far does the present movement away from this view depend on social and technological changes, the replacement of unemployment by full employment, of economic stagnation by the maintenance of a consistent, though small, rate of economic growth— all factors requiring a higher educational level among the population?

Study of the historiography of education can also be rewarding. Why has there been interest in this subject at some points in particular directions and none at others; what was it, for instance, about the turn of the century that gave rise to a new interest in study of the educational past? Foster Watson has provided one of the answers to this question, that it was the development of science that 'increasingly pressed upon the notice of students the importance of the genetic method of treatment of subjects. . . . From the very development of scientific conceptions', he added, 'there arose the new scientific demand for the study of the historical side of humanistic subjects.' In other words, people were no longer

H

satisfied with philosophic generalizations about education and the educational process; they wished to penetrate into the historical development of education itself. 'It is realized in the outer world of nature' continued Foster Watson, 'that the slightest attempts to analyse the present state of an organism leads us to the past—for what is the past but the antecedent states of the parts which in their organized form now constitute the present?'[5] Psychology was also making its own inroads on part of the philosophical field. It was again Foster Watson who drew attention to one of the pioneer psychologists, Juan Luis Vives, who was insisting that learning begins with sense impressions more than a century before Thomas Hobbes or John Locke. The idea that education could also become more scientific, and that one of the essential means to this end was a rigorous study of its history, was a particular stimulus to historical inquiry.

This was a time when W. H. Woodward brought educational developments at the Renaissance to attention, de Montmorency wrote on legal and administrative aspects of English education and J. W. Adamson began to make his major contribution to the writing of English educational history from early mediaeval times. A. F. Leach added further accounts of schools and of the development of mediaeval education to an earlier work which stemmed in large part from the findings of the Schools Inquiry Commission. There have been few names to set beside these since, though the situation is beginning to change again. Both Foster Watson and Adamson, though scholars of note, pursued their work particularly with the teacher in training in mind and were convinced of the vital importance of historical study to enlightened educational thinking. Adamson commented sadly towards the end of a long life on the fact that histories of English education are 'of the fewest', a neglect the more to be regretted 'since England, perhaps more than any other country, would be helped by an understanding of her educational past'.[6] This remains as true as ever it was but there are now fresh opportunities to close the gap.

In particular, the trend in historical studies away from predominantly political and constitutional matters towards economic and social developments with an accompanying interest in the people rather than peers is a material aid to the historian of education. If he plays his part, when history is rewritten education should take its proper place not merely as an adjunct to the historical process but as one of the chief factors conditioning men's outlook and aspirations, attitudes to which express clearly current beliefs about the human condition and the direction of social advance. So far as the history of education itself is concerned, this, too, will concentrate not so much on particular institutions or the eminent *alumni* of particular schools, but on those broad movements which have affected the majority of people, and essentially constitute the educational history of the nation.

[III]

Methods of studying the history of education in courses for the intending teacher have already been touched upon. The primary difficulty is the relative shortness of the time available by comparison with the vastness of the field as a whole. It is for this very telling reason that 'history of education' often takes the form of a concentrated course covering chiefly what might be called surface phenomena. Rarely does it extend back beyond the early nineteenth century, in the later decades of which the educational system begins to become complex and there is an unending mass of detail to outline. There remains too little time to give point to all these facts by filling in the background—the more general relations between church and state, for instance, other social factors influencing legislation, the politics and pressure groups operating when particular educational measures are under consideration, or, more fundamental, technological and industrial developments which necessitate an adaptation of education. What is likely to emerge so far as the student is concerned, is little more than an external description of events. Why these particular events took place and no other does not appear as a problem at all, though it is perhaps the question of most relevance and interest.

It is clear, from what has already been said, that to see the history of educational development as a simple linear process is to get an entirely false impression. This is so as much in the realm of ideas as in the field of practice. The remedy would seem to be that which has also been applied in the historical field generally; study in time of particular topics and study of particular periods in depth.

If the student of education suffers from the disadvantage of lack of historical training he has the advantage of some knowledge of the educational system—a knowledge most historians tend to lack. Attitudes to education as well as educational provision may have varied widely down the ages but the fundamental educational issues remain essentially the same. It is ability to distinguish the important questions from the irrelevant that provides the key to fruitful historical investigation.

This is not the place to discuss the structuring of the main studies in education of the intending teacher. It may well be that the particular contribution of historical studies—or of the historical approach generally—can best be made to a carefully thought out integrated course on education based on a series of topics. The weight given to the historical approach in this situation would depend on its relevance in each case. This matter is referred to again later; in the meantime, even if the history of education is thought of in terms of a relatively self-contained study, there is much to be said for a first approach to the past through the present, by study of issues which are of particular moment in the educational scene today. By choosing interrelated topics on the one hand, and studying these also in the context of periods covering important 'moments' of change, it is possible to arrive at a course of study which is both internally consistent and meaningful, and which can be adequately supplemented by wider reading. Such a course might well constitute part of the basic course in education.

It might be accompanied by optional studies, for instance, study in depth of a particular period. The most illuminating periods are usually those of rapid social change when educational developments also are accelerated, so that a clear picture emerges of the nature and direction of change. It is often the advances made at such times that have left the most permanent mark on educational theory and practice, for instance, the new institutions and ideas of the period 1790–1830, of the decades 1640–60, or, going further back, at the time of the Reformation. There are equivalent periods of interest in the modern age in the decades 1850–70, or 1890–1910, study of which involves picking up earlier threads and looking ahead to future developments. The object would be to study the institutional structure of education—the relation between educational theory and practice—as aspects of the social, economic and intellectual history of the age. If the view can be extended to other countries, so much the better.

Limited research projects are a useful adjunct of study on these lines. There is an immense amount of local historical material in many districts, both in local record offices and in some of the schools, not to speak of the memories of those who have taught and learned in an earlier generation whose experiences rank as history for the student of today. No specialized historical knowledge is needed to get the most out of a school log book, a school board minute book, or from the reminiscences of a teacher and much may be gained in terms of bringing the past to life. Research projects of this kind can be carried out individually or, if more ambitious, as a group undertaking.

It is as an aid to studies of this kind that the history section of the Students' Library of Education has been planned to consist of relatively short volumes at a price within the student's means. One of the main difficulties hitherto has been lack of the necessary materials to stimulate and inform a new approach to educational history. It is for this reason that there has of necessity been recourse to the lecture as the main means of imparting basic information, together with a heavy reliance on a limited group of textbooks. With additional aids there should be more scope for a variety of methods—the group discussion, individual research—though the lecture may still be the most suitable means of introducing periods or topics, of outlining methods of approach. In this matter education departments and colleges of education might well show others the way by discarding the traditional type of lecture which does little but follow the textbook and using the lecture to break new ground. There is also much scope for building up libraries and collections of other material—documents illustrating local education, photographs of schools and classrooms of different periods, prospectuses, examination papers, and anything else that throws light on what went on in the schools.

It is to be expected that courses for the B.Ed. degree will include an historical component and here there may be a place for a more extended course. More specialist and scholarly study of the history of education can find a place in diploma courses taken by practising teachers and in other courses leading to a higher degree. There is encouraging evidence of a fresh interest in historical research at this stage and it is on such researches that the rewriting of the history of education must in large part depend. Only in so far as teaching is combined with research on the part of those responsible for the subject in colleges of education and universities can there be a guarantee that it will itself be lively and forward-looking and ensure that educational history attains a new status.

Here the same considerations apply as have already been outlined. If we are to interpret the nature of education as a social function, then it is essential to study it in its origin and development as one aspect of a much wider social and economic scene. This must not mean, however, losing sight of the internal development of the educational system and its various parts, for established institutions do take on a life and develop an ethos of their own which then to a considerable extent shapes their further course; it may, indeed, be the dominant determining feature at a time when outside pressures are not very strong. At such times, it may be worth noting, established educational institutions tend to ossify, so that the concept that educational provision tends constantly to improve hardly accords with the facts. The great period of the grammar schools, for instance, was the century 1560–1660 when these were genuinely national schools—the opportunity of the ordinary local boy, farmer's or tradesman's son, reaching the university in the period 1620–40 was, certainly in Leicestershire, greater than it was to be at any future period until comparatively recently. The history of education records set-backs as well as advances; deprivation of educational facilities as well as their provision.

The problem here is to disentangle the strands which go to make up the very complex process of social change, and to assess their significance for education. At the root lie those technological developments which bring about changes in the structure of industry and the nature of production and in so doing change ways of life and work more or less fundamentally; the process is most clearly to be discerned, of course, at such periods as the 'industrial revolution' but is always operative to a greater or lesser extent. But whether or not latent potentialities are realized, to what extent and in what direction, depends on factors at the level of social organization; all industries do not share equally in, for instance, technological advance or commercial expansion, nor do these affect all classes in the same way—hence the varying programmes for, and resistances to, the corresponding educational changes, contradictory influences which also make themselves felt within the educational system itself.

Scientific and technological developments also influence the nature of education through transformation of its content. As knowledge increases, so new subjects enter the schools, though often not without a struggle sometimes extending over centuries: cosmography, splitting into history and geography; mathematics; natural philosophy, dividing into the various sciences; eventually technology itself, first developed 'on the job', becomes a subject of disciplined study in universities and, later, in technical colleges. Closely connected with the advance of knowledge are changing ideas as to the nature of learning which directly affect teaching methods and pedagogical ideas generally. If Vives was, perhaps, the first of the 'moderns' to reach towards a scientific psychology, this approach was developed by the English philosophers Hobbes and Locke, and, with the development of Hartley's associationism, profoundly influenced men's thinking about the nature of education. Thus the content and methods of education, as well as the general approach to the child and learning, are the resultant of a complex set of circumstances rooted in the social developments and intellectual movements of the time.

Also to be considered here are such factors as the pressures of increasing population and movements of population—which always have an immediate effect on educational institutions—and the varying structure of urban and rural society, down to the nature of the family and the part family life plays in education. Then there is what might be called the cultural environment, in a general sense; that is, not merely what the critic of literature or art passes as a worthy product of the age but the kind of pamphlets, broadsheets and newspapers which made up the reading matter of ordinary people at different social levels, and the kind of objects which helped to form their taste. This is to direct attention to the education which perpetually takes place in the course of daily social living, to which organized education is an adjunct.

This is a propitious time to make a new approach on these lines since such questions constantly arise for the working teacher, now that the whole child population is in school for at least ten years. In particular, perhaps, it has been forced on our attention that technological and scientific advances closely condition educational change. The controversy about the 'two cultures', the earlier efforts of an Eliot to arrive at a definition of culture, are but two examples of the rethinking that has been going on and the different forms it can take. But there is nothing intrinsically new about these discussions; rather, they reproduce in terms of today arguments that have been advanced in very similar form in the past. In other words, just as the fundamental educational issues have remained the same through the years—who should be educated, how, to what level or different levels in the service of what social or industrial needs?—so the conditioning social and economic factors continue to operate. Failure to recognize this results in mere enunciations about education rather than meaningful statements about what it is and does; these must essentially depend on knowledge of what education has been and has done, not merely in general but for different classes of the population.

In the age of Bacon, for instance, there was controversy about the relative value of liberal and scientific studies as there was also about the very nature of knowledge and so of the learning process; and new ideas on the subject (today generally accepted) were rejected out of hand in many quarters as an unwarranted challenge to current methods of education, indeed to all scholarship. The fear that entrance of 'the masses' on to the stage of politics or into the schools constitutes a threat to order, to culture, to all established standards, has been a recurring theme in history—at certain times voiced with acute anxiety, at others forgotten. All this throws light on present dilemmas and controversies and the factors which influence our thinking today.

In this connection, it was one of Clarke's suggestions that rather than outlining 'the educational outlook' of an age as if this were ever a uniform and generally accepted view, it would be fruitful to look into the educational ideologies of different social groupings: for instance, the very different attitude to education of Methodists, or Chartists, or country gentlemen in the nineteenth century. Again, there is the nature and effect of the training for different professions; if the clergy, schoolmasters, lawyers, physicians of this age showed 'a marked disposition to ally themselves with the ruling order' to what extent was this the outcome of an education on traditional 'clerkly' lines, more or less consciously designed to produce this attitude? To approach the same question from another angle is to investigate why the interests of the new manufacturing classes were ignored by the majority of established schools at this period, the kind of steps taken to provide an alternative, and the ultimate outcome both in terms of the educational system and adaptation of the curriculum in other schools. More ambitiously, Clarke proposed a general history of a new kind, under some such title as 'The Politics of Education', proclaiming the intention to interpret thought and practice since the Reformation in the light of conflicting social interests and their political expression. It is from this conflict of interests, as he consistently emphasized, that educational change has emerged—in a form tempered by the political settlement arrived at—and, too, compromises in terms of thought and practice. It is relevant to note here that this book, which still has so much to offer, was published at a time of much upheaval and heartsearching, in 1940.

If it is a main aim to make study of the history of education more rigorous—to eliminate both the lists of facts and the easy, unhistorical generalization—this should make it more stimulating and interesting. It is, after all, by entering into conflicts and controversies and seeing what they were all about—rather than leaving them aside to present educational change as a simple upward and onward movement—that those entering the field of education today are best equipped to take a positive part.

[IV]

It may be useful, finally, to assess briefly the literature of the history of education and to indicate its scope. Here another difficulty arises: education, seen as a social function, abuts onto so many fields of activity that a full discussion of relevant literature would be quite outside the scope of this essay; political, religious, and social developments are all relevant, as we have already seen. The development of the different sciences, perhaps particularly chemistry and physics, in bringing about technological change has profoundly affected the schools—as has also the evolution of philosophy and psychology. Other factors directly related to education include the role of the family, the changing demand for child labour, the organization of apprenticeship and the evolution of the professions, population changes, urban development and popular culture. The history of education can hardly be confined to schools and colleges, but it is here that social and intellectual developments are, as it were, crystallized or reflected.

There is some reason, then, for concentrating on writings strictly in the field of institutionalized education. Here alone, the student is faced with a bewildering variety of literature. If an attempt may be made to impose some order on the material available, this does not involve an attempt at a comprehensive, or, as it were, bibliographical survey. A brief round-up may help to clarify its scope, as well as pointing to the more recent trends now emerging.

It may be as well to start with textbooks on the history of education, although these are not necessarily the best approach to study. Perhaps the most distinguished of these, as well as one of the earliest in time, is J. W. Adamson's *Short History of Education* (1919), although his later detailed study of a limited period (1930) remains an outstanding work of this order.* William Boyd, in his *History of Western Education* (1921), gave the chief emphasis to educational ideas rather than to practical and institutional change and of course covered European developments, as indicated in the title.† Alongside these, the first general textbooks published in Britain, may be placed a number of textbooks covering the history of elementary and secondary education as well as later attempts to write specifically for college students and to cover the more recent period.

Reference may be made here to textbooks produced in the

* Titles of all books referred to in the text will be found listed chronologically at the end of this essay. The dates of publication are given in the text to enable identification.

† Boyd was a pupil of the philosopher Edward Caird at the turn of the century; from him he 'learned . . . that the surest way to an understanding of the present was through the study of developing thought in its social setting'. In the preface to an earlier edition, however, he describes his book as an 'attempt . . . to show educational institutions and principles in their social context'. *The History of Western Education* (1950 edn.), vi–vii.

United States which have had an influence in this country—particularly to the work of Monroe and Cubberley (1920). Monroe is distinguished as the first educational historian in the English speaking world to compile a source book (1901), though this was confined to Greek and Roman education and consisted largely of excerpts from writings about education. A. F. Leach, in his *Educational Charters and Documents* (1911), provided a source book concerned with educational institutions and their legal basis but, despite the title, the volume contains little material following the Reformation.* J. E. G. de Montmorency, a barrister who fully realized the practical importance of the study of the history of education, published significantly in 1902, his study of state intervention in English education—drawing heavily on source material largely of an administrative and legal character. Had an historian produced a real history of education some seventy years earlier, he maintained, 'England would have been spared some, at least, of her present educational troubles'. Lamenting that the provision of education had in the past been regarded simply as a burden on the rates, he stresses the revival of interest at the turn of the century. 'Within the last few years a new school of thought on the subject of National Education has arisen, and the work of reconstruction and organization has been taken up in earnest by statesmen and specialists. . . . Among its manifold aspects that are receiving consideration history is included. We may, therefore, confidently believe', he continues optimistically, 'that in the near future an exhaustive history of English education will be produced' to which his volume would be but a footnote. He expressed the hope, however, that it 'might be of some practical use to all who are interested in National Education'.† W. H. Woodward, whose book on Erasmus appeared at this time (1904),

---

* 'This book aims at doing . . . for the educational history of England what Bishop Stubbs' *Select Charters* did for its constitutional history . . . (it) will, it is hoped, at least set the early history of our educational institutions once and for all on a solid basis of historical documents'. *Educational Charters and Documents*, ix, lii.

† *State Intervention in English Education* (1902), v–ix.

makes a similar point: 'The deepening interest in educational inquiry which marks the present time will, we may confidently hope, extend to the study of the aims and achievements of the educators of the past'.* De Montmorency's book was one of a group reflecting the increased concern with the administration and control of education, symptomatic of the time. Among these were Graham Balfour's *The Educational Systems of Great Britain and Ireland* (1898), which the author describes as 'not a history of education but an account of the framework of which education is the life and spirit', Sir Henry Craik's *The State in its relation to Education* (1896), and Michael Sadler's article in the second volume of the *Special Reports on Educational Subjects* (1898). Although casting its net widely, de Montmorency's book does not contain a collection of documents and readings (though including important speeches by Brougham and Roebuck in full). English historical study still proceeds, therefore, without an adequate source book as an aid, a gap which, however, has recently been partially filled by J. Stuart Maclure's *Educational Documents, England and Wales*, 1816–1963 (1965).

Next we can define an area which has perhaps the largest quantitative output—histories of particular educational institutions. These provide a most important source for the student of educational history, ranging from such works as Mullinger's history of Cambridge University (1888) and Mallet's three volumes on Oxford (1924–7), to the many studies of the major public schools, the 500 or more histories of grammar schools, as well as histories of what might be called peripheral schools—private,

---

* *Erasmus concerning Education*, vi. Tribute should be paid here to the Cambridge University Press for the many pioneering studies in the history of education published in the early years of this century. Foster Watson, J. W. Adamson, de Montmorency, S. S. Laurie, W. H. Woodward, A. F. Leach, Irene Parker and others were numbered among their authors. In 1901, stimulated by plans drawn up by W. H. Woodward who acted as general editor, the press launched a series entitled 'Contributions to the Study of the History of Education'. These plans were, however, only partially carried out (Information from the Secretary, Cambridge University Press).

charity, elementary, even Sunday schools. Alongside these should
be listed the crop of histories of the modern universities and the
few productions covering colleges of education, technical colleges
and so on.

Every type of institution has had its historian and, of recent
years, the output of such volumes has increased greatly, especially
those celebrating the quatercentenary of grammar schools, many
of which were founded in the 1550s and 1560s. Here may be found
the groundwork of educational history as reflected in the life
of an institution. The level and purpose of these books naturally
varies considerably, from the highest level of scholarship to books
produced as an act of piety to an Alma Mater, written for a closed
'inner' group. Public school histories, for instance, have a tendency
to ignore, or explain away, important developments such as the
largely successful attempts in the nineteenth century to exclude
local boys, for whom the school was originally provided, by the
alienation of the endowment—one of the necessary conditions for
the development of local grammar schools to full public school
status. Indeed much more of the real history of public schools can
be gained from books like Graham's biography of the headmaster
of Harrow, Montagu Butler (1920), or from Parkin's life of
Thring (1898), than from official histories; in just the same way
more illuminating than a comprehensive history of elementary
education is such a book, by an inspector who had direct experience of it, as Edmond Holmes' *What is and What Might Be* (1911).
In general, biographies, correspondence, diaries, are essential
sources of educational history.

Thus much remains to be done, as Bamford's *Thomas Arnold*
(1960) has made clear. Some studies of particular schools, however,
and perhaps Lawson's history of Hull grammar school (1963) is the
best example, relate the development of the school not only to the
overall developments in the area, but also to the wider social
movements which determine the direction of change. Where this
is done, study of a particular institution serves an enlightening
function.

This leads on naturally to historical studies of particular types of institutions taken as a whole. This is a necessary and convenient approach for the historian, though it has its dangers; but here we reach the level of generalization in so far as education now begins to be interpreted as a social process—institutions as social institutions. The extent of the literature, however, is not great; with some distinguished exceptions, this approach is fairly recent. Perhaps the first study of this kind was Rashdall's great work on mediaeval universities (1895), an historical study in its own right. More recently specialist studies have been made of universities in the Elizabethan period, but nothing equivalent to Rashdall's work has yet been produced. A recent contribution, generalizing university history, is W. H. G. Armytage's *Civic Universities* (1955).

Important studies have, however, been made in other specific fields. These include M. G. Jones' study of the charity school movement (1938) and Irene Parker's monograph on the dissenting academies (1914)—both works which have stood the test of time— as well as Leach's early study *English Schools at the Reformation* (1896) (though the main thesis there advanced is no longer acceptable). Examples of other specialist studies of a group or class of institutions include Tylecote's study of Mechanics' Institutes (1957) and, an earlier work, Rich's history of teacher training (1933). A. E. Dobb's *Education and Social Movements, 1760–1850* (1919), although written nearly fifty years ago, remains a mine of unusual information, being one of the first books to attempt the approach indicated in its title and to shed some light on the educational aspirations and activities of the working class. Recently specialist studies have been made of the outlook and activities of particular religious groupings—for instance, W. A. C. Stewart's study of Quaker education (1953) and Pritchard's parallel volume on methodist education (1949). These go some way towards meeting the approach suggested by Clarke, as described earlier. Perhaps the most striking study in this category, however, is E. C. Mack's two-volume history of the public schools (1938,

1941), the first study which interpreted the inner development of what have been, perhaps, our most influential educational institutions in terms of the social pressures and conflicts to which they were subject. It is worth noting that this, the only serious attempt at an objective study of these institutions, was made by an American. Although published twenty-five years ago, it has no rival.

We may now turn to the history of educational ideas and their relation to practice. This was the first field to be at all systematically cultivated by educational historians in this country, one which for long appears to have held first place in colleges and universities. The approach is best epitomized by R. H. Quick's famous volume *Essays on Educational Reformers*, concerned particularly with the renaissance educators, Sturmius, Rabelais, Montaigne, and their English counterparts Ascham and Mulcaster, but taking in also Locke, Rousseau, Basedow, Pestalozzi, Froebel and Spencer. This book, first published in 1868, became particularly popular towards the end of the century, both in this country and the U.S.A.; it is noteworthy that Quick complains of the almost entire lack of study of the subject in this country when he wrote his volume. 'I have found', he wrote, 'that on the history of education, not only *good* books but *all* books are in German or in some other foreign language'—on these he relied heavily for this material.[7] Quick first studied for and wrote this book in a single year. It was published in only 500 copies and addressed to his fellow public school masters. He largely revised and extended the book when it was re-issued in 1890; it was then reprinted several times.

Other books of this genre were Oscar Browning's *Educational Theories* (1881), S. S. Laurie's *Educational Opinion from the Renaissance* (1903) and Woodward's *Education during the Renaissance* (1906). Laurie, Professor of the Institutes and History of Education at Edinburgh (one of the two first professorships in education) regarded the history of ideas as the key aspect of the history of education; his volume aimed at 'an analytical exposition of the doctrines of eminent writers'. 'I venture to issue these lectures', he adds, 'in the conviction that the study of the History of Education in the writings of the most distinguished representatives of various schools of thought is an important part of the general preparation of those who adopt the profession of schoolmaster'.[8]

As already noted, it was at the turn of the century that studies of this kind received a great impetus, while the tendency to treat ideas in the abstract now began to be overcome, perhaps particularly in Foster Watson's detailed and scholarly studies of the changing content of education. Foster Watson was primarily concerned with the schools as they actually existed: 'It is a history of the practice of the schools', he writes of his *English Grammar Schools to 1660* (1908), 'of their curricula, and of the differentiated subjects of instruction, in distinction from the history of the theories of educational reformers as to what ought to be taught, and how existing methods might be improved'.[9] A like concern led to the editing of texts—for instance, Campagnac's edition of Hoole's *Art of Teaching Schoole* (1913)—which received an impetus at this time. If this emphasis on practice heralded a new approach, it is noteworthy that Adamson's *Short History* (1919) was also written consciously from a more realistic standpoint. Paying tribute to A. F. Leach as 'one of the first to make us understand that the history of education is not coincident, point for point, with the history of opinion concerning what education ought to be', he continued, 'nor is it constituted by a loosely knitted collection of biographies of eminent theorizers or practical teachers, however 'inspiring' to their readers these biographies may chance to prove'. Leach's researches did a great deal to reveal the past and help students 'to trace the process of educational development'; this 'is not only a truer view of what constitutes the history of education . . . it is also a much more instructive one'.[10] Adamson implicitly criticized another school of historical writing in education when he wrote of his *Short History* that it made 'no pretence to be a 'History of Education', if the term denotes a survey of the evolution of human culture generally and in particular of

I

the schools of all known civilisations, ancient and modern, European and Asiatic'. Perhaps he had Monroe in mind here, his textbook (1905) covered education in primitive communities, in the Orient (particularly China), in Greece and Rome as well as the Middle Ages, the Renaissance, the Reformation and so on up to the modern world. Adamson's own *Pioneers of Modern Education* (1905) made an attempt to relate theory to practice and each to the changing social and political scene, but ideas still held pride of place.

It was at this period, then, that specific historical studies concerned with illuminating the English tradition in education and relating ideas to practice had their origin. It is encouraging to note that, while in the historical field generally much attention has recently been paid to the sixteenth and seventeenth centuries, this is now being followed up by parallel studies in education (1965, 1966). Reference should also be made to studies of the development of various subjects, particularly the sciences, mathematics, geography and classics, which include material on their teaching, but here much remains to be done.

A specific group of studies which will certainly expand in the future arises from the growth of interest in local history. This involves a new approach to the history of education as part of the changing local scene, an approach which is broader, therefore, than the history of specific institutions, yet limited enough to allow concentration on detailed developments, the interconnections and shifting relations between institutions, and between educational provision generally and social change. Possibly the best unit of study is a county as a whole, though this needs support by studies of developments in particular cities, especially the larger urban conglomerations. Histories of local authorities—school boards, for instance—fall in this category.

Although there are some pioneer studies to hand, mostly in the form of unpublished theses or articles in educational journals, not a great deal has, as yet, been achieved. But it seems clear that this is a fruitful and necessary field of work, one which should act as a useful corrective to the approach adopted in the Victoria County Histories which provide factual accounts of schools under various headings (grammar, charity, elementary, etc.), but rarely a picture of provision as a whole in a given period. Such accounts, together with the laborious compilation of lists of schools extant at different times are, of course, of value in providing raw material for the history of education. But until the local situation, on a county or town basis, is built up and understood as a whole, the data for generalized statements or conclusions on a national scale do not exist. As suggested earlier, this is a field in which students could most easily make a contribution.

The studies referred to so far have been histories of educational institutions or of particular aspects of education, mostly written specifically by educational historians. We turn now to a different category, to studies by historians who have treated education as part of general history. Here it must be recorded that the claims of education as an important aspect of social history have tended to be minimized by historians, though the many volumes in the Oxford History of England and of the three Cambridge series (Modern, Mediaeval, and New Modern) often treat of educational developments, sometimes alongside such topics as 'science and art' in a separate chapter. Such contributions are often illuminating, but in the absence of adequate monographs the subject tends to be treated in a general way while the pattern of these volumes imposes an approach which separates education from its social relations and obviates interpretation of its chronological development in terms of the political background.

Some historians have, however, recognized the importance of education and treated it as an aspect of social change. Examples are R. B. Schlatter's chapter on education in his *Social Ideas of Religious Leaders*, 1660–88 (1940), and A. L. Rowse's similar chapter in *The England of Elizabeth* (1950). Here we begin to approach that kind of integrated treatment which adds an extra dimension to educational history, indicating its significance in terms of the whole network of contemporary society. Reference may be made here to J. L. and B. Hammond's famous trilogy (*Village Labourer, Town Labourer, Age of the Chartists*) where certain aspects of education are given considerable emphasis. One historian must, however, be singled out, the Frenchman, Elie Halévy. In his great series covering British history from 1815 to 1914 (unfortunately uncompleted at his death) education is not only given the place it deserves, but, since educational change is here closely related to social and political change, we have here perhaps the most illuminating analysis of the historical development of education that we possess.

There is no doubt that this tendency will gain ground in the future. The modern trend in historical analysis has already been referred to. Not only is greater emphasis now given to social and economic factors, but this is now extending into investigation of the development of ideas in their social context. This, it seems, is a likely direction of historical studies in the future, one which should assist the interpretation of ideological change in the field of education.

There remains a final group of historical studies, mostly published during the last decade, where education is again treated in its social and political relations—but here the focus is on educational change, on its interpretation in terms of its social context and in the light of the contemporary movement of ideas. Professor Eaglesham's *From School Board to Local Authority* (1956), together with related articles, casts much light on the social, administrative and political conflicts leading to the passage of the 1902 Act, while Olive Banks, in *Parity and Prestige in English Education* (1955), interprets the evolution of secondary education during this century in terms of conflicting social forces and objectives. David Newsome, in his *Wellington College* (1959) and perhaps particularly in *Godliness and Good Learning* (1961), relates the changing ethos of the public school to its historical determinants, so following up and deepening the work of E. C. Mack. James Murphy's *The Religious Problem in English Education, The Crucial Experiment* (1959), a case study based on the religious conflicts in mid-nineteenth century Liverpool, breaks quite new ground, while J. F. C. Harrison's *Learning and Living, 1760–1960* (1961) uses a similar technique, illustrating the general history of education through a close analysis of developments in adult education in Yorkshire. It is this general approach that I have attempted in my own historical studies (1960, 1965) and that Joan Simon utilizes in her *Education and Society in Tudor England* (1966). It is significant that the latest textbook produced, W. H. G. Armytage's *400 Years of English Education* (1964), also uses this method, while paying particular attention to scientific and technological advance. Here again the author has had to provide his own material in the absence of effective monographs to refer to, but the fact that he makes this attempt, and points the way to further fruitful areas of study in itself can be nothing but a stimulant.

[v]

Such is the most recent trend in historical study of education, and it is to studies of this kind that we intend to add, in the Students' Library, shorter works on a variety of topics and different periods. Since the general approach marks to some extent a break with the past, these studies will involve research on the part of their authors and the presentation of new material. As such they can serve a dual function: that of assisting the study of education by students, and of contributing to providing a basis, as a series of monographs, for the re-writing of the history of education along the lines suggested by Clarke a quarter of a century ago.

Four groups of books are planned. The first is based on a chronological approach, one necessitated by the nature of history itself. This will cover the last 100 years, each book dovetailing into the other, but each concentrating on the particular crucial developments within its own comparatively narrow period, and interpreting these in the light of wider issues and conflicts.

These are designed to provide a 'way in' to the evaluation of current educational issues, as outlined in the second section of this essay. While the concentration will be on the modern period, studies will be included of important 'moments of change' in the past, in particular the Reformation and the Commonwealth, as indicated earlier.

A second group is planned on a topic basis, where a particular aspect of education of current concern is given concentrated attention in terms of its historical development. Problems of the content of education, of teacher education, of the evolution of the teaching profession, of the relations of church and state in modern education can be most usefully tackled in this manner. Such studies, using a 'vertical' approach, should help to knit those based on the 'horizontal' method of the first group, the two illuminating each other in the course of study. Ideally the two groups should 'mesh', but not significantly overlap each other.

The main emphasis of the first group will tend to be on administrative and institutional changes at different periods, so providing a basis for understanding the present educational structure and practice. Plans are on foot, therefore, for a third group concentrating more specifically on educational ideas. These will not be designed simply as an exposition of the ideas of a particular thinker, as has tended to be the practice in the past. Rather they will group educators forming a common movement of thought at a particular period. The aim will be to relate ideas to the 'soil' from which they sprang; to interpret their origin, indicate their character, and show to what extent, among which groups or strata of society, and in what form, the ideas took root in current practice. A number of groupings might be tackled in this way—for example, the Herbartians, who exercised a great influence on the training colleges and the new secondary schools at the close of the nineteenth century; more recently, the apostles of child-centred education; and, going further back, the utilitarians or 'philosophic radicals'; the group forming the English enlightenment at the close of the eighteenth century; Hobbes, Locke and their contemporaries; Bacon and the Baconians; the Renaissance educators. This group also is planned to 'mesh' with the chronological series.

Finally a smaller group will be concerned with foreign influences on English education—in the first place with American, French and German influence. Here the emphasis will be on the nineteenth and twentieth centuries, and on the effect of institutional and practical developments in these countries rather than of educational theory.

The series should, then, make possible the approach to teaching outlined earlier, whether history is regarded as a contributory study to an education course based on a series of topics, or is treated as relatively independent. In the former case the historical contribution would be regarded as one 'leg' or aspect of a many-sided approach, and here its connections with sociology, psychology and philosophy need to be made clear.

The relation between psychology and philosophy have in the past been close, and indeed it is only comparatively recently, thinking in historical terms, that the former has broken free of the latter and developed its own independent body of knowledge. Each in its historical evolution has profoundly affected educational ideas and practice, as discussed earlier. Locke, Froebel, Herbart, Dewey, all were concerned ultimately with what were then regarded as philosophical problems; their educational outlook reflected their position, as did that of those psychologists who developed the ideas of philosophers in terms of psychology.

The changing nature of educational theory and practice is, then, a proper study for the historian as well as for the sociologist, and indeed the present tendency is for the two approaches to come more closely together. The crucial pedagogical problem in the education of the intending teacher, however, is precisely the structuring of a course in 'education'—or of a series of activities and areas of study—which 'meets' the level and requirements of the students at different stages of their development. This complex and difficult task, which involves definition of education as a subject of study and is concerned both with content and method, is discussed in Chapter Seven. Whatever topics or areas of study are chosen, however, whether in the realm of theory or practice, of contemporary issues or abstractions, the historical component can act as one of the means of understanding.

No claim should be made that the study of the history of education directly affects the practice of the teacher in the classroom. Its effect must be indirect. If its primary function is to develop the 'critical self-awareness' that Clarke emphasized, this in itself implies that the student enters on the job of teaching with eyes and ears attuned to appreciate the new—with, as it were, a built-in defence against obsolete practices and prejudices. But study of this subject should take the student into areas far removed from the classroom, and encourage concern with wider fields of knowledge which should be the mark of the teacher. For Foster Watson its final justification lay in the truth that education has a humanistic end 'and to accomplish it, those actively engaged must ever keep alive within them the brightly burning lamp of humanism'.[11] Concern with immediate, day to day, practical issues is, of course, important and inevitable. Historical study can, however, give a wider perspective and a deeper understanding.

NOTES

1. Brian Jackson, *Streaming, an Education System in Miniature*, 1964, pp. 31–47.
2. 'The Study of the History of Education', *Contemporary Review*, Vol. cv, 1914, p. 86. See W. H. G. Armytage, 'Foster Watson 1860–1929', *British Journal of Educational Studies*, Vol. x, No. 1, Nov. 1961.
3. *Education and Social Change*, 1940, p. 37.
4. *World without War*, 1958, p. 197.
5. Foster Watson, loc. cit., p. 85.
6. 'A Plea for the Historical Study of English Education' in *The Illiterate Anglo-Saxon*, 1946, pp. 155–6.
7. 1893 ed., viii.
8. *Educational Opinion from the Renaissence*, v.

9. *The English Grammar Schools to* 1660, v; see also his study of the origin of modern subjects in the school curriculum (1909).
10. *A Short History of Education*, vi.
11. loc. cit., p. 90.

BIBLIOGRAPHY

Part I (books referred to in Section IV)

1868   R. H. Quick, *Essays on Educational Reformers*.
1881   O. Browning, *An Introduction to the History of Educational Theories*.
1888   J. B. Mullinger, *A History of the University of Cambridge*.
1895   H. Rashdall, *Universities of Europe in the Middle Ages*. (Ed. F. M. Powicke and A. B. Emden, 1936.)
1896   Sir Henry Craik, *The State in its Relation to Education*.
        A. F. Leach, *English Schools at the Reformation*.
1898   G. R. Parkin, *Edward Thring, Headmaster of Uppingham School, life, diary and letters*. 2 vols.
        G. Balfour, *The Educational Systems of Great Britain and Ireland* (2nd revised ed., 1903).
        M. E. Sadler and J. W. Edwards, 'Summary of Statistics, Regulations, and, etc. of Elementary Education in England and Wales, 1833–1870', *Special Reports on Educational Subjects*, Vol. 2, pp. 434–544.
1901   P. Munroe, *Source Book for the History of Education for the Greek and Roman Period*.
1902   J. E. G. de Montmorency, *State Intervention in English Education*.
1903   S. S. Laurie, *Studies in the History of Educational Opinion from the Renaissance*.
1904   W. H. Woodward, *Erasmus concerning Education*.
1905   J. W. Adamson, *Pioneers of Modern Education*.
        P. Monroe, *A Textbook in the History of Education*.
1906   W. H. Woodward, *Studies in Education during the Age of the Renaissance, 1400–1600*.
1908   Foster Watson, *The English Grammar Schools to 1660: their Curriculum and Practice*.
1909   Foster Watson, *The Beginnings of the Teaching of Modern Subjects in England*.
1911   A. F. Leach, *Educational Charters and Documents, 598–1909*.
        E. Holmes, *What is and What Might Be*.
1913   E. T. Campagnac (Ed.), *Charles Hoole, A New Discovery of the Old Art of Teaching Schoole*.
1914   I. Parker, *Dissenting Academies in England*.

1919 J. W. Adamson, *A Short History of Education*.
A. E. Dobbs, *Education and Social Movements, 1700–1850*.

1920 E. Graham, *The Harrow Life of Henry Montagu Butler, D.D.*
E. P. Cubberley, *The History of Education* (together with companion book of Readings).

1921 W. Boyd, *The History of Western Education*.

1924–7 C. E. Mallet, *A History of the University of Oxford*, 3 Vols.

1930 J. W. Adamson, *English Education, 1789–1902*.

1933 R. W. Rich, *The Training of Teachers in England and Wales during the Nineteenth Century*.

1938 M. G. Jones, *The Charity School Movement: a study of eighteenth century puritanism in action*.
E. C. Mack, *Public Schools and British Opinion*, Vol. 1, 1780–1860.

1940 F. Clarke, *Education and Social Change*.
R. B. Schlatter, *Social Ideas of Religious Leaders, 1660–88*.

1941 E. C. Mack, *Public Schools and British Opinion*, Vol. 2, *Since 1860*.

1949 F. C. Pritchard, *Methodist Secondary Education: a History of the Contribution of Methodism to Secondary Education in the United Kingdom*.

1950 A. L. Rowse, *The England of Elizabeth*.

1953 W. A. C. Stewart, *Quakers and Education, as seen in their Schools in England*.

1955 W. H. G. Armytage, *Civic Universities: Aspects of a British Tradition*.
O. Banks, *Parity and Prestige in English Education*.

1956 E. Eaglesham, *From School Board to Local Authority*.

1957 M. Tylecote, *The Mechanics' Institutes of Lancashire and Yorkshire before 1851*.

1959 J. Murphy, *The Religious Problem in English Education, the Crucial Experiment*.
D. Newsome, *A History of Wellington College*.

1960 B. Simon, *Studies in the History of Education, 1780–1870*.
T. W. Bamford, *Thomas Arnold*.

1961 D. Newsome, *Godliness and Good Learning*.
J. F. C. Harrison, *Learning and Living, 1760–1960*.

1963 J. Lawson, *A Town Grammar School through Six Centuries: a History of Hull Grammar School against its Local Background*.

1964 W. H. G. Armytage, *400 Years of English Education*.

1965 K. Charlton, *Education in Renaissance England*.
J. S. Maclure, *Educational Documents, England and Wales, 1816–1963*.
B. Simon, *Education and the Labour Movement, 1870–1920*.

1966 J. Simon, *Education and Society in Tudor England*.

Elie Halévy's *A History of the English People in the Nineteenth Century* consists of the following volumes:

Vol. I.   *England in 1815.*
Vol. II. *The Liberal Awakening, 1815–1830.*
Vol. III. *The Triumph of Reform, 1830–1841.*
Vol. IV. *Victorian Years, 1841–1895.*
Vol. V.   *Imperialism and the Rise of Labour, 1895–1905.*
Vol. VI. *The Rule of Democracy, 1905–1914.*

Vol. IV includes *The Age of Peel and Cobden* together with an essay by R. B. McCallum connecting this volume with the next. (Halévy died in 1937 before completing his study of this period.)

Part II

To the works listed may be added a short selection of books relating to different aspects of education. It can be no more than an arbitrary sample—those interested will easily find others—but it serves to illustrate different categories.

Among biographies are Graham Wallas's classic *The Life of Francis Place* (1898) and, for the same period, A. L. Morton's *The Life and Ideas of Robert Owen* (1962). For one who had much to do with Mechanics' Institutes, Thomas Kelly, *George Birkbeck* (1957). For an insight into public school life in the nineteenth century, Samuel Butler, *The Life and Letters of Samuel Butler, headmaster of Shrewsbury School, 1789–1836*, 2 vols. (1896) and Oscar Browning, *Memories of sixty years at Eton, Cambridge and elsewhere* (2nd ed. 1910)—this has material on the beginning of teacher training at Cambridge. For the universities, Mark Pattison's *Memoirs* (1885) are of outstanding interest. Light on the administration and character of elementary education in the nineteenth century may be gained from Frank Smith, *The Life and Work of Sir James Kay Shuttleworth* (1923), and, in a lighter vein, from E. M. Sneyd Kynnersley, *H.M.I., some Passages in the Life of an H.M. Inspector of Schools* (1918) and Sir George Kekewich, *The Education Department and After* (1920). For a biography of a nineteenth century 'Minister' of Education, W. H. G. Armytage, *A. J. Mundella 1825–1897* (1951). For personal experience of elementary schools as pupil and teacher (and of a training college), F. H. Spencer, *An Inspector's Testament* (1938).

Of histories of particular institutions, H. H. Bellot, *University College, London, 1826–1926* (1929) is concerned with one of the most interesting 'modern' university foundations; for one of the largest provincial universities, A. N. Shimmin, *The University of Leeds, the first half-century* (1954), and for one of the most famous forerunners of the modern universities, H. McLachlan, *Warrington Academy, its history and influence* (Chetham Society, 1943). V. H. H. Green, *Oxford Common Room* (1957) is a recent college history (Lincoln). A school history that escapes being narrowly institutional is A. A. Mumford, *The Manchester Grammar School, 1515–1915. A Regional Survey of the Advancement of Learning in Manchester since the Reformation* (1919). W. G. Walker, *A History of the Oundle Schools* (1956) is a scholarly study of a local school that developed to 'public' school status. Ralph Arnold, *The Whiston Matter. The Rev. Robert Whiston versus the Dean and Chapter of Rochester* (1961) covers attempts to secure adequate funds for a cathedral school in the nineteenth century. On adult education, J. F. C. Harrison, *A History of the Working Men's College, 1854–1954* (1954), W. W. Craik, *The Central Labour College* (1964).

Particular fields are covered in C. T. Millis, *Technical Education, its development and aims* (1925), S. T. Cotgrove, *Technical Education and Social Change* (1958), and see also Eric Ashby's stimulating *Technology and the Academics* (1958). On the origin and development of colleges of art in the early nineteenth century, Quentin Bell, *Schools of Design* (1963). D. G. Pritchard, *Education and the Handicapped 1760–1960* (1963), S. and V. Leff, *The School Health Service* (1959), E. L. Edmonds, *The School Inspector* (1962), and W. M. Eager in *Making Men: the History of Boys' Clubs and related movements in Great Britain* (1953) all deal with somewhat neglected aspects. Educational administration awaits an historian but the subject has been opened up by W. O. Lester Smith in *To Whom do Schools Belong?* (1942) recently supplemented by *Government of Education* (1965); see also L. A. Selby Bigge, *The Board of Education* (1927).

Among more specialized studies are H. M. Pollard, *Pioneers of Popular Education, 1760–1850* (1956), concerned with the impact of foreign innovators on English education, S. E. Maltby, *Manchester and the Movement for National Elementary Education 1800–1870* (1918) and, on the evolution of London grammar schools, F. Campbell, *Eleven-plus and all that: the grammar school in a changing society* (1956). For light on denominational conflicts, Marjorie Cruikshank, *Church and State in English Education, 1870 to the Present Day* (1963). Very useful for the general cultural background in the nineteenth century are R. K. Webb, *The British Working Class Reader, 1790–1848, literacy and social tensions* (1955) and R. D. Altick, *The English Common Reader: a social history of the mass reading public, 1800–1900* (1957); see also Phillip Collins, *Dickens and Education* (1963).

On earlier periods, A. W. Parry, *Education in England in the Middle Ages* (1920), A. R. M. Stowe, *English Grammar Schools in the Reign of Queen Elizabeth* (1908), W. A. L. Vincent, *The State and School Education in England and Wales, 1640–60* (1950), and H. McLachlan, *English Education under the Test Acts 1662–1820* (1931) which remains an essential source for the dissenting academies. N. Hans, *New Trends in Education in the Eighteenth Century* (1951) is on a relatively uncharted period, while B. R. Schneider, *Wordsworth's Cambridge Education* (1957) has new material on university education just before the turn of the century; for political conflicts which contributed much to the academic decline of Oxford, W. R. Ward, *Georgian Oxford, University Politics in the Eighteenth Century* (1958). A stimulating study of university education in Scotland in the nineteenth century is G. E. Davie, *The Democratic Intellect* (1961).

Regional and local studies are as yet few but see W. Boyd, *Education in Ayrshire through seven centuries* (1961), E. J. Davies, *Monmouthshire Schools and Education to 1870* (1957) and the brief survey *Education in Gloucestershire; a short history* (1954). A recent publication is N. Mackintosh, *Education in Scotland, yesterday and today* (1962), and see J. J. Auchmuty, *Irish Education; a historical survey* (1937), and *Education in Wales, 1847–1947* (1948) published by the Ministry of Education. It may be noted here that two useful historical surveys of English education are to be found in the introductory chapters (by R. F. Young) to the Hadow Report (1926) and the Spens Report (1938); the first outlines the development of higher studies in elementary schools, the second the evolution of secondary education. *Education 1900–1950*, the annual report of the Ministry for 1951, contains a useful survey of the period.

The most comprehensive bibliography for further references is *The Cambridge Bibliography of English Literature*, 4 vols, Ed. F. W. Bateson (1940), with supplementary volume, Ed. G. Watson (1957), which has sections on education. Historical works are included in G. Baron, *A Bibliographical Guide to the English Educational System* (3rd ed. 1965); a specialized list is T. Kelly, *A Select Bibliography of Adult Education in Great Britain* (1962). There are general bibliographies in S. J. Curtis, *History of Education in Great Britain* (revised ed. 1950) and H. C. Barnard, *A History of English Education from 1760* (2nd ed. 1961). For a list of textbooks and writings on education from the 15th century available in the chief School (or Institute) of Education libraries, *Union List of Textbooks and Writings on Education*. Various articles on sources for the educational historian have appeared in the *British Journal of Educational Studies* (covering primary education, grammar schools, technical education, educational periodicals, teaching of science, teacher training, handicapped children); for articles on two leading educational historians, Foster Watson and J. W. Adamson, Vol. X, No. 1, of the same journal.

Chapter Five

THE CONTRIBUTION OF PSYCHOLOGY
TO THE STUDY OF EDUCATION

BEN MORRIS

I. INTENTIONS

1. *The appeal of psychology*

There is a generally accepted, deeply rooted idea that psychology
is a study with much to offer the inquiring mind. Yet students
often come away disappointed, feeling that they have been given
very little. Performance has not lived up to promise, the subject
has flattered to deceive. Where they expect to gain an understanding of others, they encounter a stern and exacting discipline.
Where they hope for a deeper self-knowledge, they are invited to
perform experiments, sometimes on themselves, sometimes on
other students and more often than not on animals, none of which
seems to throw much light on the questions to which they may
want answers. Such questions are not infrequently about their
own inner struggles, about their relations with others and about
how to find the secret of a satisfying life. They may even be told
that for the answers to such questions they should turn to ministers
of religion, psychiatrists or old-fashioned philosophers.

Perhaps they should. For psychology to advance as one of the
sciences of man, disciplined thought and careful experimentation
are essential, and the immediate questions to be answered are
limited and precise. Their teachers are right—up to a point. Is
there not in fact, however, something to be said for what looks
at first like a naïve point of view on the part of students? While
experimental and theoretical rigour are necessary, are they enough?
Fundamentally the question for psychologists to answer is whether

or not their subject is to count as a humane study, in the traditional sense of that term. Can it do so without abandoning the virtues which it has found in what are called 'scientific methods'? What has it to offer to the student who is never likely to become a psychologist? Has it, in short, any general educational value? Where it is studied with a professional purpose in mind, such as teaching or medicine, what has it to offer?

I do not think that the answers to these questions are obvious. Is there not some truth in suggesting that psychology's proud achievement of scientific status has not in some respects come perilously near to a rake's progress, indicated by the changing focus of its definition, as the study once of soul, then of mind, and now of behaviour? Is it in fact necessary that it should abandon any role as a liberalizing component in the study of man? Many psychologists are likely to protest that they have never abandoned such intentions, and there is indeed evidence that quite a number have not. Recent books by Bruner (1960) and Murphy (1961) remind one irresistibly of earlier writers like James, McDougall, Burt and Mace, who were obviously concerned with psychology as a humane study. But a great deal of evidence can be accumulated on the other side.

These questions are of great significance for those concerned with teaching psychology to students of education. For the most part, and leaving out the larger questions in some students' minds, there are a quite limited number of things with which such students hope to be given help. Some light on teaching methods, help with class management, what to do with 'difficult' children and slow learners—this is a fairly representative list. Now these are perfectly sensible expectations. Are they fulfilled by our present courses? The trouble is that these questions are not what they seem, and that what they conceal is of crucial importance.

2. The scope of psychological study in education

Tibble (1963) has shown that psychological studies in courses of education have grown steadily in influence over the last seventy or eighty years and that, however much they may disagree among themselves, college teachers concerned with this subject are increasingly convinced of its importance. Nor can it seriously be disputed that it has had an indispensable part to play in modifications of educational thought and practice generally over this period. Tibble's account makes clear some of the ways in which this has come about. An understanding of childhood, of the difficulties, failures and achievements of children in learning, of the fundamentals of human motivation, and of the conditions under which adults and children can most successfully co-operate —all this is accepted as fundamental to the successful practice of the art of teaching. Such themes provide the solid basis on which psychological studies in teacher education have been built.

A further review of psychology teaching in education courses would have to take account of new opportunities, new pressures from within the subject itself, and also of some very old and fundamental problems, which have hitherto received but scanty treatment. The new opportunities relate principally to the lengthening of the College courses from two to three years and the prospect of a fourth year being added for students able to proceed to degree level. The new pressures arise in part from new advances in psychology and in teaching methods. One need only refer to the new approaches to reading and mathematics in primary schools, to programmed learning and to the teaching of languages in both primary and secondary schools. These developments have each of course their psychological rationale, which calls for study.

Such considerations would seem to support the view which is popular among students that the important topics for teachers are those with an obvious and direct bearing on what is called the 'classroom situation'. It is not to be supposed, reasonably, that such topics would be omitted, but difficulties at once appear when we inquire *how* we are to conceive of the classroom situation, and *what* we perceive in it. A first year junior class of fifty children and one teacher working on some modern approaches to mathematics may specify the locus of an inquiry but it does nothing to

K

define its scope. Nor does specifying objectives for teaching, the procedures these imply and means for evaluating progress do anything more than provide a rationale for the apparent task. What is ignored in this approach to psychology in education is that into one such classroom encounter is concentrated much of the essence of many lives which have their roots and draw their significance from sources far beyond it in space and time. And such considerations may be shown to be crucial for enlightened ideas of what teaching is.

There are in fact serious disputes as to what constitutes the proper fields of psychological study for student teachers. This suggests that we ought to examine critically what we mean by saying that some aspects of psychology are 'educational' and, by implication, that others are not. Even suggestions for courses of educational psychology which rightly carry weight such as those made in the recent publication of the British Psychological Society (B.P.S. 1962) do not go to the heart of the matter.

It is surely clear that in a developed and established subject like psychology, straightforward advocacy of the inclusion of this or that topic is not now enough. Different and specialized justifying reasons can be produced for a very wide range of topics. Separate treatment of each of these does not meet the case. What is needed are some more general grounds or criteria on which to justify inclusion. We can come to closer grips with the central issue by considering what is meant when it is said that psychology can be *applied* to education. The notion of application is, however, a very tricky one. It has been discussed for example by Reid (1962) who shows how differently it has to be interpreted in such cases as applying a knowledge of physics and chemistry to engineering, and applying theoretical studies to the practice of medicine, psychiatry and education.

3. *Relevance: a central problem*

Here lies the central difficulty for the student teacher. The common expectation seems to be that psychology will provide rules of procedure—for example, about how to deal with 'difficult' children or about how to teach geography. This presupposes that educational psychology has an established set of results, laws or conclusions which have only to be 'known' in order to be applied. Such conclusions do not however exist. The results of observations and experiments in educational psychology and in psychology generally always have reference to particular conditions which often bear little resemblance to the actual conditions and tasks facing teachers. Certainly, notions derived from psychological thought, observations and experiment can be seen to be related to particular approaches and methods in the classroom, for example considerations relating to incentives, to patterns of activity as opposed to the isolated elements making up an activity, and so on.

But educational procedures, while part of their rationale is to be found in psychological considerations, must also have other sorts of rationale and have to be devised to meet the particular requirement of learning particular things in particular situations. Here we attempt to induce students to *think* about what they are doing and to work out the implications of psychological thought in relation to their procedures and problems, that is we ask them to try and understand the *relevance* of psychology to their tasks. Thus the problem of what psychology contributes to the study of education is intimately bound up with the idea of how one branch of study is or becomes *relevant* to another, or to action, and in the case of psychology this question appears to have been given scarcely any serious treatment. Yet it lies at the heart of determining the nature of the contribution which psychology can make to education and of how this contribution can be made. A major part of the rest of this chapter is therefore given to a consideration of the meaning of relevance in our particular context.

In attempting to analyse the idea of relevance I will be more concerned with what may be called ways of thinking than with forms of knowledge. The difference is important. The former relates to a dialectic of thought and action while the latter is primarily concerned with the formal (logical) relations of 'subjects' or traditions of inquiry. While psychology therefore may represent an example of a combination of particular forms of knowledge (see section 3) and educational theory may not come into this logical category at all (see Chapter Two), I shall use the terms educational thought and psychological thought quite freely, implying that there is no difference in functional status between them. By 'thought' is here meant the whole reflective activity of the person, not merely cognitive activity. It embraces feeling and conation, and no distinction is implied by its use in this context between conscious and unconscious functioning. Thought in this sense is therefore always intentional, and never a bare abstraction. Educational thought and psychological thought refer to the reflective activity of educators and of psychologists respectively.

II. THE MEANING OF RELEVANCE

The question of the relevance of psychological studies to education may be broken down into a number of closely related questions. The first question is how we are to conceive of relevance, that is, what there is about two forms of thought which enable one to be relevant to the other. They can be so only if in some sense they are akin to one another, that is have something in common. Discovery of the common ground gives the answer to the second question which is concerned with erecting criteria for judging relevance. Once criteria have been obtained the two forms of thought may be explored and a kind of kinship map constructed. Here the difficulty lies in the fact that the common ground consists largely of shared presuppositions which involve value judgments. We are then faced with having to make discriminations. On the basis of these, selections may be made from the range of thought which comprises the total common ground. Thus it becomes possible in our case to define areas of psychological thought which have a high degree of relevance to educational thought. One question remains, one which is quite crucial for the student teacher. How can what has been rationally shown to be relevant become effectively relevant in a personal sense—that is, in action?

1. *Intrinsic relations*

The problem of relevance with which we are concerned arises in the first place because of the notion that education and psychology represent two forms of thought wholly distinct from one another which have consequently to be brought to bear upon one another. This notion has no doubt been nourished by the quite evident success psychology has enjoyed in becoming one of the sciences. But it grossly misconceives the nature of both forms of thought and consequently misconceives much of the relation between them. It has served to obscure the very evident fact that psychology and education have, in the most intimate sense, much common ground. This can be expressed more precisely by saying that some psychological forms of thought (and, of course, there are several, not just one) *are intrinsic* to educational thought (which is again, of course, plural). What is meant by their having intrinsic relations may be illustrated by many statements, for example 'children remember best those facts they acquire in the pursuit of some purpose'. Should this be regarded as a purely educational statement, or a purely psychological one? In fact it is a statement haunted by its own presuppositions, which are, at least, both educational and psychological. This is an illustration of what Whitehead meant when he said, 'There is not a sentence which adequately states its own meaning. There is always a background of presupposition . . .' (Whitehead 1948). In the same way educational thought is intrinsic to much psychological thought. Psychological thought owes much of what it is to the fact that, for example, educational, medical and vocational forms of thought are intrinsic to it. To exemplify this it is only necessary to refer to the pioneer work of Binet and Burt, both of whom, beginning from educational problems, jointly helped to create the whole branch of psychology concerned with the measurement of intellectual powers. Here educational thought entered into or informed psychological thought by prescribing the intentions and some of the conditions for its progress. Similarly, medical thought in terms of the work of Freud and his followers has immensely enriched psychology, and through it education.

To clarify further what is meant by one form of thought being intrinsic to another, that is *informing* it, we may suggest that psychological thought functions within educational thought (not externally to it) by helping to make some of its assumptions conscious, by helping to develop concepts essential to it and by suggesting procedures for action and for assessing the results of action. Some of Piaget's experiments on children's thinking illustrate this very well. The famous experiments on the conservation of quantity, for example, help to make conscious educational assumptions about levels of concept attainment at various ages, they help in our understanding of the way in which ideas grow and they suggest the kinds of experiences children require for the growth of general ideas. In these experiments was Piaget being in some peculiar sense a pure 'psychologist' and not an educator? Here the interrelation of thoughts is so intimate and the common ground is so obvious that it is pointless to fall back on purely logical categories and then ask from which side the entry was made. But things are not always so clear, and it is particularly with reference to psychological work which seems far removed from education that the meaning of relevance can be seen most clearly. As so often, an extreme case offers the best illustration.

Let us consider the psychology of learning as it has been developed by 'animal psychologists'. They state a number of what they consider well grounded generalizations (laws) about learning which they believe hold good thoughout the animal kingdom including man. One of these is that on the whole learning is more effective when 'reinforced' by rewards for success than by punishment for failure. Is this educationally relevant? In a certain sense parents and teachers, in many if not in all cultures, have known this for long enough without the benefit of psychology. But if they have been 'good' parents and teachers, they have known it in a sense quite different from that of the so-called law. Rewarding a child with a sweet and punishing him with a slap may look like direct applications of the findings of animal psychologists, but in fact they are nothing of the kind, for they are procedures intimately related to the ties of feeling which unite parent or teacher and child, and to culturally sanctioned ways of expressing these. Moreover, there is no good reason at all for supposing that what is happening in the child's case resembles in any precise sense what psychologists mean by 'reinforcement'. Any analogy is an extremely sketchy one. This truth is even more evident when reward and punishment are in terms of praise and blame.

A psychological theory of rewards and punishments in a human context has to take account of enormously more than it has in an animal context, and the idea of reinforcement if it is to be relevant at all, has to be put in the form of a generalization which is capable of being *interpreted* within a psychological theory of inter-personal relations. In being so interpreted the presuppositions on which it is based change their character. It is therefore only by a process of assimilation involving transformation that the kind of psychological thought represented by 'the law of rein-forcement' becomes relevant to education. In this way it may contribute its mite to a whole nexus of already existing thought about the regulation of interpersonal relations which is common ground for education and psychology. To what extent in the present instance the addition is significant seems to me to be a complex question and in some respects an open one.

Equally illuminating and much more significant are the observa-tions and experiments of ethologists like Lorenz (1952) and of psychologists like Harlow (1961) who have explored adult-infant interaction in a range of animal species. These have rightly attracted the interest of psycho-analysts, particularly Bowlby and Ambrose (Foss 1961) because of the light they may throw on parent–child relations. Here the analogies are much closer than in most animal learning experiments because the situation in both cases have important features in common. Yet the human and animal situations are by no means identical and for these experiments, whether in humans or animals, to have educational significance for the care of children their findings again have to be reinterpreted in the context of the realities of child care. Such studies are contributing to a psychology of mother–child relationships through a transformation which makes them educationally relevant.

This whole discussion brings out the fact that psychological forms of thought which are educationally relevant are continually being created by the coming into being of common ground between education and psychology. This fundamental point may be expressed by saying that psychological and educational thought do not enter into one another *indifferently*—both are subtly transformed in the process into something new. This something new may with justice be called 'educational psychology'. Thus psychology which is educational is a form of thought continually being created and modified by the intrinsic relations developed by educational and psychological thought. It can never be completely defined, althought it may from time to time be characterized by reference to a finite list of topics.

It may be felt that here there has been something of a sleight of hand. What we are calling educational thought, because it is intentional, has value judgments built into it, whereas surely psychological thought as a branch of 'science' involves no such value judgments! The idea of their science being deeply infected by value judgments is anathema to most scientists and particularly to scientific psychologists. In fact psychological thought always intends to count as truth, which is a value (Peters 1959), but it is certainly true that much psychological thought proceeds, and in fact must proceed without *explicit* reference to the values built into educational thought. The distinction merely serves, however, to strengthen the point which has been made. When it functions within educational thought, psychological thought shares the value judgments (whether explicitly or implicitly—it makes no difference) made by educational thought, and is directed by the conditions which these prescribe.*

2. *Shared presuppositions*

The sharing of presuppositions between education and psychology is therefore a necessary, although not a sufficient, condition of their mutual relevance. These presuppositions may be of a number of kinds, but because educational thought is itself intrinsically valuative many of the major presuppositions it shares with psychology are essentially valuative. The value judgments made by educational thought however, are themselves very various and some of them would be felt by educators to be much more 'valuable' in another sense (referring to superior or more inclusive kinds of value judgments) than others. The former would be regarded as having more cogent justifying reasons. For example, the advocacy of the use of examinations as incentives to learning is felt by not a few educators to involve presuppositions which include value judgments whose justifying reasons are poor compared with the reasons for advocating intrinsic interest as an incentive.† This point is of great importance, for in the whole range of presuppositions shared by education and psychology, there are not a few which would be rated so low by some educators (again by reference to a superior criterion of value) as to be properly excluded from being called 'educational'.

This is well illustrated by the following quotation: 'Growing up consists in learning how to behave, and learning how to behave means acquiring the proper responses to the batteries of social stimuli which compose our social order' (Warner and Havighurst 1946). Among the many presuppositions of this statement is one which entails a view of man as an organism responding to stimuli— that and nothing more. On this view the shared life of human beings

* Many ambiguities and disagreements in ideas about the nature of educational psychology spring from confusions about what is matter of fact and what is matter of value (Archambault (Ed.) 1965).

† Among the reasons in support of intrinsic motivation are the results of empirical inquiries (Bruner 1962).

is nothing but a complex of stimuli and responses. It is not difficult to see at least one form of psychological thought which shares this presupposition. It is in fact nakedly clear that in this instance educational thought has taken into itself a view of man inherent in many forms of behaviourism. Is this instance of a psychology which is 'educational', in the very general sense in which this term has so far been used, to be given a prominent place, or indeed to be included at all, in a scheme of psychological studies for student teachers? Clearly some appeal will have to be made to some more general category of values in order to answer this question.

We can now see how, in principle, it should be possible to reach decisions as to what to include and what to omit from 'educational' psychology. The work falls into two stages. Firstly, everything in educational and psychological thought with any claims to shared presuppositions (and adjudicating here would often be difficult) would have to be mapped. Secondly, all that is eventually agreed to be common ground would have to be judged in terms of a generalized criterion of value. This is of course a gigantic and unending task. In order to illustrate essential principles, however, it can be approached through an example.

3. *Outline of a map of kinship*

A suitable starting point is suggested by the various major dichotomies which have haunted educational thought in the western world for centuries. We might begin with the most deep seated of them all—society and the individual, which for psychology becomes translated nowadays into the concepts 'socialization' and 'individual development'—and go on to its derivative (at several removes) 'adult centred' and 'child centred'. Beyond this, and again derivative at several further removes, we have 'authority' and 'freedom'. One illustration must suffice however, and 'socialization' and 'individual development' contain enough of the presuppositions of the others to serve our purpose.

In order to make the contrast as sharp as possible let us take the quotation just given from Warner and Havighurst as exemplifying a 'hard' meaning of the term 'socialization'. Socialization may mean at least two things. It may refer only to the acquisition of social habits, etc., without specifying what part the individual, considered as an agent, plays in this—a 'soft' meaning of the term —or it may imply that the individual undergoes a process akin to conditioning, to ensure that he responds to stimuli in an approved manner—a 'hard' meaning. At classroom level it might be translated as meaning that teaching consisted in a set of techniques for imparting knowledge, skills and attitudes. On this view education is a *process* and consists in doing things *to* people. It is a purely adult-centred definition and one leaning so much to the side of authority as to convey an authoritarian ethos. Ultimately individual men exist for the sake of society. Such a view demands a particular kind of purely social psychology in which the individual has only a very minor role to play, that of a mere instance of a class of objects, of which all the instances are more or less alike. The 'individuality' or uniqueness of the individual is at a discount. This kind of psychology is largely concerned with mass behaviour and with the conditions under which men will tend to behave uniformly. It is therefore an easy ally for all kinds of authoritarian control whether in the classroom or in society at large. Moreover, it emphasizes techniques of control, and it draws its explanatory concepts from a variety of doctrines which stress the notions of drive and of reinforcement of desired responses by some form of conditioning. Any form of teleology is profoundly distasteful to it and the general form of thought to which it is most easily assimilated is one which we may call mechanistic. Men are no doubt organisms with drives, but the behaviour of an organism is as far as possible to be reduced to a mechanistic model.*

The opposing view would be one which asserted the claim of individuality to be the supreme educational end. On this view

* Continuing controversy about explanatory concepts in biology is shown clearly in what seems an almost inherent antivalence about 'causal' and 'teleological' categories. 'The story goes around among biologists that teleology is a woman of easy virtue, whom the biologist disowns in public, but lives with in private' (Polanyi 1965).

education is concerned with individual experience and the development of powers. The educator's task is to do things *for* people (in the sense of 'for the sake of'). Hence it is essentially child centred and leans heavily towards 'permissiveness'. Ultimately, society exists for the sake of individual men. Psychologically, all that is important about an individual is his unique characteristics and he may essentially be studied in isolation from his fellows. The appropriate kind of psychology is one largely concerned with the discovery and nourishment of individual talent, and social situations derive their significance from the differential effects they have upon individuals. It is the natural ally of abstract doctrines of freedom, and in the recent past it has tended to draw its explanatory concepts largely from notions among which that of purpose or goal directed activity plays a leading part. The individual is activated by instincts or drives which, provided they can be given socially approved expressions and can be brought into harmony with the needs of others, find their ultimate justification in his development as a unique being. Some form of teleology is often presupposed and the general mode of thought to which such a psychology is most easily assimilated is what we may call an organic one. (The influence of McDougall and of some aspects of Freud are clear.)

4. *Grounds of discrimination*

What characterizes these two views is, on the one hand, a rigid separation of society and the individual, and on the other, the ease with which both can be assimilated to more general forms of thought; the first to a mechanistic form, the second to an organic one. In neither case is there any real recognition that man is by nature social, that his very being depends on its nourishment by others in all its modes, that it is through our relations with one another that we constitute our own personal natures, and that our values all derive from the life we share in common. There is also no explicit appeal to man's rationality, to his capacity for dispassionate reflection, for imagination, logical thought, judgment and decision and also for sympathy, moral conviction and self knowledge.

There is no sense anywhere that his being is grounded in a self (as it is) through its relations with other selves. Thus man is conceived as having no intentions, but only as being subject to stimuli or to drives. He is incapable of action, he can only behave.

In making such criticisms I am asserting that there is a view of man which is more adequate to all that we know about him. Such a view would give us firm grounds on which to make discriminations among views of education, and their correlative forms of psychological thought. I would suggest that the necessary presuppositions of such a view are to be found in a form of thought which John Macmurray calls the form of the personal. Among other characteristics such a view is fully transactional. A psychological form of thought which is fully transactional demands the rejection of a social psychology which is so riddled with the errors of partial truths that persons as such play no part in it. And, on the other hand, it demands the rejection of a psychology based on the study of individuals in isolation. Correlative to such a form of psychological thought is a form of educational thought which sees 'in every relation between teacher and taught a full transactionalism, the teacher being taught, the student teaching, the two learning and teaching in reciprocity' (Gardner Murphy 1961).

The form of the personal is what Macmurray calls a philosophical mode of thought with which he contrasts the mechanistic (mathematical in his terminology) and organic forms.

As science moves from an established physics to the foundation of a scientific biology, we find that philosophy moves from a mathematical to an organic form. We should expect then that the emergence of a scientific psychology would be paralleled by a transition from an organic to a personal philosophy. The form of the personal will be the emergent problem. Such a new phase of philosophy would rest in the assertion that the self is neither a substance nor an organism, but a person. . . . the purely individual self is a fiction . . . the unity of the personal cannot be thought as the form of an individual self but only through the mutuality of personal relationship (Macmurray 1957).*

* It should be noted that in the above quotation I have omitted passages which, while essential to Macmurray's argument, seemed to me would have diverted attention from my immediate purpose. I do not claim fully

This is of course a fundamental position and for its justification one must read Macmurray's Gifford Lectures. We are concerned, however, with the form of the personal as it emerges in psychological thought. The first of our sets of presuppositions (those subsumed under the notion 'socialization'), being deeply embedded in a mechanistic form of thought, cannot be assimilated to the form of the personal without transformations so radical as to alter them almost out of recognition. The second set (subsumed under the notion of 'individuality'), while being thoroughly permeated by an organic form, can in part and in some respects be assimilated without major transformation to the form of the personal.

Only a few of the signs that psychological thought has reached the level of the personal can be given here. One is that the concepts of 'individual' and 'society' disappear, being transformed into the notions of 'persons' and 'community' (i.e. persons in relation). Another is that the self is recognized fully as an agent and not just as a sufferer of experiences or even as a mere knower,

---

to have understood Macmurray, but I have attempted to use in relation to our present problem some of the things I have learned from him which would appear to be relevant to it. He is concerned with what he calls philosophical forms of thought, we are concerned with psychological forms. But in my view one can no more hold this as a rigid distinction, than one can the distinction between educational and psychological forms of thought. One of the difficulties here is the definition of 'science'. If this necessarily involves psychology in treating men as 'objects' on the mechanistic or organic model, psychology must be behaviouristic, and it can never assume the form of the personal. But this cuts it off from large bodies of thought which may rightly claim to belong to it, including much of psycho-analysis, which is now obviously assuming the form of the personal (see Guntrip 1961). If this means that such activities have to be classed entirely as 'arts' and not 'sciences', it would seem to me that these distinctions have begun to outlive their usefulness. Here I would substantially agree with Burt (1964), though not necessarily for the reasons he gives, that psychology requires thought forms of its own, and that it cannot usefully be made to conform to a behaviouristic model, let alone a purely hypothetico-deductive one. To give only one example, Cheshire (1964) has shown that hypothetico-deductive models are quite inappropriate to psycho-analytic argumentation and that there are other, perfectly reputable models which are appropriate to it.

and that the scope and limitations of its agency are realized only in relation to the agency of others. Freedom is always relative to the freedom of others, and true freedom resides only in full mutuality. Psychological thought reaches the level of the personal when it makes the self the ultimate referent of its discussions. This does not in the least imply that in some sense we are ultimately dis-embodied beings or souls unaffected by our nature as animals. The self is simply the most inclusive psychological concept of our being. We are none the less 'embodied' beings and intrinsically related to others. In a sense we can say we are selves from the beginning but fuller realization of the self depends on others, on our education. At the level of the personal, education is neither doing things *to* people nor *for* them, but *with* them. As Pilley (1953) points out, anything we learn or invite others to learn represents a human achievement and we constitute our own minds through studying the achievements of others.

5. *The task of discrimination*

The whole object of this analysis has been to provide a position from which we could begin to discriminate among the many forms of psychological thought which clamour for inclusion in the study of education. The standpoint of the personal provides such a position. For the task of discrimination the relations of the various generalized forms of thought to one another must be correctly conceived. Their relationships may be described as not unlike those holding between the different parts of the soul in Aristotle's view of it. 'He suggested that there are three levels of soul—the rational, the animal and the vegetative. The lower is a necessary condition of the higher: but the higher modifies the way the lower operates and cannot be sufficiently explained in terms of it' (Peters 1959). However, Aristotle's categories are not ours, vegetative is not the same as mechanistic and the rational is only one aspect of the personal. It is necessary also to distinguish forms of thought from levels of what Aristotle calls soul or being. Mechanistic and organic images of man are partial images, not wholly false, but far from wholly true, resulting from the failure of thought to reach the level of the personal.

Such partial images reflect much of the reality of human existence. Hence the tremendous temptation to fall into the error of supposing that a description of what men habitually do is an adequate account of their essential nature, defining this nature as what they are capable of becoming as evidenced by what would commonly be acknowledged to be their highest achievements. Men seldom succeed in living wholly at the level of the personal. Their rationality and intentionality, which are marks of the personal, are often impaired or distorted, and sometimes distorted out of recognition, by the operation of what are, in isolation, quite rightly called 'animal drives', 'social factors', etc. This obviously happens in a fit of rage, it occurs more subtly when we are moved by unconscious jealousy and more painfully and drastically in a mental illness. When rationality is so impaired men's freedom is impaired or even destroyed, for they fail to respect one another as persons. In this condition a man is alienated from his fellows and from himself, i.e. his nature as personal. He treats others as only organisms to be directed or conditioned, or as instruments of his own pleasure, or as mere objects to be exploited or manipulated for his satisfaction. Freud, who has been our greatest student of human alienation in the psychological sphere (as Marx has been in the politico-economic), spent his life in trying to discover the inner conditions under which men cease to exploit one another and can claim, or regain, their freedom. It was not for nothing that psychiatrists were once called alienists.

Mechanistic and organic forms of thought have their proper place in science; there would be no sciences without them and advances are often made by pushing to the limit the categories of explanation they employ, as for example in cybernetic theory. It turns out to be very instructive indeed to consider brain functioning in terms of the mathematical theory of communication systems (McKay 1964). It is quite another matter however in an educational context to prefer to think, for example, of the laws of learning as necessarily involving the concepts of conditioning and reinforcement when it is essential to represent *acts* of learning in quite other terms. This is not to say that what we describe as conditioning processes do not enter as components into learning sequences which taken as a whole are something quite different. But to prefer to think in terms of partial truths may be to be tempted to act upon them. We may teach children through procedures which are largely ones of conditioning—it happens every day. In so doing, and when we have other procedures at our disposal, we necessarily dehumanize them in some measure. We fail to treat them as persons. But this is not to say that experiments with simplified forms of learning have nothing to teach us.

Conceptions of this kind are by no means new, as the reference to Aristotle shows. The difficulties which many people have with them and in interpreting them rightly are chiefly due to habits long established by traditional scientific thought. In studying man by scientific methods, we are most of the time investigating only partial aspects of him, that is, functions isolated for purposes of study. This is essential if we are to understand them. But they cannot be fully understood unless, later, they are studied in the context in which they belong, that is, in relation to the higher order systems (more inclusive functions) they subserve. To investigate the basis of blinking for example, a mechanistic model may be all that we need. Why we blink at all requires an organismic one for a full explanation. Whereas a deliberate wink is something quite different from a blink (Peters loc. cit.). If the blink becomes a tick, we will need the organismic model at least, and may indeed require to see this symptom in relation to the man as a person. As Laing (1960) puts it 'Man as seen as an organism or man as seen as a person discloses different aspects of the human reality to the investigator. Both are quite possible methodologically but one must be alert to the possible occasion for confusion.'

Moreover what we are dealing with is a hierarchic system. In the living being we speak of a hierarchy of functions in which (in Aristotle's terms) the lower order functions are essential to the

L

higher, but incapable of fully explaining them. Their full integration discloses to us the nature of the being as a whole. Our conceptual systems about ourselves therefore need to be cast in the form of a dialectical hierarchy, in which the all inclusive concept is that of the person. In attempting to conceive of man on either a mechanistic or organismic model we are necessarily involved with 'concepts out of context'. For the particular purposes of scientific study this may not matter, but in medical affairs it may often be serious, and in educational ones it always is.

In constructing schemes of psychological study in education there is therefore no question of jettisoning all the hard won psychological knowledge of man in his various partial aspects, gained through the scientific study of him. On the contrary, the task of discrimination is to use the form of the personal to discover, from among what is cast in mechanistic or organic forms, those concepts and systems of concepts which by suitable transformation might be made to fit a fully human image of man. The kind of transformation required is one which enables them to be seen functioning in a more inclusive context. This kind of transformation is always going on. Perhaps the most notable example at the present time is the way in which psycho-analytic thought is undergoing transformation from an originally largely organic form to one that is unmistakably personal (Guntrip loc. cit.).* Tasks of this order can only be patiently accomplished. They are, in one sense, never ending. It would be absurd to suppose that we could, without more ado, transform all that we need from psychological thought into the needed image of man. Our task is to use the concepts we need and try always to see their significance in the most inclusive context possible. What is needed is a principle in terms of which this can continually be carried out. The form of the personal provides this principle, and it turns out that it also

* Notable contributions to this transformation have been made in Britain by Fairbairn (1952), Guntrip (1961), Klein (1960), Laing (1960) and Winnicott (1964 etc.), and in U.S.A. by Bettelheim (1961), Erikson (1959 & 1964), Hartman (1958), Rapaport (1951) and Schachtel (1963).

provides what I have taken to be the final criterion for the relevance of psychological thought to education. Such thought becomes · fully relevant in so far as it comes to share presuppositions with educational thought which has assumed the form of the personal.

6. *Educational thought in the mode of the personal*

Before proceeding to show how this analysis can help in ordering psychological thought in the service of education, we need as a guide some more explicit indication of the nature of educational thought when it assumes the form of the personal. The following is offered as suggestive of some of the salient characteristics of educational thought at this level.*

Education is a joint enterprise in which older and younger people in all societies engage. The study of education is concerned with the ways in which we come to be constituted by, and come to constitute ourselves through, our relations with others. All that we learn, we learn in its beginnings from others. This we do through being involved in joint enterprises with them. There are always unconscious relationships involved, and much that is referred to as imitation comes under this heading. Gradually we acquire powers through which we can consciously guide our efforts, and pre-eminent among these powers are the power to use language and the power of imagination. Through the imaginative use of language we learn to interpret more fully the actions of others, their response to our actions, and their interpretation of events and things which make up the world of shared experience.

Apart from the works of nature, what we have to interpret are the works, that is the achievements, of men. A crucial achievement of man is the achievement of a balance, always a rather precarious balance, of co-operative relations over hostile ones. This achievement has its roots in a positive balance of affection over anxiety and hostility in our early relationships, and from this stems our

* Apart from psycho-analysis and other obvious influences, I owe much in my own efforts to think in this mode to John Pilley, Emeritus Professor of Education in the University of Edinburgh.

capacity to accept the foundations of the moral order of our community. This moral capacity grows as we consciously learn how to discriminate between love of self and love of others, and to act on this knowledge. Through reflection on our relations with others we learn to make the discriminations and decisions which constitute moral achievement.

All that we learn, if it is to become personal to us, we have to learn in part through first hand exploration and discovery, guided by our teachers. This applies to all modes of activity. This direct cultivation of creative imagination we gradually learn to supplement through studying the achievements, that is the discoveries, of others, and this we do largely through language, spoken and written. In this way, in reflection, and through acquaintance with the minds of others, we augment our powers of imagination, sympathy and reason.

In education, the relation between pupils and teachers is transactional, it takes the form of a partnership, and the main task of the teacher is to understand how this partnership can come to bear the stamp of a mutuality which transcends the inequalities inherent in relations between adults and children. This notion is derived from reading Macmurray. It is also virtually identical with what Erik Erikson, the psycho-analyst, posits as *the* problem of man in our time (Erikson loc. cit.).

7. *Sources of the problem of relevance*

The problem of relevance may now be restated in terms of its sources. The first is a major misconception of the interrelations of educational and psychological thought. The teaching of psychology in education courses has to lead to a growing awareness on the part of students that these studies are closely relevant to one another only when they share major presuppositions about the nature of man. It is absurd to expect students, and particularly young students, the majority of whom have only modest intellectual gifts, to sort out entirely by themselves the complexities in educational and psychological thinking. To leave them to flounder is not to encourage them to think for themselves. Without shrewd guidance they will at best achieve an inadequate grasp of what is at stake, at worst they will be utterly confused, and even permanently alienated from psychological study. Such guidance does not aim at their acceptance of a particular standpoint, but at helping them to see what the problems are, and how they may be tackled.

The second source is that, even given that various kinds of affinities begin to emerge between their studies, what is learned will not be felt to relate to action unless it is genuinely assimilated. A course of psychological study in education must not therefore be only a means of teaching the 'content' of psychology, it must make a contribution to students' personal education. This is to state the further problem of how such studies are made personal. It is the problem of the relevance of theory to practice.

III. WHAT IS MOST RELEVANT?
SOME REQUIREMENTS FOR AN EDUCATIONAL PSYCHOLOGY

1. *The necessary foundation*

This long analysis of the idea of relevance has been undertaken in order to exhibit certain principles which seem to be fundamental to the construction of a psychology which is fully 'educational'.

a. The relevance of psychology to education depends on a sharing of their presuppositions. From this it follows that (i) there are large areas of psychological study with prima facie claims to relevance, i.e. those dealing directly with children, teachers and, in the narrower sense, educational questions; (ii) there are other larger areas within which relevance to education may be established by suitable transformation of thought forms, often making use of analogy. As we have seen, great care has to be taken in doing this, a care related to the second principle.

b. If the shared presuppositions are to be ones assimilable to a fully personalized image of man, then all areas of psychological thought in principle relevant to education require some measure of transformation to render them so assimilable.

c. Since educational thought, particularly in its personalized form, necessarily includes considerations which go far beyond the immediacy of any situations in home or school, a correlative psychology must in principle also do so.

d. A constant scrutiny of its presuppositions is a necessary task for such an educational psychology, and in this particular task it must explicitly avail itself of the help of other foundation disciplines: e.g. philosophy, sociology, and history. Failure to do this necessarily entails its offering itself as purely a technology, afraid or unconcerned to avow the presuppositions necessarily built into it through its intrinsic relations with educational thought.

An example of such failure, which is at the same time a grave warning, is close to hand. The psychology of mental measurement, through failure to scrutinize adequately its presuppositions, developed into a technology concerned with establishing and measuring the more or less fixed intellectual abilities with which it supposed children to be endowed at birth, irrespective of the cultural and educational milieu in which they developed. In this country the growth of this technology was nourished by convictions, having deep ideological roots, that education required rigid systems for classifying children in terms of such abilities. Because it appeared to achieve practical success in carrying out such classification, educational psychology tended to become identified with the technology of mental measurement. We are now witnessing the slow crumbling of this technology, and of its supporting ideology, as the presuppositions of both become exposed to radical criticism.

These general principles suggest the foundations on which an educational psychology should be built, and point to the tasks with which it must be continually concerned if it is to remain educational. In the first place it has to be conceived as a humane general psychology, concerned primarily with man, his achievements and the vicissitudes of his life, and it has to be focused on human development in the context of interpersonal relations within a given society. Such a general psychology will be very close indeed to that also required as one of the foundations of education for a wide range of 'welfare' professions (certainly for the education of social workers and possibly also of doctors), and of a reformed general education. Secondly, those themes which have a prima facie relevance for the educational profession have to be conceived as arising within such a general psychology. (This is of course a requirement of dialectical logic and does not specify a pedagogical order of treatment.)

Such a viewpoint has radical implications. A strictly scientific psychology in the current sense will form an important component in such a general psychology, but it cannot dominate it. Change will be required in the sense in which the term 'scientific' is to be used, and forms of thought which are not scientific at all, notably philosophical, historical, and literary forms, must be built into it. This means that psychology must cease conceiving of itself as a kind of physics, or even a kind of biology (useful as physical analogies may be and much as it requires biological studies) and be prepared to construct its own thought forms borrowing whatever it requires from other disciplines.* For example, clinical psychology has always availed itself of historical thought, as well as scientific thought, and as a form of knowledge history cannot be reduced to science (Gallie, 1964).

The criterion required for a general psychology of this kind is not that it be 'scientific', but that it be an intellectually reputable study, an entirely different thing.† Moreover in many of its recent

---

* Among other things this entails a recognition of the logical impossibility and the practical absurdity of trying to maintain a purely behaviourist position (Peters 1959). To say this is not to deny the right, and indeed the necessity, of some branches of psychology to pursue a programme of behaviouristically defined studies. It is only to deny the right of anyone to define psychology as a whole in terms of such studies. Of course, it might be agreed that 'psychology' refers only to purely 'scientific' studies. In that case other relevant studies of the kind referred to here would require another title. This semantic manœuvre might well have an impoverishing effect on 'scientific psychology' itself.

† As used in certain contexts and in a certain tone of voice, the term 'scientific' has the flavour of an article of faith, and as so used is indistin-

developments, psychology has come to have, and must continue to develop, extensive intrinsic relations with sociology. None of this entails any break with tradition, rather it means that the claims of tradition and of critical thought must be reasserted within psychology. But one consequence would be a fairly radical reorientation in the general education of psychologists. Such a reorientation has recently been suggested by Harding (1956).

The tasks with which a reformed educational psychology must be continually concerned, if it is to be and to remain 'incorrigibly humane', to use R. B. Perry's phrase (Perry 1940), are a search for sources through a wide range of studies, a critical consideration of its main concepts and their interrelations from the standpoint of the form of the personal and a pedagogically sound ordering of its themes.

2. *Sources*

The next step is to indicate the kinds of sources which *the teacher of psychology to students of education* needs to draw upon. The field is a vast one and as a guide two further general principles seem to be required, both derivable from what has been said. The first we might call a principle of catholicity or liberality and the second a principle of stringency. Without a liberal principle our attention can easily become fixed on what is apparently and narrowly relevant, and without stringency we would inevitably be lost in an immense range of studies. These principles must be closely related, each continually modifying what is suggested by the other. The judgments which emerge, if they are to be wise, will obviously have to take account of experience and common sense.

Our focus has to be on childhood and youth and on the interaction of adults and young persons in the educational contexts provided by a particular society. These are both points of departure and points of return, but they do not prescribe what is to be

---

guishable, logically and psychologically, from other religious and quasi-religious utterances. This is ironical, for those who so use it are inclined to dismiss religious thought as concerned entirely with illusions.

traversed in between. A major objective is to exhibit human development, including adulthood as it normally occurs in our society.* But such development cannot be properly interpreted without reference to studies dealing with departures from the normal involving temporary or permanent impairment of function, with development in cultures other than our own, and with some aspects of animal behaviour. Our interpretation of the normal has to be illumined by reference to the stresses and strains through which it has to be maintained, and here Carstairs (1964), Murphy (1947), Storr (1963) and Winnicott (1964) are valuable sources. Studies of childhood and youth in other cultures are indispensable in making conscious the presuppositions inherent in our own child rearing and educational practices. In this field the writings of Margaret Mead (see bibliography), spread over many years of pioneer endeavour, those of Gorer (1949), and the more recent studies represented, for example, by Erik Erikson (loc. cit.) are indispensible. The animal studies of, for example, Lorenz (loc. cit.), Harlow (loc. cit.) and the Russells (1964) are highly suggestive of functional patterns either common to man and some of the higher animals, or of considerable relevance to certain problems of the human species.

There is great need also of the wisdom which careful readings in the classics of psychology could provide and here one thinks inevitably of selections from Freud (1962), James (1901), Prince (1906), McDougall (1934) and a reading of Brett's *History of Psychology* (Ed. Peters 1953) will suggest others. A notable addition to modern texts is one by Miller (1964) which focuses study on the work of seven eminent psychologists including Binet, Freud and Pavlov. Selections from the Gestalt school (Ellis 1950) and some of the writings of our own near contemporaries and teachers like Allport (1961), Bartlett (1932), Burt (1936), Harding

---

* The range must be the 'Seven Ages of Man' (see *New Society*, Nov./Dec. 1964). Relations between young and elderly, essential to both, have been much neglected in our society See also Barker, Kounin & Wright (1943) and Hoffman (1964).

(1941), Luria (1960), Mace (1962), Murray (1938), Richards (1949) and Thouless (1958) are valuable. Such sources would seem indispensable background to the collections of modern readings which have appeared under the editorship of Cohen (1964), and Iliffe (1959), and to modern evaluations of theoretical and experimental work in the psychology of personality such as those of Hall and Lindzey (1957), Wepman and Heine (1964), and P. E. Vernon (1964).

But our general sources have to be much wider than the writings of the great psychologists or of modern compendia, and critical studies of research. Relevant studies include not only case studies of children (there are many in some of the modern texts of child development and educational psychology), but autobiographical, biographical and literary studies including novels which enhance our understanding of human life in direct personal form. Here there is a very wide field of choice. One need only mention such a source of writings on childhood as that provided by Oakeshott (1960), great novels like those of Doestoevsky, and the more recent seminal study of Luther by Erik Erikson (1959). Beyond this, psychological study can be greatly enriched from mythological and religious sources. Leaving aside the more controversial question of the interpretation of some aspects of religious thought (but reference to Buber (1947), James (1906) and Tillich (1955) at least can scarcely be omitted), much is to be gained from the study of fairy tales, of myths (for example, that of Narcissus (Grace Stuart 1956)—the Oedipus myth is of course taken as fundamental), and of tales from the Odyssey. Only by taking into account material of this kind and relating it to studies by projective test methods (e.g. Symonds 1949), can the pervasive influence on thought of phantasies derived from unconscious themes fundamental to personality functioning, be properly appreciated.

While many of the sources already indicated provide a basis from which the development of the person can be seen in relation to, and in terms of, his interpersonal relations and his life in a community of persons, it is essential to augment this from sources concerned explicitly with the study of interpersonal relations in groups and with inter-group relations. The social psychology of the classroom and of the school is a growing study which brings into focus the relations of adults and young persons, and of adults concerned with young persons. References to some of the classical studies in group behaviour and to recent pioneer work in education will be found in Morris (1965). Studies of small groups and of behaviour in interpersonal relations have also to be seen against the wider background of general social psychology, and here Newcomb and Hartley (1958) is an excellent source book.

The study of such distinct functions as perception, imagination, and thought has always had an important place in general psychology and it goes without saying that education students must be helped to grasp some of the more important general principles in these fields, as well as having to pay close attention to individual differences in such functions. M. D. Vernon (1962) provides an excellent guide to present directions in the study of perception, and Wolters (1933) is still unsurpassed as an introduction. There is also a clear revival of interest in 'productive thought' and imagination, books by Koestler (1964), McKellar (1957), Rugg (1963) and Wertheimer (1961) providing a background to the recent studies in creativity by Getzels and Jackson (1962), Torrance (1962) and Hudson (1966). It is important also to link such studies with the work of educators concerned directly with fostering children's creative powers such as Cizek (1942), Hourd (1959) and Robertson (1963). It should be noted that the work of Hebb (1961) has played a powerful part in freeing cognitive psychology from the rigid bonds of the doctrine of innate abilities (Vernon 1950), and a massive preoccupation with the classification of such abilities to the neglect of how abilities function in the individual. The most easily accessible summarized account of the whole field of cognition is that of Thomson (1959).

The effects of fresh thinking in the cognitive field are as yet only being partially realized. As soon as thought is studied functionally as it occurs in people, it becomes increasingly difficult to ignore the fact of unity in the mental field, and the critical and intimate relations between thinking and feeling become recognized. Moreover it becomes apparent that the divorce between thought and feeling as a convenience of study seems to be easily linked with an actual divorce between these functions and this is apparent in the attitudes of some intellectuals including psychologists. Hence a diet of highly 'scientific' psychology concentrating on purely cognitive functioning can be seen to be not unconnected with the need of individuals to defend themselves against the realities of the life of feeling. The teacher student is in great need of being made aware of the dangers inherent in the arbitrary nature of the separation of cognitive and orectic functions, both for himself and for his pupils. Separate study of these functions, though necessary, has to be strongly complemented by studies of the creative life of mind. Here recourse should be made to studies of perception like those of G. S. Klein (1951), to the more articulate among artists and innovators of all kinds (see Koestler, loc. cit.) and to psycho-analysts interested in the psychology of art. Milner's essay (1956) is a crucial one for educators and her essay on psycho-analysis and art (1958) is a valuable guide to other sources in this field.

Among modern studies of fundamental relevance to educational thought about the development of the individual, pride of place should undoubtedly go to Piaget's voluminous writings, to Susan Isaacs' pioneer studies, and to Schachtel, Vygotsky and Witkin. The influence of Piaget is already extensive, but he is a writer badly in need of commentary and elucidation by others. Here Flavell (1963) is an important work of reference and recent publications by the Froebel Foundation (Isaacs 1961) and Lunzer (1960) provide useful clarification. Even here, however, there is scope for fairly extensive critical interpretation in order to relate psychological and educational presuppositions. Cultural relativity is an important issue in respect of some of Piaget's particular findings, if not in respect of his findings regarding the general processes of intellectual development. As a result of Piaget's work, experiments devised to discover, for example, whether certain forms of concept attainment may be accelerated by particular educational procedures, are being undertaken. Such an experiment into the attainment of arithmetical concepts is now being carried out in Bristol by one of my colleagues, Mr. J. G. Wallace. The results of such experiments if positive will clearly require critical discussion as to whether, and under what circumstances, such acceleration is desirable.

Susan Isaacs' books on intellectual (1930) and social development (1933) are still fundamental sources. Schachtel's work (loc. cit.) is likely to have a profound influence in bringing psychoanalytic studies more fully within the framework of general psychology through his critical consideration of the functions of affect, perception, attention and memory in relation to what he calls the metamorphosis of the individual from autocentric to allocentric modes of activity. Moreover his approach is based on the fundamental concept that the human individual is from birth an active being, and not just a reactive one. In the recently translated work of Vygotsky (1962) western psychology has been given a much needed stimulus from Russia to reconsider the relations of thought and language, and this has raised the problem of connecting his work with that of Piaget. Witkin (1962) and his collaborators have carried out important new studies of the ways in which people differ in their preferred modes of perceiving and have related these modes to a varied array of other personal characteristics. In this country Hudson (loc. cit.) has opened up a new field of inquiry, through his distinction between convergent and divergent modes of thinking, which has connections with other work on creativity mentioned above.

One field which is usually considered to be of pre-eminent concern for students of education is that of the psychology of learning, and reference may be made to any recent text book. Here, however, we encounter a major paradox. The studies which strictly deserve the title 'modern learning theories' are of remarkably little direct interest to teachers, since they largely comprise efforts by experimental psychologists to devise a systematic general theory from experiments on extremely simple forms of learning in the lower animals, particularly the white rat, and pigeons. Whatever ultimate value such work may prove to have, its immediate relevance for human learning is extremely limited since the latter is largely dependent on social influences and on the capacity to develop symbolic functions, particularly language (Mowrer 1960). The most important considerations in human learning would seem to derive from the tendencies of the young toward empathy, imitation, and identification (Mead 1964), coupled with their emerging capacity to understand, to criticize and to create through the use of language and other media. The treatment of children's learning needs to be based on the assumption that it must be regarded not merely from the behavioural standpoint, but also from the point of view of the experiencing learner and of those who guide him. It is important to remember too that concepts like 'reinforcement' have to be reinterpreted in the context of relations with others and in the light of personal levels of aspiration. The importance of social influence on the functioning of language in the mental development of children has recently been underlined by the work of Bernstein (1961) in this country.

One recent development which is supposed to have its rationale in the work of psychologists mainly concerned with animal learning, and which is of considerable significance to education, is of course 'programmed learning'. There is, however, little necessary connection between this development and 'modern learning theories', although the contingent connection, through the development of 'teaching machines' and the interest of such psychologists in computor-like devices, is real enough, and education students should certainly be aware of the work of, for example, Skinner (1961). Basically, programmed learning depends on the logical analysis of subject matter into very small learning steps (a development from Herbart!) so as to secure that pupils will experience a maximum of success and a minimum of failure and be able to correct their own work as they proceed. While its practical significance must not be minimized, critical studies of the role of this form of instruction for various purposes and at different stages have scarcely begun to be made. Smith and Moore (1962) is a useful guide to this rapidly developing field, and Leith, Peel and Curr (1964) provide a practical handbook.

It is a remarkable fact that experimental psychologists have as yet given little attention to devising experimental and critical studies of learning as it takes place in the classroom.* This is an aspect of educational psychology which may well begin to claim more attention as preoccupation with the technology of mental measurement diminishes. It should not be supposed, however, that the vast amount of work which has been done on measurement is without important implications for general educational policy and for educational guidance in the hands of teachers. The problem here is for students of education to understand how this work relates to the psychology of individual differences and the extremely clear account of this complex field given by P. E. Vernon (loc. cit.) is likely to remain an indispensable and reliable guide. It is in fact to the field of educational guidance that the major work of educational psychologists over the last forty or fifty years is most relevant and it is in future closer collaboration between teachers and psychologists in developing comprehensive guidance services that this work is likely to find its ultimate justification (Wall 1955 and 1956).

It is of course assumed that work in psychology will be linked to that in teaching method wherever possible and in particular it will be important to do this in relation to the learning and teaching of the basic skills in the primary school. Within the general context of guidance there must also be room for consideration of learning difficulties and of the problems of emotionally disturbed children which the pioneer work of Burt (1931, 1937), Schonell (1948), the Gluecks (1959) and many others has done so much to clarify. Moreover, there will obviously be many opportunities for cross

* For developments in treatment of 'learning theory' and of emphasis now being given to research relevant to classroom practice see Hilgard (1964).

reference from these specialist topics to the work done on the development of personality and on individual differences. In their broadest forms psychological studies of development and learning contribute one essential component to the study of curriculum construction (Olson 1957).

It is one of the aims of the Students' Library of Education, of which this is the initiating volume, to make available a series of studies in the psychology of education of direct use to students in education courses. These it is hoped will supplement texts in child development and educational psychology. Among these monographs will be ones dealing with children's learning, programmed learning, language, and measurement in education. Of the large number of texts which now exist it is unfortunately true that not very many can be wholly recommended in terms of the criteria set forth in this chapter. Some notable exceptions are Gabriel (1964), Jersild (1963) and Stone and Church (1957) on development, and among more general texts those of Cole (1950, 1953), Cronbach (1963 edition only), McFarland (1958) and Valentine (1960). From the many experimental studies in educational psychology now available in the professional journals, the discerning tutor can draw much valuable material, but in relation to initial studies in education great stringency is required in selection. It is assumed that the psychology course will include an introduction to observation, experiment and measurement, and these are topics coming within the scope of the monograph studies now being planned. It is, of course, beyond the scope of this chapter to comment in detail on the growing importance of research in education, much of it psychological research, but mention should be made of the admirable summaries of research published in 'Educational Research' by the National Foundation for Educational Research.

3. *Critical reviews of concepts*

The interrelation and criticism of leading concepts in psychology is a very large task, and much help is needed from the philosophy of mind (Chapter Three), but one or two general points need stressing here. From the point of view of this chapter, the Self appears as a fundamental, and superordinating concept for personality study. It is a significant fact that for years general psychology, particularly in America, has tried to do without such a concept. One is here irresistibly reminded of Polanyi's comment about biologists and the concept of teleology (p. 145 footnote). Many psychologists tend to treat the concept of the Self in a similar manner. Allport's advocacy of its re-introduction is therefore an important one (Allport 1955). The different meanings of this term (and of personality) are a source of much confusion at present but the modifications of Freud's thought now being attempted by Guntrip (loc. cit.) and other students of Fairbairn, notably Sutherland (1963) are pointers to further clarification. In educational studies the work of Staines (1958) on children's self concepts has not yet received the attention it deserves.

No adequate psychology is nowadays possible without an appreciation of the idea of unconscious functioning. Freud himself is of course by far the best source,* but the rendering of this and allied concepts of psycho-analysis in terms which relate it properly to general psychology has still to be fully accomplished, by psychologists and philosophers alike. Winnicott (loc. cit.) is a gifted expositor of its psychological interpretation and MacIntyre's analysis (1958) from a philosophical standpoint needs study. However, in common with most philosophers, even those most favourably disposed to psycho-analysis, he fails to grasp the real significance of the concept of man's 'inner world'.† Lastly we need

* The metaphors of Freudian thought have to be interpreted to students. They have also to learn how the reification apparent in concepts like that of super-ego is necessary to convey the stability and partial autonomy of such a function, as well as its origins in inter-personal relations.

† A term used by Freud in his last book (Freud 1949). It is now a commonplace in the thought of Klein and Fairbairn, and finds echoes in ordinary language. Thus recently a reviewer could describe Sartre as 'a man totally uninhabited by his father' (Rycroft 1964). To render this kind of comment into impersonal generalities, as some philosophers would have us do, is simply to take the guts out of it. The personalization of the

M

to reconsider carefully such pervasive concepts as motivation (Peters 1958) and needs and drives. These are fundamentally organic, and to become concepts within a psychology of persons, ought to be replaced in general theory, possibly by older terms like desires, the passions, strivings. When we are absolutely *driven* by hunger, sex or aggression, the self has surrendered its sovereignty and drive is in such a context descriptively correct. But normally, and most of the time, we have desires and may even be gripped by passions, such as love and hate, without the self surrendering to them. Desires and feelings are among the constitutive components of all rational activity, and the self is always in part guided by unconscious desires. Moreover in creative work, the self may relinquish purely conscious rational control altogether, and be wholly guided by unconscious aims, without losing its sovereignty (Milner, loc. cit.). The notions of social and personal 'adjustment' are also ones which, as commonly used, are at variance with ideas of the life of community as fundamentally transactional. The search for an active mutual accommodation, ideally for mutuality, is the idea which now needs effective expression. The current revision of psycho-analytic concepts is aiming at representing man, not as

---

'inner world' in psycho-analytic thought is not crude metaphor but direct reference to what is manifested personally in us. It may be noted that the concept of an 'inner' or 'representational' world is now strongly emerging in general psychology. The terms 'internalization of experience' and 'internalization of social norms' are now common. Piaget speaks of thought as internalized action. Tustin (1953) makes the observation that an essential mode of functioning of the human 'organism' is to build up an internal analogue or simulacrum of the external world. This conception is intrinsic in cybernetics in which brain functioning is conceived in terms of neural mechanisms which in part simulate external events and elaborate and transform them into symbols. Mowrer (loc. cit.) regards theoretical constructs of this kind as essential to understanding how the simpler concepts of S-R theory may be linked with a theory of complex behaviour. While neurological models will obviously play a part in future development here, it is important that psychological models should also be constructed. Bartlett's 'schemata' are surely forerunners of a more fully developed psychological model of man's internal world, in which the personalized 'internal objects' of psycho-analysis are likely to be prominent features.

seeking instinct satisfaction or the satisfaction of needs or reduction of drives, but as fundamentally seeking personal relationships. Such relationships are of course subserved by his various desires, passions and strivings, which in turn are subserved by biological drives. A reductive analysis of this kind while essential as a step in understanding has to be seen in the context of a continuous attempt to act at a fully personal level.

IV. HOW RELEVANCE IS MADE PERSONAL

To determine what is relevant is a necessary but insufficient basis for an educational psychology. What is relevant has to become part of thought issuing in action, that is, it has to be made fully personal. In part this aim can be achieved through an adequate relationship of the various studies fundamental to education, to one another, and to educational theory. It may be further facilitated by an ordering of the major themes in psychological study in such a way that they are seen to relate to the wider context of personal living and to the more immediate context of teaching in the school community. Essential to its achievement is enlightened teaching of a kind which involves students in observation, experiment, discovery and discussion, including critical discussion of the terms they are learning to use. Such teaching must also be careful to secure that the psychological principles it uses in relation to children's learning are exemplified in the students' own studies and in the community life of the college as well. But over and above all this there are problems peculiar to studying psychology in the way necessary to make it into personal knowledge.

The crucial point may be made plain by saying that it is not enough to understand *about children*, one has to come to understand *them*. Such a kind of understanding is based primarily on an understanding of one's self. No matter how much this understanding requires (as it does) to be augmented by all sorts of relevant study, its primary source lies in the understanding one has, and can gain of one's own 'childhood', that is of the child still active within oneself. This may be generalized to the whole question of interpersonal relations at all levels of development, to what Oakeshott has called 'the art of human understanding' (1958). Understanding here is of a different kind from that referred to when we talk about understanding a problem or procedure. This latter kind of understanding requires much more analysis in order to determine what kinds of action are to count as pointing to understanding (Williams 1964). But in understanding people we come to the limit of what clarity of logical thought can do for us. Such clarity is essential but not sufficient. Something else is required.

What is required is the cultivation of the kind of sympathy through which we are able in imagination to *identify* with others, to experience something of their joys and sorrows, their problems, failures and achievements. Moreover we have to learn to do this without surrendering our own identity and independence. This cultivation of the power of detached but sympathetic identification lies at the heart of making the study of psychology truly personal (Morris 1958 and 1961). Some of this power is necessarily implied unless we are prepared to refuse to recognize the inevitable self reference in psychological study. To do so is to affirm that psychology in a professional context is the study of other people only. Its applications must then be essentially manipulative and constitute a denial of human mutuality (Morris 1955).

The capacity to accept such self reference is very variable indeed and constitutes (often unrecognized) a major difficulty which education tutors have with their students and indeed with themselves! Detached but sympathetic identification may be cultivated in various ways but primarily, in an education course, through studies of children and adults very different from oneself. It is relatively easy to 'understand' those like oneself, though such understanding will be intimately related to one's own self knowledge or lack of it;* it is much more difficult to understand

* It is notorious of course that we can often perceive the 'projection' in, for example, various forms of scape-goating behaviour in others, while entirely failing to identify it in our own behaviour.

others quite unlike oneself, whether they are of another temperament, or from a different social background or from another culture altogether. The latter provides the supreme test. Here literary studies and reflection on personal experience come into their own as the essential complement of 'objective' disciplines.

The professional task of education students, like that of others whose concern is primarily with people, means that their major resources lie in their capacity for making and sustaining fruitful relationships. In this they are necessarily exposed to a continuous reactivation of the unconscious foundations of their own personalities, in the case of teachers the reactivation of their own childhood by their pupils. The anxieties attendant on self knowledge are intensified, and defensive behaviour of various kinds is always prominent. Flight into impersonal study is one form of defence, and equally flight from a disciplined rationality is another. Neither by a cold logical understanding nor by getting into a cosy huddle with children can the teacher fulfil his professional role. But defences are important: something of value is being defended, namely the integrity of the personality, in particular its inner core, the ego. We all need our defences respected. We can relinquish those which inhibit further development only by being helped to achieve more adequate forms of personal integration.

In their professional work, teachers and student teachers alike have a peculiarly difficult task, for they have to learn to combine sympathetic understanding with detachment, and intellectual objectivity with moral conviction. In helping students, particularly with psychological studies which may impinge directly on cherished moral values, the teacher of psychology has to bring to bear in his relations with his students not only a wide and disciplined understanding of his subject, but also the detached sympathy and wisdom which an imaginative study of it can give him. The major contribution of psychological studies to education lies in their potential power to deepen and augment our perception of what we are doing in education, and our understanding of one another as we attempt to carry out together the tasks with which we are faced. It is in terms of such conceptions that we gain an understanding of the relation of theory to practice.

CONCLUSION

A plea is made in this chapter for psychological studies in education to be based on a humane general psychology in which the more specialized studies related closely to classroom and school will take their place. Such a psychology can still have its roots, so far as the teaching of it is concerned, in topics natural for the student teacher. Some separate treatment of the main themes of psychology is certainly required, but throughout the education course it must be constantly linked with educational theory proper and with the other foundation disciplines of education.

The structure, scope, content and treatment of psychological studies in education must obviously vary with the backgrounds of the students and with the length of the course. Scope and treatment, for example, are bound to vary between a one-year course for graduates in training as teachers, and three-year and four-year courses for students in colleges of education. Yet it should be possible to apply similar principles. In the introductory stages for example there is much to be said for an approach involving the close integration of psychology with the other disciplines. A course beginning with a co-operative treatment of themes such as children and their families, teaching and teachers, and the school as a community and an institution within society, could do much to give education studies the manifest relevance for students which they often seem to lack. Such an approach moreover provides for the essential discipline of observation, inquiry, reflection and interpretation which is a necessary prelude to the more differentiated and formal treatment of various fundamental themes within the separate contributary disciplines. As differentiation and formal study increase, however, there will always be a constant need for the kind of reintegration which is relevant to educational action.

BIBLIOGRAPHY

Allport, G. W., 1937, *Personality. A Psychological Interpretation.*
— 1955, *Becoming.*
— 1961, *Pattern and Growth in Personality.*
Archambault (Ed.), 1965, Best, E., *Common Confusions in Educational Theory* (section on 'Language of Educational Psychology').

Barker, R. G., Kounin, J. S. and Wright, H. F., 1943, *Child Behaviour and Development.*
Bartlett, F. C., 1932, *Remembering.*
— 1958, *Thinking.*
Bernstein, B., 1961, 'Social Class and Linguistic Development: a Theory of Social Learning'. In *Education, Economy and Society*, ed. A. H. Halsey, *et al.*, pp. 288–314.
Bettelheim, B., 1961, The Informed Heart.
British Psychological Society and A.T.C.D.E., 1962, Report of the joint working party on teaching educational psychology in teacher training.
Bruner, J. S., 1960, *The Process of Education.*
— 1962, *On Knowing.*
Buber, Martin, 1947, *Between Man and Man.*
Burt, Cyril L., 1931, *The Young Delinquent.*
— 1936, *The Subnormal Mind.*
— 1937, *The Backward Child.*
— 1964, 'Consciousness and Space Perception'. In *British Journal of Statistical Psychology*, Vol. XVIII, Part I, pp. 77–85.

Carstairs, G. M., 1963, *This Island Now* (also Pelican, 1964).
Cheshire, N. M., 1964, 'On the Rationale of Psycho-dynamic Argumentation'. In *British Journal of Medical Psychogogy*, Vol. XXXVII, Part 3, pp. 217–30.
Cizek, 1942, see Viola.
Cohen, J., 1958, *Humanistic Psychology.*
— (Ed.) 1964, *Readings in Psychology.*
Cole, L. E., 1953, *Human Behaviour.*
Cole, L. E. and Bruce, W. F., 1950, *Educational Psychology.*
Cronbach, L. J., 1963, *Educational Psychology* (2nd ed.).

Ellis, W. D., (Ed.), 1950, *A Source Book of Gestalt Psychology.*
Erikson, E. H., 1959, *Young Man Luther.*
— 1964, *Childhood and Society.*
— 1964, *Insight and Responsibility.*

Fairbairn, W. R. D., 1952, *Psycho-analytic Studies of the Personality.*
Flavell, J. H., 1963, *Development Psychology of Jean Piaget.*

Foss, B. M. (Ed.), 1961, *Determinants of Infant Behaviour*, Part I.
— 1963, *Determinants of Infant Behaviour*, Part II.
Freud, S. 1933, *Introductory Lectures on Psycho-analysis* (2nd ed.).
— 1945, *The Interpretation of Dreams* (3rd ed.).
— 1946, 'A note on the Unconscious in Psycho-analysis' (1912). *Collected Papers*, Vol. IV.
— 1949, *Outline of Psycho-analysis* (1938).
— 1962, *Two Short Accounts of Psycho-analysis:* (a) *Five Lectures on Psycho-analysis*, 1909; (b) *The Question of Lay Analysis*, 1926, Penguin.

Gabriel, J., 1964, *Children Growing Up*.
Gallie, W. B., 1964, *Philosophy and the Historical Understanding*.
Getzels, J. W. and Jackson, P. W., 1962, *Creativity and Intelligence*.
Glueck, S. (Ed.), 1959, *The Problem of Delinquency*.
Glueck, S. and Glueck, E. T., 1947, *Juvenile Delinquents Growing Up*.
— 1950, *Unravelling Juvenile Delinquency*.
— 1959, *Predicting Delinquency and Crime*.
— 1962, *Family Environment and Delinquency*.
Gorer, G. and Kickman, J., 1949, *The People of Great Russia*.
Guntrip, H., 1961, *Personality Structure and Human Interaction*.

Hall, C. S. and Lindzey, G., 1957, *Theories of Personality*.
Halmos, P. and Iliffe, A. H. (Eds.), 1959, *Readings in General Psychology*.
Harding, D. W., 1941, *The Impulse to Dominate*.
— 1956, 'Education Through Psychology'. In *Bulletin of British Psychological Society*, No. 28.
Harlow, H. F., 1961, 'The Development of Affectional Patterns in Infant Monkeys'. In *Determinants of Infant Behaviour*, Part I, ed. B. M. Foss.
— 1965, with Harlow, M. K. (1) 'Romulus and Rhesus'. In *The Listener*, Feb. 11, pp. 215–17; (2) 'An Analysis of Love'. In *The Listener*, Feb. 18, pp. 255–7.
Hartmann, H., 1958, *Ego Psychology and the Problem of Adaptation*.
Hebb, D. O., 1961, *The Organization of Behaviour*.
Hilgard, E. L. (Ed.), 1964, *Theories of Learning and Instruction*. Sixty-Third Year Book of National Society for the Study of Education.
Hoffman, M. L. and L. W. (Eds.), 1964, *Review of Child Development Research*.
Hourd, M. L. and Cooper, G. E., 1959, *Coming Into Their Own*.
Hudson, L., 1962, 'Intelligence, Divergence and Potential Originalty'. In *Nature*, Vol. 196, p. 601. 1966, 'Contrary Imaginations'.

Iliffe, A. H., 1959, see Halmos and Iliffe.
Isaacs, N., 1961, *The Growth of Understanding in the Young Child*.
Isaacs, S., 1930, *Intellectual Growth in Young Children*.
— 1933, *Social Development in Young Children*.

James, W., 1901, *Principles of Psychology*.
— 1906, *Varieties of Religious Experience*.
— 1911, *Talks to Teachers on Psychology*.
— 1919, *The Will To Believe*.
Jersild, A. T., 1963, *The Psychology of Adolescence* (2nd ed.).

Klein, G. S., 1951, 'The Personal World Through Perception'. In *Perception; An Approach to Personality*, ed. R. R. Blake and G. V. Ramsey, pp. 307–55.
Klein, M., 1960, *Our Adult World and its Roots in Infancy*.
Koestler, A., 1964, *The Act of Creation*.

Laing, R. D., 1960, *The Divided Self*.
Leith, Peel and Curr, 1964, *A Handbook of Programmed Learning*.
Lorenz, K., 1952, *King Solomon's Ring*.
— 1956, Contributions to: *Discussions on Child Development*, ed. J. M. Tanner and B. Inholder, 4 vols.
— 1957, 'Companionship in Bird Life'. In *Instinctive Behaviour*, ed. C. H. Schiller, pp. 83–128.
Lunzer, E. A., 1960, *Recent Studies in Britain Based on the Work of Jean Piaget*.
Luria, A. R., 1960, *The Nature of Human Conflicts*.

Maccoby, E. E., Newcomb, T. M. and Hartley, E. L. (Eds.), *Readings in Social Psychology*.
McDougall, Wm., 1934, *The Energies of Men* (2nd ed.).
Mace, C. A., 1962, *The Psychology of Study*.
McFarland, H. S. N., 1958, *Psychology and Teaching*.
McIntyre, A. C., 1958, *The Unconscious—A Conceptual Analysis*.
McKay, D. M., 1964, 'Information Theory in the Study of Man'. In *Readings in Psychology*, ed. J. Cohen.
McKellar, P. H., 1952, *A Text Book of Human Psychology*.
— 1957, *Imagination and Thinking*.
Macmurray, J. 1957, *The Self as Agent* (Gifford Lectures 1953).
— 1961, *Persons in Relation* (Gifford Lectures 1954).
Mead, M. 1928, *Coming of Age in Samos*. Pelican 1963.
— 1930, *Growing Up in New Guinea*. Pelican 1963.
— 1939, 'Sex and Temperament'. In *From the South Seas*.
— 1944, *The American Character*.
— 1950, *Male and Female*.
— 1956, *New Lives for Old*.
— 1964, *Continuities in Cultural Evolution*.
Miller, G. A., 1964, *Psychology. The Science of Mental Life*.
Milner, M., 1956, 'The Sense in Non-Sense, Freud and Blake's Job'. In *New Era in Home & School*, Vol. 37, No. 1.

Milner, M., 1958, 'Psycho-Analysis and Art'. In *Psycho-Analysis and Contemporary Thought*, ed. J. D. Sutherland, pp. 77–101.

Morris, B. S., 1955, 'Guidance as a Concept in Educational Philosophy'. *Year Book of Education.*

— 1958, 'Personality Study: Its Aims and Implications for Students of Education.' *Sociological Review Monograph* No. 1, pp. 75–86.

— 1961, 'Personal Growth Through Professional Education'. In *Proceedings of the VIth International Congress on Mental Health.*

— 1965, 'How Does a Group Learn to Work Together?' In *How and Why do We Learn?*, ed. W. R. Niblett.

Mowrer, O. H., 1960, *Learning Theory and Behaviour.*

— 1960, *Learning Theory and the Symbolic Processes.*

Murphy, Gardner, 1947, *Personality. A Biosocial Approach to Origins and Structure.*

— 1961, *Freeing Intelligence Through Teaching.*

Murray, H. A., 1938, (and others) *Explorations in Personality.*

— 1953, (with Kluckhohn, C.) 'Outline of A Concept of Personality.' In *Personality in Nature, Society and Culture*, ed. C. Kluckhohn and H. A. Murray (2nd ed.).

— 1962, 'A Prospect for Psychology'. In *Science*, Vol. 136, No. 3515, pp. 483–8.

National Foundation For Educational Research. *Educational Research.* 3 parts per annum from 1958.

Newcomb and Hartley, 1958, See Maccoby, Newcomb and Hartley.

Oakeshott, E. M., 1958, 'Means by which Students of Education may learn about Personality Development.' In *Sociological Review Monograph* No. 1, pp. 51–60.

— 1960, *Childhood in Autobiography*. (Readers Guides, 4th series, No. 1).

Ogden, C. K. and Richards, I. A., 1949, *The Meaning of Meaning.*

Olson, W. C., 1957, *Psychological Foundations of the Curriculum*. UNESCO Educational Studies and Documents No. 26.

Perry, R. B., 1940, in *The Meaning of The Humanities.*

Peters. R. S., 1953, *Brett's History of Psychology.*

— 1958, *The Concept of Motivation.*

— 1959, *Authority, Responsibility and Education.*

Piaget, J., see Flavell.

Pilley, J., 1953, 'Educational Theory and The Making of Teachers'. In *Educational Theory*, Vol. III, No. 1.

Polanyi, M., 1965, 'Modern Minds'. Encounter, May.

Prince, M., 1906, *The Dissociation of A Personality.*

Rapaport, D., 1951, *Organization and Pathology of Thought.*

Reid, L. A., 1962, *Philosophy and Education.*

Richards, I. A., 1949, see Ogden and Richards.

Robertson, S. M., 1963, *Rosegarden and Labyrinth*.

Rugg, H., 1963, *Imagination*.

Russell, W. M. S., 1964, (1) 'The Wild Ones'. In *The Listener*, Nov. 5, pp. 710–12; (2) 'The Affluent Crowd'. In *The Listener*, Nov. 12, pp. 753–5.

Rycroft, C., 1964, 'Words. Jean Paul Sartre'. Review in *New Society*, Dec. 3, p. 25.

Schachtel, E. G., 1963, *Metamorphosis*.

Schonell, F. J., 1948, *Backwardness in the Basic Subjects* (4th ed.).

Skinner, B. F., 1961, *Science and Human Behaviour* (2nd ed.).

Smith, W. I. and Moore, J. W. (Eds.), 1962, *Programmed Learning*.

Staines, J. W., 1958, 'The Self-Picture as a Factor in the Class-Room'. In *British Journal of Educational Psychology*, Vol. XXVIII, Part II, pp. 97–111.

Stone, L. J. and Church, J., 1957, *Childhood and Adolescence*.

Storr, A., 1963, *The Integrity of the Personality*.

Stuart, G., 1956, *Narcissus*.

Sutherland, J. D., 1963, 'Object Relations Theory and the Conceptual Model of Psycho-analysis'. In *British Journal of Medical Psychology*, Vol. XXXVI, Part 2, pp. 109–24.

Symonds, P. M., 1949, *Adolescent Phantasy*.

Thomson, R., 1959, *The Psychology of Thinking*.

Thouless, R. H., 1958, *General and Social Psychology* (4th ed.).

Tibble, J. W., 1963, 'Psychological Theories and Teacher Training'. In *Year Book of Education*, pp. 85–94.

Tillich, P., 1955, *The Courage To Be*.

Torrance, E. P., 1962, *Guiding Creative Talent*.

Tustin, A., 1953, 'Do Modern Mechanisms Help Us To Understand The Mind?' In *British Journal of Psychology*, 44, pp. 24–37.

Valentine, C. W., 1960, *Psychology and Its Bearings on Education* (2nd ed.).

Vernon, M. D., 1962, *The Psychology of Perception*.

Vernon, P. E., 1950, *The Structure of Human Abilities*.

— 1964, *Personality Assessment. A Critical Survey*.

Viola, W., 1942, *Child Art*.

Vygotsky, L. S., 1962, *Thought and Language*.

Wall, W. D., 1955, *Education and Mental Health*.

— 1956, (Ed.) *Psychological Services for Schools*.

— 1962, (with F. J. Schonell, and W. C. Olson) *Failure in School*.

Warner, W. L. and others, 1946, *Who Shall be Educated?*

Wepman, J. M. and Heine, R. W., 1964, *Concepts of Personality*.

Wertheimer, M., 1961, *Productive Thinking*.

Whitehead, A. N., 1948, *Essays on Science and Philosophy*.

Williams, J. D., 1964, 'Understanding and Arithmetic II. Some Remarks on the Nature of Understanding'. In *Educational Research*, Vol. VII, No. 1.

Winnicott, D. W., 1964, *The Child, The Family and The Outside World.*

— 1965, *The Family and Individual Development.*

— 1966, *The Maturational Processes and the Facilitating Environment.*

Witkin, H. A. and others, 1962, *Psychological Differentiation.*

Wolters, A. W. P., 1933, *The Evidence of Our Senses.*

Chapter Six

THE SOCIOLOGY OF EDUCATION

WILLIAM TAYLOR

Although the term sociology is now over a hundred years old, and it is possible to produce a list of thinkers who have made contributions to sociological understanding that goes back to antiquity, the organization of sociology as a university study is of comparatively recent origin. There were only five established chairs of sociology in British universities in 1962; by the end of 1964 their number had increased to twenty-nine. Sociologists, who for years had been defending themselves against the view that their subject had no independent existence or that its methods would never earn it scientific status, have suddenly found themselves in demand to start and staff new departments, to train new generations of students, and to provide advice for government, industry, churches and schools. Part cause, part effect of this new-found respectability and academic status, are the efforts sociologists are making to free their studies from the realms of moral philosophy and social improvement from which they originated. Sometimes the efforts result, on the one hand, in fact-grubbing and methodological embellishment, and, on the other, grandiose and diffuse system-building of a kind that has attracted a good deal of lay criticism. Sometimes they encourage a form of spurious professionalism and unjustifiable verbal prolixity that does little to earn the respect that, on the whole, contemporary sociological studies deserve. For such studies, with all their faults, are exhibiting a degree of vitality and a capacity to penetrate lay thinking about society that is both encouraging and impressive. They are serving the practical and intellectual needs of a type of society which is itself new—an affluent, industrial society in which for the first time the majority of the population possesses a substantial surplus, beyond biological need, of both leisure and income, in which speedy transportation and mass communications are in the process of altering our perspectives of time and distance, and in which the effects of the work of Darwin, Marx, Freud and others on our image of ourselves and our social relationships are all-pervasive in everyday social life and language. The very newness of this world, and the immanence of social change within it, are often underestimated. Too much social and educational discourse is still based on a model of change that envisages a movement from one stable, long-term structurally integrated pattern, towards some equally stable long-term replacement, via an essentially temporary and 'abnormal' anomic period of revolution or transition. A good deal of present day discussion of the reorganization of secondary education is influenced by a model of this kind. But since the beginning of this century there has never been a period of stability during which some reorganization of some kind or another has not been going on. The Hadow reorganization of 1926 was still incomplete in some areas twenty years after the Education Act of 1944. Some former all-age schools were reorganized straight into the comprehensive pattern, missing out the bipartite stage altogether. One is inclined to agree with Glazer (1960) that 'carry through a revolution in the schools—any revolution, in any direction, and education will improve, at least in the short run'. To recognize the immanence of change highlights questions quite different from those characteristic of earlier, non-industrial periods. In Gellner's terms (1964): 'In the twentieth century the essence of man is not that he is a rational, or political, or a sinful, or a thinking animal, but that he is an industrial animal. It is not his moral or intellectual or social or aesthetic, etc., etc., attributes that make man what he is; his essence resides in his capacity to contribute to, and to profit from, industrial society. The emergence of industrial society is the prime concern of sociology.'

Modern sociology tends to be less concerned with the grand sweep of history than with the detailed analysis of social structure and process; less interested in the traditional social problems of poverty, delinquency and vice than in the more generalized patterns of institutional disintegration and change that provide the settings for such problems. Its methods are largely empirical, rational, descriptive and analytic. Whilst not without value orientation— the improving and reforming spirit of the early social surveys is still present, not least in the sociology of education—it is concerned to avoid hortatory and inspirational pronouncement, and tends to be more influential at the level of policy rather than of practice, in influencing structural development rather than individual behaviour, touching the administrator and the legislator rather than the social worker and the teacher.

Many of those who call themselves sociologists and have been trained in university departments of sociology have an interest and commitment at two related levels. Much of their personal research and study may be concerned with one of the specialisms within the field of sociology—with the sociology of industry, religious behaviour and institutions, survey and research methods, political sociology or the sociology of education and so on. But in their work in these areas they share a common concern with such features of social structure, organization and action as class and stratification, the role of the family, the dynamics of social change and the nature of bureaucracy. And, to the extent to which they are serving not only a field of practical activity but also the development of their discipline, they also share a desire to facilitate a two-way traffic of influence between the refinement and elaboration of these broader concepts of sociological inquiry and work in a particular field of research. It is important to emphasize the need for this two-way traffic, not just in the case of the professional sociologist and research worker, but also for the student who wishes to know something of the sociological contribution to the understanding of his own professional activity and expertize. For example, to study the facts about educational opportunity that have been made available by a series of official committees and in several private research projects during the post-war years, without any understanding of what is implied by the terms 'social class' or the broader aspects of stratification, and without an awareness of the way in which technological innovation has altered the occupational structure and the nature of skill, is to omit any possibility of appreciating the impact of the facts and figures that have been discovered, or of assessing their significance to the work of the teacher and the school. In the college and department of education there is no time for the course in general sociology that could provide the context for a later study of the sociology of education; but at least the effort can be made to provide some of the sociological background that enables the results of specialized studies to make sense. The educator of teachers must choose among the themes and approaches offered by sociologists those that seem most relevant to the needs of the students and the schools; but the criterion of relevance must be illuminated by a proper understanding and respect for the nature of the sociological contribution, by a willingness to take what is offered on its own terms, and to accept the limitations of the evidence that exists. The requirement that the college or department lecturer should be a specialist in a particular field is not to suggest that the lecture course and other work done by students should themselves be highly specialized. Rather the intention is to ensure that an informed selection can be made from the contributions of the specialism to the development of educational theory and a rationale for practice, in which the integrity of the original discipline can be properly respected.

The scope of the sociology of education

Looked at from the point of view of the professional sociologist, the sociology of education has a place alongside other specialisms such as the sociology of religion, sociology of industry and sociology of economic life. Sociologists of education are interested, first of all, in the way in which schools, colleges and universities are related to other institutions and structural features of the societies in which they exist. At the broadest level, this involves asking questions about the link between industrialization, technological change and educational provision. There are clearly important links between, on the one hand, the methods of production that a society employs, the scale of its consumption and other economic activities, the organization of work and occupational opportunities, and, on the other, the values that characterize its educational efforts, the type of schools that it possesses and the qualifications that these provide. But this relationship is neither simple nor one-way. There is nearly always some kind of educational lag that reduces the effectiveness of educational institutions in fulfilling the demands of industry and commerce for skill and knowledge of particular kinds—and the type of skill and knowledge required is not always well understood by those who are making these demands. Structural and traditional brakes in the educational system itself, and a legitimate concern with educational and intellectual values that transcend the immediate needs of the economy, will all affect the way in which schools and colleges react to the pressures of employers and the labour market. In any case, educational institutions have a multi-dimensional relationship with other aspects of social structure. Technological need and manpower demands may clash with certain features of the system of class and status stratification that permeate the relationship of individuals and groups and the work of schools and teachers. The sociologist of education wants to know how educational institutions deal with such competing pressures, how closely associated are certain types of curriculum and educational provision with given levels of adult employment and status.

A concern with matters of this kind inevitably raises questions about the role that schools fulfil as agents of social mobility, the extent to which children of varying social origins are provided with opportunities to find the place in society for which their 'abilities and aptitudes' fit them, and the degree to which the generally accepted principle of 'equality of opportunity' has meaning within a system that differentiates as well as selects and deals with pupils

N

whose performances are not determined wholly by heredity. The image of a ladder of opportunity, in which the ladder itself is static and progress depends upon the actions of the climber, can be replaced by the more dynamic notion of a series of escalators; the structure of the escalator itself does something to determine the direction and rate of progress of the individual who boards it; some opportunity for self-determination remains, but this is most easily exercised in one particular direction. Such a metaphor is more appropriate than the ladder to the realities of educational provision, in which structural features and institutional goals and values can be as important as individual endowment and effort in facilitating and blocking social and occupational movement—it also fits in with such concepts as 'sponsored' and 'contest' mobility (Turner, 1961).

To understand the dynamic relationship of the school and society, and the way in which individual educability is influenced by the efforts of teachers and the range of curricular offerings, it is necessary to study the schools themselves in considerable detail, to examine them as self-contained if not autonomous microsocieties, with their own patterns of social structure, methods of social control and processes of social change. In this respect a descriptive study of outward appearances, of the goals and aims that teachers set themselves, the ideological obfuscation that surrounds much educational discourse, is of interest only as a feature of a more systematic analysis of intention and outcome, formal and informal structure, norms and values. The behaviour of students and pupils, teachers and administrators, and the historical development of particular educational roles all need close attention if the way in which schools and colleges work is to be understood.

Since the focus of all educational efforts is the acquisition of knowledge, skills, and ways of behaving by individuals, the sociologist must also concern himself with the factors that make it more or less easy for the pupil or student to profit from education and with the influence of home background, peer group and neighbourhood on attitudes towards and response to schooling.

Among these social determinants of educability will be the structures and processes of the educational institutions themselves, and the demands that exist for certain types of training and qualification. In these studies of individual educability the sociologist brings to bear his total understanding of the relations of school and society and joins his efforts with those of the social psychologist and psychometrist.

In this country, the dominant tradition in the sociology of education has been that of social inquiry and documentation that begins with the work of Booth at the beginning of this century. During the twenties and thirties the London School of Economics sponsored inquiries into the provision of educational opportunity, beginning in 1926 with Lindsay's *Social Progress and Educational Waste*, and continuing with studies by Grey and Moshinsky and others. Lindsay's study examined the problem of 'how far the education ladder is effective; whether it in fact is, as has been described, a greasy pole; and what are the main difficulties that beset the path of the child, the parent, the teacher and the local education authority' (p. 7). He concluded that 'proved ability to the extent of at least 40 per cent of the nation's children is at present being denied expression, that the full extent of unproved ability is not yet known, only because a sufficiently comprehensive test has not yet been applied, and that of a very conservative estimate of 20 per cent who may be described as below average ability, social environment, in many cases remedial, is the main contributory cause.' The political and economic conditions of the thirties did not encourage reforms designed to alleviate this situation—the problem became one of finding enough jobs for the educated, and the spectre of the political dangers of an unemployed intelligensia was sometimes invoked in the discussion of educational change. But the Second World War again highlighted the wastage of talent that, despite the existence of the special place and scholarship system, had characterized our educational arrangements during the first three decades of the century. The requirements of both national need and social justice emphasized the necessity of further reform, and the 1943 White Paper and the 1944 Education Act attempted to meet this by providing a wider range of opportunities in secondary and higher education and by removing some of the grosser financial handicaps to a longer period of education for those from homes of humble means. The criteria employed to discriminate between those who could benefit from such extended education and those who could not were based largely on the work that psychologists had done during the inter-war period on the classification and measurement of abilities, and reflected the recommendations of the consultative committees regarding the wider use of objective and standardized tests as a means of reducing the effect of such educationally irrelevant factors as home background, wealth, the occupational level of the parents and different qualities of primary schooling. But it soon became clear that, however carefully designed the selection procedures might be, such factors continued to exercise an important effect, and a good deal of the empirical work undertaken since the end of the Second World War has been concerned with the manner in which this is exercised (Floud and Halsey 1957, Douglas 1964).

Some of the most valuable work of this kind has been done by official committees, which have adopted an increasingly empirical approach to the problems posed by their terms of reference. Nothing is more striking in this respect than a comparison between some of the inter-war reports on education, in which a great deal of practical advice and sound educational analysis was larded with unsupported sociological and psychological generalizations, with, for example, *15 to 18*, the 1959 Report of the Central Advisory Council, or the *Report* of the Committee on Higher Education, 1964, and its five substantial volumes of statistical appendices.

Within recent years there has been an expansion in the range of sociological studies of education undertaken, although work on opportunity and educability still has a prominent place. The work of particular types of schools has received more attention. Banks (1958), Taylor (1963), Stevens (1961) and Wilkinson (1963) have provided a series of very different but essentially sociological analyses of the place of Grammar, Modern and Public schools within the educational and social system. Although dominated by considerations of educational opportunity, some of the publications of the Institute of Community Studies (Jackson and Marsden 1963, Jackson 1965, Young 1965) have helped to throw light upon the way in which schools function and their relationships with the communities they serve. The community studies sponsored by the University of Liverpool have also made contributions in this respect (Mays 1962). The extent of genuine sociological analyses of the work of teachers is very limited—Tropp's (1958) study of the development of the teaching profession and Wilson's (1962) consideration of the role of the teacher are both useful, and there have also been one or two analyses of the work of particular role-incumbents in schools and elsewhere (Burnham 1964, Taylor 1964). The social determinants of educability are also receiving attention; among recent studies Bernstein's work on language development has been of particular importance (Bernstein 1964, 1965). One of the most interesting and potentially fruitful recent developments has been the application of organization theory to an understanding of the internal dynamics of the school (Hoyle 1965, Etzioni 1961, 1962). Little work has been done in this area, and Willard Waller's thirty-year-old *Sociology of Teaching* (Waller 1932) provides a still valuable source of insight and experience of the social relations in classroom, assembly hall and workshop.

Official concern with the expansion of higher education has stimulated interest in the patterns of university and student life, and there is now a growing list of such studies (Healey 1964, Kendall 1964). Once again, the English student has a considerable transatlantic literature to draw upon, including some sources where secondary and higher education are considered alongside one another in relation to the demands of the economy and social change (Clark 1962, Reisman 1958).

The volume of research and studies specifically in the sociology of education in this country is still small. Out of 173 papers and publications in this field listed in *Sociological Abstracts* for the first six months of 1964, twelve were written by authors working in this country against 108 for the United States. It is perhaps fortunate that many of the sources that are most useful for the college of education course in the sociology of education are not concerned with this particular specialism at all—for example Brown's *Social Psychology of Industry* (1954) provides many of the most important concepts and ideas necessary for organizational analysis, and Goffman (1961), Leavitt (1963) and March and Simon (1958) are all valuable sources in this respect.

Sociology of education in the training of teachers

Partly because of a shortage of qualified lecturers, sociological studies have played only a small part in courses for intending teachers. Few graduates in sociology have gone into school teaching, and since classroom experience has been an essential condition for appointments in colleges and departments of education, most of the work in sociology of education in such institutions is undertaken by those with interests rather than qualifications in the subject. There were in 1964 only a dozen members of staff of university departments and institutes of education and twenty-four lecturers in colleges of education in England and Wales with first degrees that included sociology (Taylor 1965). But the newness of the subject and the shortage of suitably qualified staff is only one part of the explanation of the comparative neglect of sociological studies in the education of teachers, and there are other factors that require some attention.

Some of those who are concerned with the teaching of 'Education' in colleges and departments have a certain distrust of the disciplines that underly the study of educational processes and institutions, feeling that these get in the way of the sort of synoptic understanding that the teacher needs in the face to face classroom situation. There exists a good deal of sympathy for the point of view expressed by a lecturer in the following statement:

The Education tutors in this college are of the firm opinion that the approach through specialist avenues does not fulfil the aims and ideals of teacher training. The core of the education course in our opinion should be a study of children in the complex situations of life. In this way students will see that the true interrelationships of the various branches of education, and the essential sociology, philosophy and psychology will receive their due attention. We consider that the departmentalizing of education into a number of specialisms would present students with the difficulty of forming a synthesis. (Quoted Maguire 1963.)

The organizational concomitant of these views has been the group-based education course—sometimes rather unkindly referred to as the 'mother hen' system—in which the work in education for a given number of students is undertaken by a single tutor, who may possess qualifications or training in none of the fields involved, with or without the assistance of year-group lectures by others with more specialized interests. Such a form of organization has its advantages, principally of close personal contact and supervision of study, and it would be wrong to dismiss it out of hand. But it is the argument of this volume that, given the improved educational level of students,* the increasing complexity of educational processes, and the growth of understanding about social and psychological phenomena, such an approach to the study of education and the preparation of teachers can no longer be justified. The fact that universities are today experimenting with new types of course, based upon new combinations of elements drawn from established disciplines, has sometimes been employed as a justification for an integrated approach to educational studies in the colleges. But, as Reisman (1958) has pointed out, integrative and interdisciplinary programmes can have very

---

* Throughout this chapter I am referring to both students in colleges of education following three-year courses and post-graduate students pursuing one-year courses. Although the amount of time available is rather different in the two cases, and there are also differences in the level of maturity of the 18-year-old school leaver and the 21-year-old graduate, the principles on which courses need to be based are the same.

different meanings at various levels of the educational hierarchy; in the colleges they would often seem to be less a considered effort to lower disciplinary barriers than a rationalization of a situation in which there is an inadequate supply of specialist lecturers with relevant teaching experience, and a mistaken belief that students who are not in the first rank intellectually will find a synoptic approach more congenial.

Another reason why sociological studies have not caught on as quickly as they might in colleges and departments of education is the difference in perspectives of the educator and the sociologist. Much of the basic work in sociology of education in this country has been the responsibility of persons outside the colleges and the departments, and, whilst it has quite obviously had a good deal of practical relevance for the work of the administrator and the teacher, it has not been initiated primarily to answer a series of educational, as distinct from sociological questions. The sociologist and the educator have rather different purposes in view. The sociologist is interested in education because it is one of the central activities of industrialized societies; he studies schools, colleges and universities, curricula and teaching methods, in order to improve his understanding of the structure and institutions of such societies and the ways in which the young are inducted into full membership of them. The educator is interested in the contribution that specialist studies make to the practical activity of educating; he wants to make use of the findings of the sociologist, and when he himself undertakes sociological research and inquiry it is nearly always with a useful purpose of some kind or another in mind. The distinction is not absolute, for there are some people working in the field whom it would be difficult to restrict to the one category rather than the other. But it does help us to distinguish between the sociology of education, which is usually an activity and an orientation of sociologists (who may also be educators) and educational sociology, which is an activity principally of educators. It has been suggested by Brim (1958) in his review of the field in the United States, that 'sociological research in education can contribute both to the growth of general sociological theory and to the solution of practical operating problems of the educational institution.' Unfortunately, however, too little research of a kind that might make such dual contributions has been undertaken. In particular, the didactic orientation of educational sociology, as distinct from the sociology of education, has limited its usefulness as a contribution to the growth of sociological understanding of educational processes (Floud 1964).

Educational sociology has enjoyed a good deal of popularity in the United States, where it has long played a part in courses for intending teachers. But, although in its more rigorous forms it has brought a good deal of sociological insight to bear upon educational problems, it has tended to be hortatory rather than empirical, inspirational rather than objective, and synoptic rather than analytic. The authors of a well known text state the scope of educational sociology in the following terms (Cook and Cook 1950):

To us, in years of work with school and community groups, educational sociology is the application of sociological knowledge and technique to educational problems in the fields of human relations and material well being. Our concern has been with the total educational process in school and outside wherever people learn, and our business has been the practical one of helping them to solve issues which interfere with the achievement of group goals. It has been to bring insight on group life situations, to advance in season and out what we should call group process education in field programs and in classroom teaching. (p. 10.)

Such an approach is likely to have a more immediate appeal to the intending teacher than others that follow more closely the pattern of academic sociology of education, and there are signs that, where sociology is coming to be included in teachers' courses in this country, it is being adopted with the normative orientation that characterizes a good deal of such work in the United States. This may be encouraged by the growing concern with educational-cum-social 'problems', and the need to give students some understanding of these in order that they may be better able to face up to difficulties in the classroom and neighbourhood. The effect of the Newsom Report, and such studies as those of Professor Mays (1962) in Liverpool, has been to stimulate interest in recruiting sociologists to the staff of colleges with a view to providing more emphasis upon the 'welfare' functions of the teacher. That such an emphasis is important there is no doubt; as Jean Floud and others have pointed out (Floud 1962), there is a real need for the improvement of this aspect of the schools' task, and for teachers who possess some of the insights of the trained social worker. But there is a danger that the sociological element in the education course will become too closely associated with this welfare role, and take on the colour of earlier American concern with community integration, guidance and social therapy, at the expense of the potentially more valuable understandings of social process and change that it can provide. Sociological studies may be seen as contributing to technique rather than understanding, to skills rather than knowledge; and whatever the apparent short-term advantages of such technique and skill, they are no substitute for the knowledge and understanding that alone enable the individual to make sense of a professional task in which ambiguity and indeterminancy are more conspicuous than order and coherence.

Another danger of the 'problem centred' course is that the problems selected may not be those that permit systematic analysis of social structure and behaviour, but instead reflect an emphasis upon the practical and the 'socially significant'. This approach is typified by the subject matter of a recent book by F. W. Garforth, whose *Education and Social Purpose* (1963) was not written 'as an introduction to educational sociology, though indirectly it might serve as such'. The author suggests that 'a complete survey of the many problems in contemporary Britain which concern the educator is impossible. The following, therefore, have been selected for consideration; mass media, the dehumanization of man by his own inventions, the decline of religion, internationalism, the increasing importance of science and technology, and the welfare state.'

Such a choice of topics illustrates the normative orientation to which reference has already been made. And whilst such a choice might be defended by many of those engaged in teacher education, who claim that the social responsibilities of the teacher require some form of commitment and concern with values, it is unfortunately all too likely that a concern with topics of this kind will legitimize the sort of normative analysis of some of our present discontents that characterizes a good deal of contemporary social comment.*

Although superficially attractive in the context of a course that is often pressed for time, which must show itself to be practical if it is to convince students of its usefulness, and which needs to take account of the social responsibilities of the teacher, educational sociology has serious weaknesses. In the first place, the unsystematic nature of much teaching in this field, based on topics, 'burning issues' and the like, does little to provide the student with what Oakeshott (1963) calls a 'language' by means of which he may acquire a better understanding of the society in which he lives, the social pressures to which he is subject, and the social roles that are involved in his work as a teacher.† The language and sociological manner of thinking is not best acquired by a consideration of the

* 'When the citizen is protected by health services, pension schemes and subsidies against so many of life's misfortunes, he is inclined to belittle his responsibilities and rely increasingly on the state as the universal provider. This is bad for himself and for society; bad for himself because it impairs his status as a person; bad for society because the renunciation of responsibility by the many leads to a concentration of power in the hands of the few, and this is a denial of democracy. Moreover, when so much is given to the citizen in cash and services, the fact that ultimately wealth can only be created by work is obscured from him. The failure to grasp this elementary principle of economics has been a major cause of inflation and of the depreciation of our currency. It is a fact, not only of economics, but of life itself, that a man reaps what he sows; but the welfare state encourages us to think that we can reap without sowing anything.' (Garforth 1963, op. cit.)

† '. . . the distinction between a language (by which I mean a manner

literature of our contemporary moral concerns, by an exploration of the mass media, the social services or the leisure facilities of the neighbourhood. Secondly, the concentration upon problems, the implicit notion that the teacher of socially underprivileged children in a poor neighbourhood can 'use' more sociological understanding than his colleagues in other types of school, diverts attention from the structural contexts within which the genesis and nature of such problems and concerns can be appreciated and without some knowledge of which no rational understanding of social process can be achieved. Thirdly, educational sociology, in so far as it departs from the rational and empirical basis of contemporary sociological study, runs the risk of introducing a metaphysic that is unlikely to be helpful in facilitating a gathering together of the various strands that constitute educational study into a viable educational theory.*

Sociology and the culture controversy

A further, and perhaps more fundamental reason for the limited use of sociological studies in the training of teachers is to be found in a certain species of criticism that rejects the assumptions about society and education on which the sociology of education is alleged to be based. Sometimes this acts as a rationalization of the objections that have already been mentioned. The clearest statement of this kind has been made by Bantock (1963) who suggests that 'the fact that more and more people want to *describe* the various ways in which it makes sense to think of the school as a social institution, even the growing sociological interest itself, with

* My use of the term 'educational theory' follows that of Hirst op. cit.

of thinking) and a "literature" or "text" (by which I mean what has been said from time to time in a "language") . . . is the distinction, for example, between the "language" of poetic imagination and a poem or novel, or between the "language" or manner of thinking of a scientist and a text-book of geology or what may be called the current state of our geological knowledge.' (Oakeshott 1963.)

its more technical awareness, springs partly out of, and partly in its turn stimulates, an interest which very easily slips over from being simply descriptive to being covertly normative.' (p. 21.)

A covertly normative approach of this kind is to be found, according to Bantock, in many of the post-war studies of educational opportunity, which we have already seen as the dominant element in English sociology of education; reference is made to Glass's statement that 'such problems are central to the study of social structure, they are of direct concern both for the development of sociological theory *and for the formulation of social policy'* (Bantock's italics). The current 'obsession' with class factors in educational provision strikes Bantock as 'a curiously outmoded centre of concern, relevant amidst the rigidities of the nineteenth century but hardly fundamental in view of today's fluidities' (Bantock 1965).

There are, of course, a number of value judgments implicit in studies of educational opportunity. Few sociologists would argue that sociology can be 'value free'; values enter in to the selection of problems and to the interpretation of findings, if not to the choice of methods and the collection of data. Research that is undertaken with the exclusion of value as its central concern is often of little use either theoretically or practically—the value-free is often the valueless. With respect to the sociology of education in England, it has been admitted that 'socialist influence on the choice of problems remains strong' (Floud and Halsey 1958). But all that Glass, Floud, Halsey, Douglas and others have done in relating educational provision to the needs of complex industrialized societies is to recognize that it is industrialism that provides the rationale for the work of specialized educational institutions on a mass scale. They provide no critique of industrialism and its effects upon the content of education because this is not part of the terms of reference of the type of study in question. That such a critique is important and necessary there is no doubt. Reisman (1964) has drawn attention to the fact that an advanced industrialized economy and a high level of personal consumption have as yet no competitors as models for the future of our own and other societies. But it is not the function of empirical studies of the working of the school system within our existing social framework to suggest new models, even assuming that these could be found. Reisman goes on, 'In other words, we have become a conservative country, despite our worldwide reputation for seeking novelty, in that we are unable to envisage alternative futures for ourselves'.

Few of the studies in the sociology of education that have been carried out in this country during the past twenty years would make any claim to be, in Bantock's terms, 'simply descriptive'. What Bantock and others seem to dislike is not the fact that such studies imply value-judgments, but the character of those judgments; the objection is not so much that studies of educational opportunity have a prescriptive element, but to the nature of what is prescribed. Bantock contrasts what he calls 'political' life-chances—the opportunity to acquire certain qualifications, to obtain particular types of employment, to be socially mobile—with 'cultural' life-chances—the demand that 'every child shall, as a socio-cultural personality, have the right to that enlargement of his nature which a variety of educational provision can afford'. Because many children have already been formed by 'historical socio-cultural forces', the attempt to offer them a share in 'high culture' is unlikely to be successful. Indeed, their 'satisfactions may spring out of a fuller exploitation of such cultural possibilities as form part of their world . . . the radio, cinema, TV and so on.' Some of the wastage that occurs in Grammar school and University 'springs out of unpalatable cultural provision; and some of the so-called successes acquire only a veneer of high culture', sufficient to get them through examinations but not to 'inform their actual living'. Bantock claims that his own priority is 'pop' culture, which, in so far as it drives straight to the affective core of the individual life has a power to make or mar individuals in a way that is 'much more potent than class' (Bantock 1965, ibid.).

The cultural conservatism of this point of view contrasts strongly with the radicalism that has characterized much work in the sociology of education. But the difference is not merely one of political temperaments; there are involved here attitudes to the character of industrialized society that feature in a wide range of contemporary social and literary discussion, and which are highly relevant to the reception given to the sociologists' attempt to understand the relationships of the school to society and to communicate this understanding to intending teachers. There seems to be a broad division between those who can accept the social pluralism and lack of cultural consensus associated with a highly complex, technological, town-dwelling, mobile, self-conscious and consumption oriented industrial society, and those who see these as inimical to social health and the fostering of individual sensibility and irrelevant to the content of educational provision. On the one side, there is an acceptance of the fact that vocational and instrumental purposes influence a good number of our present attitudes to education, coupled with the desire to communicate the elements of a common culture (with its roots in what has been called 'high culture') to children in all types of school. On the other, there is a move towards devocationalized and rehumanized education, an attempt to strengthen relationships that it is claimed have been attenuated by industrial–bureaucratic society and to protect high culture, the property of an élite, from the threats inherent in massification. Those holding the first view have been called 'contemporaries'; those supporting the second, 'moderns'.*

Too much must not be made of this distinction between those who accept and those who reject the dominant values of industrial society, and hence who take up particular positions *vis-à-vis* the attempt to achieve a clearer understanding of that society and the role of educational institutions within it. Such acceptance and rejection are not usually clear-cut, and attitudes on such general

* For statements of the position of 'moderns' and 'contemporaries' in political and social contexts see Gellner op. cit. (for the contemporaries) and Marcuse (1964) (for the moderns). See also Trilling (1963), Snow (1963) and Spender (1962).

issues are seldom consistent either internally or in point of time. Nevertheless, it can be suggested that teachers and those responsible for training teachers, in so far as they take up a position of any kind on such questions, lean towards the modern rather than the contemporary. Several influences may help to account for this. One is the traditional moral function of the school and the college, the duty that the teachers have inherited from the nineteenth century to accept some responsibility for the improvement of society. (Willard Waller (1932) refers to the school as a 'museum of virtue'.) At present, the teacher is very much aware of the comparative ineffectiveness of his work in this respect, especially against what he takes to be the enormously greater power of the mass media. There is little evidence on which to support or deny this assessment—see, for example, the carefully formulated conclusions of Himmelweit (1962) and the review of the literature of the influence of television in Halloran (1964).

Added to this the teacher may gain from the behaviour and attitudes of some of his more difficult pupils the impression that the family is doing little to co-operate with or assist the purposes of the school, that recent social changes have tended to undermine the positive approach to work that was allegedly characteristic of an earlier period. Something of what Galbraith (1965) calls 'social nostalgia' seems endemic in much of the literature of teacher education. Such feelings enhance the teachers' sense of powerlessness, and are not calculated to encourage positive proposals for change and reform, or alterations in the methods and content of teaching. Furthermore, the teacher does not feel that he has been the beneficiary of recent social change—the debates associated with salary claims and awards since the Second World War have shown teachers as possessing a strong sense of relative deprivation.

Drawing upon her researches on teachers' attitudes, Himmelweit refers to the way in which teachers, 'relative to their financial and social position, are a highly conservative group'. She concludes that 'Teachers whose task it should be to build on the past and to provide the child with a perspective with which to evaluate and respond to the challenge of the future, too often accept as un-alterable an unsatisfactory *status quo*, too frequently look at the novel with distaste and too often perceive progress as restricting rather than liberating. They are in the rear-guard rather than the *avant garde* of progress.' (1961.)

Any general rejection of the possibility or desirability of struc-tural change is likely to encourage a tendency to fall back upon the satisfactions of interpersonal contacts in classroom and school, study and hall of residence. Teachers and teacher-trainers are traditionally—and to a degree, rightly—concerned with the dy-namics of interpersonal behaviour, with what Stewart has called 'the existential and inspirational aspects of the teacher-pupil re-lationship such as may be found (discussed) in Buber and Highet —and indeed at some point or another in almost any English writer on principles and aims of education' (Stewart 1953). But too exclusive a concern with the interpersonal increases the like-lihood that teachers will too readily and uncritically respond to analyses of the 'dehumanized', impersonal, instrumental relation-ships that some observers see as the dominant characteristics of present day social arrangements. The importance of the primary group, of the intuitive and the intangible in face to face contact and group life, may be elevated to the status of a creed. What are perceived as 'academic' and 'intellectual' approaches are suspect, the attempt to apply a rational analysis of social process to the teaching situation regarded as doomed to failure. With this is likely to go a stress upon the feeling aspects of education, an agreement with Jaspers that 'we cannot, with the logicians, escape into a set of clearly defined symbols to avoid the difficulties of an existence experienced as metaphorical. Indeed, to be truly logical, we must capture the logic and the language of that existence itself.' (*Tragedy is not enough*, p. 110. Quoted Niblett (1954) p. 101.) Bantock makes virtually the same point in a more practical way 'It is odd that we ignore the methods of those who have most touched the "masses" in our time—the advertisers, the political dictators, and the purveyors of cheap art in its various forms.

O

These people sell a myth, a symbol, a dream. We must seek to direct the powers they have unleashed into better channels.' Bantock (1963) p. 106.

Such orientations find little sustenance in the social arithmetic and structural and institutional studies that characterize the work of sociologists of education. The sociologists' attempt to analyse and to categorize the dynamics of social relationships is seen as either unhelpful, or, because of the assumptions about the contemporary world that seem to be entailed, positively dangerous. When, as often seems to be the case, the concerns of teacher educators polarize around, on the one hand, the search for some metaphysic of 'meaning' and, on the other, the provision of practical classroom technique, there is little room for the middle range of explanation and theory that the sociologist may be able to provide. In part, of course, the problem is one of the confusion of these metaphysical, middle-range and skill elements. Comte, referring to what he called the 'theological', the 'metaphysical' and the 'positivist' approaches stated 'Any one of these might alone secure some sort of social order; but while the three co-exist, it is impossible for us to understand one another upon any essential point whatever'. (Quoted Lundberg (1947) p. 35.) Yet work at this level is essential if the individual teacher is to have an adequate intellectual basis for his techniques and for his beliefs and commitments. How can sociology contribute to these middle-range studies?

Sociology and the education course

The preceding discussion will already have indicated some of the materials that might constitute part of a course in sociology for intending teachers. It has been argued that 'educational sociology', for all its apparent relevance to the needs of the student, has serious weaknesses which limit its usefulness as a contribution towards a more developed educational and sociological understanding. But a survey of the range of research work and study that constitutes the more rigorous and cumulative 'sociology of education' in universities and elsewhere does not immediately yield a list of topics and approaches suitable for the college and department of education course. Several factors have to be taken into account. The time available in the initial training course is very limited and attention has to be given to subject and method courses as well as to the various elements that make up the study of education. The capacities of the students must also be considered; the type of high-level abstraction that is involved in a good deal of sociological theory is quite beyond the comprehension of most eighteen year olds—and even of the more mature postgraduates in university departments of education and fourth year B.Ed. candidates. Few, if any, will have any previous acquaintance with an objective and critical examination of the social institutions and social forces that have moulded their own lives, and the task of converting their continuing social experience into conscious thought is not always readily or enthusiastically undertaken. The need for the various threads that make up the study of education to have some consistency, and to be organized in such a way that the relevance of the one approach to the other and the methodological limitations of each are taken into account, is also an important consideration. It has already been suggested that group-centred teaching and the attempts on the part of a single individual to undertake the teaching of all the relevant disciplines, either synoptically or in distinct sessions, is not helpful in this respect. The most appropriate form of organization would seem to be some form of team teaching, whereby the lectures and other work in the various fields of educational study are undertaken by specialists, with follow-up by group tutorial work that focuses on the examination of particular educational problems. A pattern of this kind helps to ensure that the specialized contribution of the field of study in question is not lost, that its limitations are recognized and that its integrity is respected (Taylor 1964 [ii]).

There are two main ways of introducing the student to the sociology of education that preserve the essentially sociological orientation that such studies should possess. The first and most familiar is by giving initial consideration to the structure of the society in which schools function, tracing the development of industrialization and its effects upon the type of culture that the schools transmit and the means by which this is done, explaining the nature of social class and stratification, social control and social change in broad terms, and then siting the performance of educational functions within this complex of structural relationships, seeing how the activities of schools, teachers and pupils respond to, and in turn, help to modify, the pressures of the wider society. A second approach—and that outlined in rather more detail here— starts with the school itself and works outward.

The familiar classroom situation may provide the point of departure. In order to explain what goes on in classroom and school it is necessary to introduce a whole range of sociological concepts, such as role and norm, status and rank, legitimacy and authority. Questions need to be asked about why the teacher and the pupil are there—what the formal purposes of their activity may be said to be, and how far the realities of what goes on conforms to these purposes. An elementary application of structural–functional analysis—the limitations of which will need stressing—can be made in the discussion of such topics as examinations, punishments and the enforcement of school uniform. The notion of latent function directs students to look beneath the surface of things to find out how far the institutional styles and procedures that are adopted for dealing with day to day problems, for 'keeping going', hinder or advance the formal aims that are set.* The way in which sub-groups within the institution interact with one another, the manner in which conflict is dealt with, the significance of the institutional folk-lore and gossip† that can be heard in common room and corridor, these can all be examined, and there are

* 'It is characteristic of sociology that in every field it investigates it tends to look away from the formal elements—formal ends, formal structures, formal organizations—and to search out those ends, structures and regulations that are unacknowledged and often unknown to people working in the field itself'. Glazer op cit.

† For a discussion of the role of gossip see Burns and Stalker (1962).

excellent opportunities for making explicit the student's own experience in these areas. The way in which the college or depart-ment itself works and the importance of various sub-groupings within the student body, the existence and influence of recog-nizable 'student cultures', all provide ample material, and school practice gives chances for observation and reflection upon staff and pupil behaviour in terms other than those of teaching pro-ficiency and formal learning. In work of this kind it is possible to draw upon studies that have been made of other forms of institu-tional organization, in factories, hospitals, army units and so on, with a view to stressing the generalized character of the patterns of interaction that are displayed in face to face and group situations.

What is required here is that we should start from what is already familiar or what is becoming familiar to the student and encourage him to look at this experience in an unfamiliar—a sociological—manner. For example, in Durkheim's *Moral Edu-cation* (1925) there is a very full discussion of the role of rewards and punishments in school from a systematically sociological point of view. Durkheim also brings out the characteristics of the social environment of the classroom that differentiates it from the family, and considers such issues as the rights, duties and obligations of teachers and pupils. Most students are very much preoccupied with questions of authority and control, and the essentially practical focus of these chapters is likely to give them a lively appeal. On the other hand, the very familiarity of the relation-ships and social processes to which Durkheim refers may make it too easy for students to reduce what he has to say to 'common sense', to a 'restating of the obvious', and for them to reject the need for such abstract notions as are employed in this discussion. This conceptual reductivism has to be resisted, for it is one of the chief means by which the student accommodates himself to what is, rather than what might be, and blunts his capacity for the higher-order understanding that can best inform his practice. The student's rejection of the abstract may be linked with what Klein (1965) has called 'cognitive poverty', which she sees as characteristic of groups in which tradition plays an important part: 'abstract thought is by definition about possibilities, not actualities. In so far as people are traditional, actualities do govern their lives. If they were to give a sufficiently strong allegiance to what they felt to be possibilities, changes would be going on. The lack of interest in possibilities is one of the things which keeps them traditional.'

The possibilities of the familiar situation can only be seen if the student can be brought to think about the elements of this situation in a novel way, if he can be encouraged to articulate and reorganize these elements in a systematic manner. In many respects, this is more difficult than getting him to think about, say, the social life of the Samoans or the attitudes of the Arapesh, but there may be little carry over from such anthropological exercises to the concrete classroom problems of mid-twentieth century Britain.

From an examination of the way in which schools work, the type of authority structure that they possess, the goals and the purposes that they recognize as legitimate, there should grow an awareness that the teacher is rarely able to make 'purely educational' decisions, that the family, the employer and the local community all have certain expectations regarding what schools and teachers should do and the type of pupils that they should produce. A fuller appreciation of the social role of education, therefore, is dependent on moving outward from the school to examine the influences that these external agencies have and the manner in which it is exercised. The family deserves special consideration, not so much as a socializing agency in its own right—it is to be hoped that the child development work in other parts of the course will focus psychological insights on this aspect of family influence—but in the way in which it helps to shape the child's responses to the efforts of teachers and the structure of formal educational agencies. The particular patterns of language development and habit training, the hopes of parents for the educational and occupational futures of their offspring, the existence or otherwise of a climate of achievement in the home background all play their part as 'social determinants of educability'. So too do the more straight forward differences in housing provision, the educational level of parents, sibling position and so on. The importance of all these factors can only be appreciated within a more general understanding of the structure of the contemporary family and the ways in which it has changed over the past fifty years. A brief outline of comparative family structure could be followed by an examination of variations in family pattern in this country, both within and between different socio-economic and regional groups. The fundamental importance of the family is reflected in a wealth of superficial critical material regarding its contemporary 'decline' and 'moral disintegration'. The analysis of these judgments in the light of such empirical evidence as exists, and the effort to distinguish a tenable value judgment from a statement that ignores or contradicts significant evidence, can all add to the value of this part of the course.

In discussing changes in family life and their impact on the school it is necessary to look again at the impact of industrialism and urbanization, and to emphasize the pervasiveness of these major shifts in the pattern of society on the roles of parents, teachers and community agencies. The need for the teacher to have a knowledge of the home background of pupils and to seek ways in which she may co-operate with parents, is often stressed in the college education courses. Yet it is all too easy to gloss over the very real differences in function that characterize the parent's and the teacher's role, and hence to give a false impression of the ease with which a basis for mutual co-operation in the interests of the child's development can be attained. The sociology of education course provides an opportunity to examine parent–teacher relations in a more systematic way, to indicate how the clash between the more objective and achievement-oriented criteria of the teacher and the subjectivity of the parent can lead to difficulties, to show how the efforts of some schools to wean children from the values of home and neighbourhood, and to cultivate independence in the child, may go against the deeply felt, if only half understood, concerns of parents to retain children within the family orbit and to ensure generational continuity.

Neighbourhood and community studies are already common in colleges of education, involving students in lengthy and time consuming series of visits, observation walks, interviews and the like. Such activity is only useful if the preparation and follow-up provides a systematic framework within which such experience can be categorized and discussed; all too often this aspect of such work seems to be given inadequate attention. 'Concepts without percepts are blind; percepts without concepts are empty.' To study the neighbourhood is at once to bring up questions of equality and inequality, social class and status, differential life chances and the influence of community traditions. Treatment of these topics provides an introduction to the basic patterns of social stratification, some knowledge of which we have seen as an essential part of a developed sociological understanding. To examine the factors that influence an individual's occupational status and social position entails looking at the role of the school as an agent of social selection and differentiation, at the manner in which job selection is made, at the questions raised by the concept of the meritocracy and the provision of equal opportunities for all. Such work can well be linked with the discussions of equality that form part of the course in philosophy.

Recent official reports on education in this country provide a wealth of material of a kind that can be used in connection with studies of this type. Such reports also need to be examined with respect to the assumptions they make about the role of particular types of educational institution and about the society in which these institutions operate.

In treating the topics outlined in this chapter there is a constant emphasis required on the two-way flow of influence between the individual and the group, between the specialized institution and the wider society. In catching and holding the dynamic role of the teacher and the school for the purposes of analysis and discussion, there are needed not only facts about numbers and wastage, opportunity, family influence and teacher status and so on, but also—and perhaps more importantly—theories and generalizations by means of which these elements can be systematized and conceptualized. If a cafeteria style offering is to be avoided, it is essential that throughout the consideration of topics such as those outlined here the student should be in contact with some of the theoretical constructions that are relevant to an understanding of the social role of education. An individual's judgments and practices in educational situations are derived less from his knowledge of facts and findings than from the theories that, consciously or unconsciously, he supports; there is in this sense a far closer link between theory and practice than between fact and practice, despite the beliefs of many students and teachers to the contrary. For an example, one only has to consider the impact upon teachers' attitudes about streaming by ability and the limits of individual educability of such theoretical typologies of children as were widely canvassed in the inter-war period and in official reports such as those of the Norwood Committee. The choice in the training of teachers is between good theories and bad theories, not between theories and no theories at all. With this in mind, it is necessary to select carefully from the range of typologies and theoretical constructs that have been employed in sociological and educational analysis, with a bias in favour of those contributions that have shown themselves to be both cumulative and productive of further exploration and study. What the 'founding fathers' of sociology had to say about the work of schools and teachers is often a good deal more relevant to the conditions of today than later formulations. A systematic exegesis of those aspects of the sociology of education that fall within the conceptual framework provided by one particular theoretical scheme may well be more illuminating and profitable than an attempt to sample for the whole range of empirical studies in this field.

Sociology and the aims of the education course

It is clear that the quality of the teacher's judgments on social life outside the school are not uncorrelated with the quality of his thinking about 'specifically educational' issues. Generally speaking, the person who is prejudiced, irrational and bigoted in his political and religious beliefs is unlikely to be open-minded, rational and flexible in his educational attitudes. One of the attributes of the 'professional' is a commitment to a task that goes beyond the delimitation of specific duties and obligations, and involves a larger area of behaviour than is taken up by the performance of routine tasks. To be really effective, a professional education needs to be as much concerned with the total pattern of the individual's thinking as the 'liberal' education with which it is often contrasted. In this respect, sociological study may make a contribution in sensitizing the student to the interplay of social forces upon the development of his own personality, life chances and values. Tutors concerned with sociology share with psychologists the advantage of being able to call upon the students' experience of life in the family and the community, school life and day by day experience of society as course materials. The sociological element of the education course can help in clarifying these experiences and utilizing them in the development of what Wright Mills called the 'sociological imagination'—'a quality of mind that will help (men) to use information and to develop reason in order to achieve lucid summations of what is going on in the world and what may be happening within themselves.' (Mills 1961.)

Another gain from the pursuit of sociological studies is in respect of the methodological issues involved. The problems of objectivity and judgment, the basic procedures of scientific method and the extent to which these can be applied to the study of human behaviour, the use of survey techniques, questionnaires and interviews, all need to be considered if the student is to understand how information on social behaviour is gathered and how the findings of empirical work are to be evaluated. One of the dangers to be avoided is the assumption on the part of students that educational and sociological research yields—or, to be really fruitful, *should* yield—'rules' for the improvement of teaching. If this assumption is made, research findings may be seen as unhelpful when in fact their usefulness needs to be evaluated on quite other grounds. As Scheffler (1960) has pointed out, the improvement of practice is not facilitated by artificial attempts to close the gap between the here and now interests of teachers in fostering certain types of learning in children, and the research workers' interest in developing a theoretical approach for explaining such learning. 'The more enquiry is restricted to local and practical spheres, the less capable it is of attaining general, theoretical grasp, and hence of guiding and explaining practice.' Hegel was clear as to where the emphasis should lie, 'theoretical work accomplishes more than practical work. Once the realm of concepts is revolutionized, reality cannot hold out against it'. (Quoted Jaspers 1946.)

Sociological study may also help the student to achieve a more realistic evaluation of the role of the school and the teacher in social change. There has been a tendency in the past either to over-rate this influence, or—especially on the part of the teacher himself—to assume that schools can play only an insignificant part in influencing the direction of change. Reference has already been made to the teachers' sense of helplessness in the face of what they take to be the immensely more powerful forces of the mass media and the administrative machine. In fact, the decisions of teachers can have a very important effect upon the way in which the educational system functions. An example of this is the way in which teachers in secondary modern schools introduced external examinations and vocational courses into their curricula during the 1950s, in direct contradiction to official views regarding the type of incentive and teaching approach that should be characteristic of such schools. The ideals surrounding the concept of secondary education for all during the immediately post-war years placed an emphasis upon individual and school 'achievement' rather than competitive 'success' in social terms.* In

* '. . . one can have created a good organization, a serviceable shoe, a competent symphony, but these *achievements* do not necessarily carry with them *success* . . . an achievement is a kind of objectification or

responding *selectively* to the pressures of parents, employers, educationists and officials, teachers reveal their capacity for bringing about transformations of function within an unchanged structural context.

The justification for the inclusion of sociological studies in the course for intending teachers does not rest upon any observable link between the pursuit of such studies and the improvement of classroom technique and practice. Rather it is dependent upon the requirement that the teacher should first of all be capable of thinking logically and rationally about the whole range of social phenomena that he encounters in his personal and professional life. It is this rational intellect, the ability to sort out fact and value judgment, the respect for evidence, the capacity for making valid generalizations, that has been valued, over and above a training in teaching method and classroom skill, by those responsible for appointing teachers in 'superior' schools—and it is perhaps because the teacher training that we have provided has not been seen as contributing significantly to the further development of this rational intellect that such training has tended to be held in poor esteem.

It follows from all that has gone before that the chief rationale for the inclusion of sociological studies in courses for intending teachers is that they provide one of the indispensable elements of the knowledge that is essential for the formulation of sound educational principles and practices. Any attempt to create a premature synthesis, to discuss educational theories without due consideration of the logically and methodologically differentiated studies that underlie them, is likely to lead to confusion in the student's mind regarding the differences between, say, philosophical and sociological forms of judgment, and a consequent inability to analyse and think clearly about the complex educational

---

realization within a particular field of productive activity. The existence and validity of an achievement are independent of the social acceptance and fate of its author. "Success" on the other hand, is a realization in the field of social (inter-individual) relations.' Mannheim (1951) p. 233.

situations in which he finds himself. The synthesis that college and department tutors often consider it is their duty to provide, in so far as it is a viable gathering together of philosophical, sociological, psychological and historical strands, and a considered evaluation of these with respect to the performance of an educational task or the resolution of an educational problem, is largely personal in nature, and cannot be presented to students or lectured about in the ready-made form in which it may exist in the tutor's mind. If, as is frequently asserted, we want to give students more help in making up their own minds on these difficult issues, then we need to provide them with the means by which a defensible point of view may be formulated. Sociological studies of education are one of these means.

BIBLIOGRAPHY

Andreski, S., 1964, *Elements of Comparative Sociology*.

Banks, O., 1959, *Parity and Prestige in English Secondary Education*.
Bantock, G. H., 1963, *Education in an Industrial Society*.
— 1965, *Education and Values*.
Bernstein, B. B., 1965, 'A socio-linguistic approach to Social Learning'. In J. Gould (Ed.), *Penguin Survey of the Social Sciences*.
— 1964, 'Elaborated and Restricted Codes'. In *American Anthropologist*, Dec. 1964.
Brim, O. G., 1958, *Sociology and the Field of Education*.
Brown, J. A. C., 1954, *Social Psychology of Industry*.
Burnham, P. S., 1964, *The Role of the Deputy Head*. Unpublished Thesis, Leicester University.
Burns, T. and Stalker, 1962, *The Management of Innovation*.

Clark, B. R., 1962, *Educating the Expert Society*.
— 1964, 'Sociology of Education'. In R. E. L. Faris (Ed.) *Handbook of Modern Sociology*.
Clark, B. R. and Trow, M., 1961, *Determinants of College Student Subcultures*. (Mimeographed.)
Cook, L. A. and Cook, E. L., 1950, *A Sociological Approach in Education*.

Douglas, J. W. B., 1964, *The Home and the School*.
Durkheim, E., 1925, *Moral Education*. (Trans. E. Schnurer.)

Etzioni, A., 1961, *Complex Organizations—A Sociological Reader*.
— 1961, *A Comparative Analysis of Complex Organizations*.

Floud, J. E., 1964, 'Sociology of Education'. In W. L. Kolb and J. Gould (Eds.), *A Dictionary of the Social Sciences*.

Floud, J. E., 1962, 'Teaching in the Affluent Society.' In *British Journal of Sociology*, 13.

Floud, J. E. and Halsey, A. H., 1957, *Social Class and Educational Opportunity*.

— 1958, *The Sociology of Education*.

Galbraith, J. 1963, *The Liberal Hour*.

Halloran, J. D., 1964, *The Effects of Mass Communication*. Television Research Committee, Working Paper No. 1.

Halsey, A. H., 1965, 'Educational Organization. In *International Encyclopaedia of the Social Sciences*.

Himmelweit, H., 1961, 'The Teaching of Social Psychology to Students of Education and Social Work.' In P. Halmos (Ed.), *Sociological Review Monograph No. 4*.

— 1962, *Television and the Child*.

Hoyle, E., 1965, 'Organizational Analysis in the field of Education. In *Educational Research VII*.

Healey, J., 1964, *Summary of Current Research in the British Universities concerning aspects of the University Process itself, and cognate topics* (mimeographed).

Jackson, B., 1964, *Streaming—An Education System in Miniature*.

Jackson, B. and Marsden, D., 1962, *Education and the Working Class*.

Jaspers, K., 1946, *Mission of the University*.

Kendall, M., 1964, *Research into Higher Education: A bibliography*.

Klein, J., 1965, *Samples from English Cultures*.

Lindsay, A. D., 1936, *Social Progress and Educational Waste*.

Leavitt, H. J., 1961, *Managerial Psychology*.

Lundberg, G. A., 1947, *Can Science Save Us?*

Maguire, J. M., 1963, 'Sociology for Teachers'. In *Education for Teaching*, May.

Mannheim, K., 1951, *Essays on the Sociology of Knowledge*.

March, J. G. and Simon, H. A., 1958, *Organization*.

Marcuse, H., 1964, *One-Dimensional Man*.

Mays, J. B., 1962, *Education and the Urban Child*.

Mead, M., 1961, 'The School in American Culture'. In J. E. Floud, A. H. Halsey and C. A. Anderson, *Education, Economy and Society*.

Mills, C. W., 1961, *The Sociological Imagination*.

Niblett, W. R., 1954, 'On Existentialism and Education'. In *British Journal of Educational Studies*, 2.

Oakeshott, M., 1963, *Rationalism in Politics*.

Pilley, J., 1955, 'Liberal Education in the making of Teachers'. In *British Journal of Educational Studies*, IV.
Parsons, T., 1961, 'The School Class as a Social System'. In J. E. Floud, A. H. Halsey and C. A. Anderson, *Education, Economy and Society*.

Reisman, D., 1958, *Constraint and Variety in American Education*.
— 1964, *Abundance for What?*

Scheffler, I., 1960, *The Language of Education*.
Shils, E., 1963, 'Mass Society and its Culture'. In H. M. Ruitenbeck (Ed.), *Varieties of Modern Social Theory*.
Snow, C. P., 1964, *The Two Cultures and A Second Look*.
Spender, S., 1962, *The Struggle of the Modern*.
Stevens, F., 1961, *The Living Tradition*.
Stewart, W. A. C., 1963, 'Karl Mannheim and the Sociology of Education'. In *British Journal of Educational Studies*, 1.

Taylor, W., 1965, 'The University Teacher of Education'. In *Comparative Education*, 1:3, June.
Taylor, W., 1963, *The Secondary Modern School*.
Taylor, W., 1964 (i), 'The Training College Principal'. In *Sociological Review*, 12:2 July.
Taylor, W., 1964 (ii), 'The Organization of Educational Studies'. *In Education for Teaching*, Nov.
Trilling, L., 1963, 'Commitment to the Modern'. In *Teachers College Record*, 64.
Tropp, A., 1958, *The School Teachers*.
Turner, R. H., 1961, 'Modes of Social Ascent through Education'. In J. E. Floud, A. H. Halsey and C. A. Anderson, *Education, Economy and Society*.

Vivian, F., 1964, *Human Freedom and Responsibility*.

Waller, W., 1932, *The Sociology of Teaching*.
Wilkinson, R., 1963, *The Prefects*.
Wilson, B. R., 1962, 'The Teacher's Role—A Sociological Analysis'. In *British Journal of Sociology*, 13.

Young, M., 1965, *Research and Innovation in Education*.

Chapter Seven

SOME APPLICATIONS

J. W. TIBBLE

The foregoing chapters of this book have been mainly concerned with investigating the nature of education as a subject of study in courses for intending and practising teachers. This chapter deals with some of the implications and applications of our views on the nature of the subject: in particular, the relation between theory and practice in teacher education, problems of staffing and organization of courses, and the relation of the study of education to the other study ingredients in the course as a whole.

What are the implications of the definition of the study of education as 'practical theory' for the relationship between theory and practice in the context of the education course? The study of education can, of course, be undertaken without any direct reference to the students' practical experience and without aiming at the development of practical teaching skills. This is indeed usually the case in advanced diploma and higher degree courses in education. The aim of the course is fuller understanding of 'the collections of knowledge used in the formulation of principles for practice', and the acquiring of techniques and skills relevant to this understanding. What is asserted by the central position taken up in Chapter Two is that these principles, properly understood, are 'for practice'. 'The whole point is the use of this knowledge to determine what should be done in educational practice. In the process the theory draws on all the knowledge within the various forms that is relevant to educational pursuits but proceeds from there to grappling with practical problems' (p. 48). This 'grappling with' refers, of course, to the students' activities in lecture room,

P

seminar and library, and not to his activities as teacher in a classroom. Now in the courses of initial education in colleges and departments of education we have to recognize a double obligation: not only to introduce students to the study of education as 'practical theory' but also to provide an apprenticeship to their practical work as teachers, to help them to acquire what we judge to be the necessary skills, insights and attitudes of the teacher's craft. This second obligation is, indeed, fully accepted by the colleges and departments. As we saw in Chapter One, the education courses developed, historically, out of the nineteenth-century pupil teacher apprenticeship and until well into the present century the 'study' element amounted to little more than management and method. The colleges and departments accepted and continued this practical bias; the organization and supervision of school practice is a major responsibility of all education lecturers and usually involves other members of college staff. Few would question the validity of this emphasis on practical skills; what we may well question is the form it takes, its continuance more or less unchanged since practising schools were superseded by general school practice, without fundamental consideration of its function in relation to the rest of the education course.

This relationship between theory and practice is not a simple one; it may be useful to refer the reader back to references in previous chapters which have a bearing on this discussion. Professor Hirst refers to this relationship towards the end of Chapter Two:

Throughout this chapter educational theory has been regarded as a body of theory which issues in principles for practice. But principles are one thing, practice is another and nothing whatever has been said of the relationship between them. The link has in fact to be forged by the making of particular judgments in individual cases according to the relevant principles and the facts of the situations. If it is the job of educational theorists to formulate the principles, it is certainly vital for educational practice that teachers and others who both take and implement individual decisions fully understand the principles and their bases. But they must in addition be equipped to adequately distinguish the features of the particular situations in which judgments have to be made. Granted all this there remains the formation of the judgments themselves, a process which, for all its importance, is still little understood either logically or psychologically. (p. 56).

In Chapter Three Professor Peters warns against any expectation of short term and easy transfer of effect from courses of study to practice, 'The process is a long one which can only be set in motion in such special institutions. Those, therefore, who begin to think in these ways if they study philosophy, literature, history, psychology, and sociology in colleges of education will only gradually have their view of children, schools, and subjects transformed' (p. 79). Nevertheless, it must be embarked on, for it is no longer possible for teachers to pick up their art entirely on an apprenticeship system from experienced practitioners. 'The importance of this learning on the job under skilled direction must not be minimized. Indeed I think all would agree that it must be the lynch-pin of any system of training.' But it has severe limitations since 'Education no longer has agreed aims; procedures are constantly under discussion and vary according to what different people conceive themselves as doing in teaching the various subjects; fundamental questions concerned with principles underlying school organization, class management and the curriculum are constantly being raised; and in the area of moral education the task is made more perplexing by the variations of standards which characterize a highly differentiated society.' (p. 81.) Furthermore, education is increasingly a matter of public concern and scrutiny and the teacher needs to be sufficiently versed in the sciences ancillary to his task to defend his opinions and justify his practices in an informed and intelligent way. He has to learn to think for himself about what he is doing and can no longer rely on an established tradition. (p. 82.)

Later on Professor Peters has some comments on the implications for methods of teaching philosophy. To avoid the danger of a corpus of inert ideas, he suggests:

Philosophical questions must gradually be differentiated out from the practical and personal problems encountered in schools. These problems—e.g. those of discipline, teaching methods, and the organization of the school—have psychological and social aspects as well. It would be desirable, therefore, if the different forms of thinking which contribute to educational theory could be differentiated out gradually in relation to a common corpus of practical problems. Gradually, as the student develops in maturity and begins to get accustomed to the different ways of thinking about these problems, he or she will be able to go deeper into the contributing disciplines and will be ready for formal courses in them. (p. 84.)

He distinguishes three principles underlying the teaching of any branch of educational theory: relevance to practical problems and interests of teachers in training, possibility of linking with other disciplines and desirability of leading on to the fundamental problems in the discipline itself: he goes on to suggest topics which meet these criteria.

Professor Simon, writing in Chapter Four on the history of education, says there are no direct short term links between this aspect of educational theory and practice. 'No claim should be made that the study of the history of education directly affects the practice of the teacher in the classroom. Its effect must be indirect. If its primary function is to develop that 'critical self-awareness' that Clarke emphasized, this in itself implies that the student enters on the job of teaching with eyes and ears attuned to appreciate the new—with, as it were, a built-in defence against obsolete practices and prejudices.' (p. 126.) He can become aware of 'the body of educational theory which lies behind the practical day to day business of teaching and school organization'—the latent theory referred to by Professor Taylor in a later chapter. For there is nothing more stultifying in any profession than the assumption of a sharp and obvious distinction between practice and theory, the former needing no justification because it 'works', the latter the domain of cloudy theorists and speculation. John Dewey dealt trenchantly with this false opposition.

Professor Taylor, dealing with the most recently developed of the forms of knowledge bearing on the study of education, one only now in process of full acceptance in the universities in this country and by no means fully established in colleges of education, stresses that the subject of study should be the sociology of education and not some watered down hybrid, educational sociology or the social background of education, as is likely to appear in the syllabuses. It should lead to an understanding of such sociological concepts and techniques as are relevant to educational issues. Granted this, the opportunities for making links between theory and practical experience are plentiful, whether the first or the second approach outlined in Chapter Six be adopted. In outlining the second approach, starting with the classroom and school situation and making explicit the student's own experience, Professor Taylor makes a general point about the value of using what is already familiar and is becoming familiar to the student and encouraging him to look at this experience in an unfamiliar—in this case sociological—way. (pp. 202-6.) In particular this will help to make him aware of the latent assumptions underlying practices—like dead metaphors in a language. 'An individual's judgments and practices in educational situations are derived less from his knowledge of facts and findings than from the theories that, consciously or unconsciously, he supports; there is in this sense a far closer link between theory and practice than between fact and practice, despite the beliefs of many students and teachers to the contrary.' (p. 207.) The justification for including sociological studies in the course does not rest on any observable link between the pursuit of such studies and the improvement of classroom techniques and practice but rather on the development of a capacity to think about the whole range of social phenomena he encounters, the ability to sort out fact and value judgment, the respect for evidence and the capacity to make valid generalizations. (p. 210.)

Professor Morris makes a similar point with regard to the relation between psychology and educational practice. This is indeed the field where the student is most likely to expect prescriptions from theory to practice. Such expectations, however, are based on a misconception of the nature of both psychology and education and we may suggest that the concept of 'Principles of Education' as historically developed in the education courses has helped to foster this misconception. The relationship is subtler and more complex and one of our main aims should be to help the student to understand this. 'Here we attempt to induce students to think about what they are doing and to work out the implications of psychological thought in relation to their procedures and problems, that is we ask them to understand the *relevance* of psychology to their tasks.' (Chapter Five, p. 137.) Professor Morris's discussion of the nature of relevance as a basis for establishing criteria of choice of studies and methods of treatment is pertinent to our present topic. The relating of psychology and education is not, he suggests, a question of extrinsically relating two distinct forms of thought; some psychological forms of thought are intrinsic to educational thought. 'We may suggest that psychological thought functions within educational thought (not externally to it) by helping to make some of its assumptions conscious, by helping to develop concepts essential to it and by suggesting procedures for action and for assessing the results of action.' (p. 140.) By this process both are subtly transformed into something new—educational psychology.*

Mechanistic and organic models, however appropriate they may be in other areas of psychological inquiry, Professor Morris finds inadequate for the determination of relevance in the field of educational psychology; he suggests that a more appropriate criterion here is to be found in the mode of the personal as defined by Professor Macmurray. This does not mean discarding or

---

* It may be useful for the reader to consider whether this is to be understood as making a special case for the relationship between psychology and education, or whether the same may not apply also to the relationship between the other forms of thought and education, at any rate when the relationship has been as fully established. On the latter interpretation, Professor Morris's discussion of relevance in Chapter Five could be read as a gloss on the meaning of the term 'practical theory' as applied to education.

ignoring the other models. 'On the contrary, the task of discrimination is to use the form of the personal to discover, from among what is cast in mechanistic or organic forms, those concepts and systems of concepts which by suitable transformation might be made to fit a fully human image of man. The kind of transformation required is one which enables them to be seen functioning in a more inclusive context.' (p. 152.)

This concept of transformation, relevant for the determination of content and method in this study of educational psychology, has also a direct bearing on educational practice and the relation between theory and practice; this is made explicit in Part II, Sections 6 and 7 of Chapter Five. Professor Morris returns to this theme in Part IV at the end of the chapter, 'what is relevant has to become part of thought issuing in action, that is, it has to be made fully personal.' (p. 169.) This is to be achieved in part by the ordering of the themes of the course so as to relate them both to the wider context of personal living and to the more immediate context of teaching in the school community and by involving students in observation, experiment, discovery and discussion. But over and above this, 'cultivation of the power of detached but sympathetic identification lies at the heart of making the study of psychology truly personal. Some of this power is necessarily implied unless we are prepared to refuse to recognize the inevitable self reference in psychological study. To do so is to affirm that psychology in a professional context is the study of other people only. Its applications must then be essentially manipulative and constitute a denial of human mutuality.' (p. 170.)

This review of the earlier chapters emphasizes that the relating of theory and practice is indeed of fundamental importance both for our ordering of the theory courses and for the arrangements made for the gaining of practical experience. At the same time, the relationship, as all our contributors agree, is not a simple matter of learning to use appropriate prescriptions for action; it implies a subtle, complex and long term process of which the end product will be certain qualities of thought, feeling and attitude, informed by study, supported by evidence and reason but capable of spontaneous translation into action in classroom and school situation in response to the ever moving flow of events. The teacher can and should think about his work 'out of class' where it is possible to ruminate, have second thoughts, consult books, discuss with other teachers; but in the classroom he must do most of his thinking operationally; a response of some kind has to be made; he must be able 'to think on his feet' as one experienced teacher put it. For anything learned in the theory course to be applied, other than spasmodically and superficially, in this setting, it needs to have been transformed into habitudes and sentiments, to have become personalized. This is a long term process and quick results cannot be expected. But a start can be made and a foundation laid in the college and department courses and we are concerned here with the conditions which will best promote this development.

There is general agreement that in the theory or study courses the fullest use should be made of the students' previous experience of life, from the earliest recollections of home and family through the various stages of schooling and influences outside home and school. To these will be added present experience of the college community, visits to a range of educational and other institutions, participation in play groups, youth clubs, etc. This recollecting, pooling and comparing of one's own and others' experience will provide under the tutors' guidance initial training in the techniques of observation, the collection and organization of data, discrimination and interpretation. This would lead, in the next stage of the course, to the selection of topics for further and more systematic study. The criteria for the choice of these topics, it is suggested, should be (a) that they are seen by the students, not just by their tutors, as relevant for the study of education as practical theory (b) that there exists in one or more of the basic disciplines areas of organized thought and inquiry bearing on the topic and (c) that they will provide opportunities for further practice by the student in the basic techniques introduced in the earlier stage of the course. As we saw in Chapter One, many of the questions included in Principles papers can be criticized on the grounds that they can be answered in some cases without any special knowledge of the topic, 'in the light of common sense', or in other cases by the regurgitation of lecture and text book material. Some of the selected topics could appropriately be dealt with within the orbit of one of the forms of thought, psychological, philosophical, sociological or historical; some, however, would provide opportunities for relating contributions from several or all of the forms.

This would lead in the third stage of the course, and certainly in the projected B.Ed. courses, to more systematic and rigorous study in one or two of the contributory disciplines. Of the connection between theory and practice at this level, Professor Peters writes:

At this level of teaching the philosophy of education there is a constant tension between attempting to illuminate and clarify concrete issues so that teachers can go about their business in a more clear-headed way, and drawing them deeper into the discipline so that they can begin to develop a distinctive form of thought which will entail a more vigorous overhaul of their fundamental beliefs and ideals. The effectiveness of teaching philosophy at this level will be revealed both in the autonomy and critical experimental attitude which teachers begin to show in the later stages of teaching practice, as well as in their desire to return to the philosophy of education in a more vigorous way when they are established as teachers. (Chapter Three, p. 87.)

The same point could be made in reference to the other forms of thought.

If it is important, though not for the most obvious reasons, to incorporate relevant practical experience of the learner in the theory courses, it is equally important that the provision for practical experience should facilitate reference from theory to practice. It cannot be said that the most usual arrangement, periods of block practice in schools with supervision by college tutors, forbids this; but the traditional methods operating here certainly make it difficult. For one thing, as a time and motion study of the tutors' activities would show, much time is spent in transit from college to school and from one school to another; of the time spent in school much will be taken up with sitting in classrooms watching students at work. The actual contact with the student is often limited to a few hurried words between lessons or a few comments made in a note book. On the assumption that the tutor's main function as supervisor is to assess the students, this makes sense; but not on the assumption that the tutor's main function is to help the student to see all that is involved in the transactions of the classroom, to think about what he is doing both as he does it and in advance and in retrospect and to compare these views, to widen the scope of habitual observation and deepen insight.* A second criticism of the present system might be that even where the tutor is devoting time to helping a student, the help given is seen in terms of comments and advice on practical matters that could be just as well, probably better, given by the class or subject teacher to whom the student is attached. In this case, tutor and teacher are either duplicating each other or possibly contradicting each other in their influence on the student. What is being suggested here is that the supervision of college tutor and school teacher should be complementary, the latter being given much more responsibility for the specific practical help and guidance a student needs in working in this school with these children, the former concentrating on the relating of the student's practical experience to his learning in the course as a whole and in particular developing his awareness of relevance as described by Professor Morris.

To illustrate this, reference may be made to two recent innova-

---

* The difference between an experienced teacher and most student teachers in their early stages is (a) that the former, whilst concentrating on some particular piece of classroom business is also aware of the total situation, i.e. he seems to have 'eyes in the back of his head' and (b) the former interprets any behaviour cue more adequately on a time scale, i.e. in terms of past and future behaviour; thus he is able to anticipate and prevent learning difficulty or disciplinary trouble. Most students need much help and practice in the acquiring of these skills.

tions in the field of practical work supervision. The first is the introduction by a number of colleges of periods of study practice or group practice interspersed with the more usual block practice. In these, groups of students with a college tutor and in some cases also a class or subject teacher, work together in a school, usually for a day or half-day a week. Since the participants see each other at work and share a common task, this provides ample opportunity for discussion both in the planning of the work and in retrospect, working out the implications of what has been done, arriving at judgments and so on. Furthermore, very close and specific linkage can be made between the practical work on the project and aspects of the study courses in college. Studies of individual children or of group behaviour, the use of statistical techniques, evaluation of methods of teaching and learning and discussion of values have greater relevance for the student in this setting because the application process is being made explicit. Pioneer work in study practice and the exploration of its possibilities was undertaken by the education department at St. Luke's College, Exeter, under the direction of Mr Gerald Collier, and later by Mr Leonard Downes. The projects took a wide variety of form and involved members of the college staff in other departments.

A second kind of experiment is currently being tried out in the Leicester School of education and involves the use of a form of tutor supervision borrowed from another field of training, that of social workers and educational psychologists.* The supervision is based not on the tutor's impressions of a 'lesson' obtained by sitting in as a non-participant observer (in social case work it is usually not possible to have such an observer present without altering the whole situation) but on a written or oral account by the student, doing his best to recall what was significant and to

* Professor Morris refers (Chapter Five, p. 157) to the possibility of common courses in the education of teachers, social workers, doctors, etc., and in fact the experiment referred to originated in the discussions of a working party set up to explore the possibilities of such interprofessional training. The working party was an offshoot of larger scale conferences held at Keele, Leicester and Nottingham between 1958 and 1961.

evaluate it. The tutor, perforce, must start where the student is, not expect the student to adjust to his viewpoint as in the more usual school practice supervision. The tutor's aim is, by comment and question, to help the student to become more aware of all the implications in the situation, including orectic factors. Specific advice is rarely given, the student is led to produce his own suggestions and interpretations. In this setting the connections between theory and practice can be more fully explored in a form which is necessarily attuned to the student's stage of development and capacity for insight. It avoids on the one hand the assimilation of inert ideas and on the other the practice of techniques uninformed by theory. There are two further by-products of this method; it reduces in both students' and tutors' minds the preoccupation with assessment and puts the emphasis on understanding. This is not to decry the necessity for and value of the assessment of performance in any field of effort; but surely our aim should be the development of the student's capacity for self assessment and this, as experiment is showing, is more likely to happen in the supervisory setting described above. In the traditional system assessment is felt by the student to be the tutor's business; and indeed the letter grades assigned are not supposed to be divulged to the student, being part of the confidential examination machinery, so it is difficult to see what possible use this process may have for the student.* The by-product is that fuller responsibility is placed on the school staff for the day to day assistance of the student in practical matters. It therefore satisfies the frequently made demand of practising teachers and their associations for school based training; but without, be it noted,

* The question whether it is really necessary, at any rate in its present elaborate form, for other reasons is one that needs reconsideration. In fact it was taken over by the institutes from the earlier procedures of the Joint Boards and before that, of the Board of Education. Minor simplifications in grading have been made by some institutes but the interests vested in long established routines make fundamental review difficult. It might be suggested indeed that the system persists because it suits the tutors rather than benefits the students.

diminishing the supervisory responsibility of the college tutor. The two sets of influences become complementary.

These suggestions about the structure of the study courses and the relation between theory and practice have implications for the staffing of departments of education in colleges and universities. To put into practice the proposals outlined above, the staff as a whole would need to meet the following requirements: there would have to be a sufficient number with qualifications in the contributory forms of thought, i.e. graduates in philosophy, psychology, sociology or history (possibly also in the future, B.Ed. graduates) who have undertaken further study in the relating of these disciplines to education; all members of staff should be capable of team teaching and interested in the relating of their own basic discipline to the others, not only in the planning of courses but in the execution thereof and they should also have had some training, possibly included in their advanced course work, in the special skills involved in the relating of theory and practice.

A review of the present situation indicates that we are very far from being able to meet these requirements.

Firstly, the recent rapid expansion of the colleges has meant heavy demands for education lecturers as this is a subject all students must take. There is another special difficulty which arises because roughly 80 per cent of these students are expected to be prepared for work in primary schools and it is thought desirable that those, or a good many of those preparing them should have had experience of primary school work. At present only a small minority of primary school teachers are graduates. Some may have taken one of the advanced diploma courses in education or educational psychology which the institutes of education offer, as full or part-time students. Possibilities for further study at higher degree level are limited for non-graduates either by the regulations of the university in question or by the application of the regulations. Only one or two universities accept non-graduates to higher degree courses as freely as they do graduates. In both cases they must have adequate qualifications in the study of education at an advanced level. Turning now to those who *are* graduates, it is unlikely that they will be graduates in one of the contributory forms of thought, with the exception of history. Graduates in psychology, sociology and philosophy are not in general prepared to, as they see it, abandon their subject while they acquire experience teaching other subjects. They would not, on our present assumptions, be likely to be appointed to posts in the colleges without teaching experience. Psychologists and sociologists are anyway in short supply and it will be some time before the recent expansion of these departments in the universities affects this situation. Some way round this series of obstacles must be found if the training needs of the professions are to be adequately met. The development of B.Ed. courses providing for the study of education at the undergraduate level is the first requirement for a long term solution. It will of course be some time before any of the first graduates qualify, pursue courses of further study, acquire some teaching experience, and so become available to the colleges. Meanwhile, the expansion of advanced diploma courses and the admission by more universities to higher degree courses of non-graduates who are well qualified in education would do much to help. One might also suggest the employment by the colleges of some assistant lecturers with first degrees in psychology, sociology or philosophy but without teaching experience. The large education staffs now common in many colleges would be able to carry them; the opportunity to teach their specialism (for which so few opportunities exist) would no doubt attract some of them and they would, in the setting of work described above, quickly learn a good deal about education.

Secondly, experience of team teaching would have to be acquired on the job. There is little of it yet in schools. The secondary schools operate on a basis of specialist subject compartmentation, the primary schools on a basis of all-purpose teacher compartmentation. The colleges, presumably for reasons arising from recruitment, adopt the one system in the field of the special studies and very often the other in the field of education. Professor Taylor refers to the 'mother hen' system of organizing education courses whereby one tutor has charge of a group of students for everything for a year and sometimes the whole course. This is a practice which has persisted from an earlier day and it is quite inadequate even in the context of three-year courses, much less of B.Ed. courses. The value of tutorial groups, especially for the close relating of theory and practice, is not in question. But the theory course as a whole must include contributions from the basic disciplines by specialist tutors. Team planning and teaching is then essential to avoid compartmentation of the other kind. The latter is common in the university department courses and team teaching is equally needed there.

Thirdly, the need for some preparation of members of staff newly appointed to colleges of education has been recognized and some institutes have organized short courses or made informal arrangements for help to be given. Perhaps a lack of recognition in the profession as a whole that there are special skills involved in the training of teachers, combining with the exigencies of expansion, has helped to militate against a full scale and regular provision of such courses. The special feature of the college course, which it shares with other branches of professional training, is that the student is both pupil and teacher, passing from one to the other and back again within the rhythm of the course. What he learns as pupil and the way he learns it and his problems in learning it are relevant (or should be relevant) to his work as teacher with his own pupils. The special skills of the tutor derive from his recognition of this situation, and the use he makes of it to facilitate transfer from the learning to the teaching situation. Study practice and the alternative supervision scheme outlined earlier are essentially devices for ensuring maximum transfer. And they certainly require special skills on the part of the tutor. Some training in these skills could well be incorporated in the full- and part-time advanced diploma courses, from which many students do proceed to college posts. The Leicester experiment has included this provision as part of the diploma course in the sociology and psychology of education. An account of this appears in *Education for Teaching*, November, 1965.

What of the relationship between the study and practice of education and the rest of the college course? All students select one or more (but rarely more than two) main or special course subjects which are studied primarily not as subjects to be taught but as part of the students' cultural and liberal education, much as these same subjects are studied in a university course. For students who are preparing to be secondary school specialists, obviously this study also has a vocational value. But the majority of students are preparing to be class teachers in primary schools and need to be able to cope with the whole range of the primary curriculum. To meet this need, most students take what are usually called curriculum courses, covering the basis subjects of the primary school curriculum. No-one is happy about these courses. The root problem is the early specialization which has become, with the development of sixth form courses, the general practice in English grammar schools. As a consequence any given student will have ceased to study a good many of the curriculum subjects some years before entering college. When they are resumed, much remedial work needs to be done. Students are at varying stages of achievement, the time for study is inadequate when what is left from education and special subjects has been divided out among the curriculum courses, there is uncertainty about whether the emphasis should fall on content or method, there is uncertainty about whether these courses should be under the general direction of education tutors or specialist tutors, and both specialist tutors and students may well resent having to 'go back' and work at the relatively elementary level of these courses. Reform of the grammar school programme to provide a broader curriculum up to the age of eighteen would help; but so far it has proved an intractable problem. Failing this, what can the colleges do? The difficulty is that the colleges are themselves part of the system which produces the problem. They are themselves as fully committed to specialization as the grammar schools and the universities. Of necessity many special subject staff are former grammar school specialists: that is what they know how to do and what they want to go on doing. The colleges, understandably, have seen the improvement of their status in terms of a closer approximation to university conditions and standards. What one might legitimately question is whether the model chosen (and with regard to the special subject courses, this model is undoubtedly that of the Honours or special university course) is the most appropriate one. One might suggest, bearing in mind the needs of the primary curriculum, that an older model like the Oxford Greats or a newer one, on the pattern of the Field of Study courses now operating or being planned in most of the new universities, would be more appropriate. Essentially these courses involve relating a number of subjects in a field of study as described by Professor Hirst in Chapter Two. Such subject fields do exist in the college courses; geography is essentially this kind of a subject, art and crafts is another; environmental studies, linking history, geography, biology, sociology have been recently introduced. If all special subjects were of the field type and a student chose two of these, it would reduce the area to be covered by the curriculum courses. The fundamental question being raised here is whether the college special study courses should be regarded as identical in nature and function with the subjects in university arts and science courses or whether they should in some respects differ because they are ingredients in a course of professional education. Current discussion on the nature and structure of the B.Ed. courses has forced this issue into the open, both as a general issue and as a particular one with reference to the inclusion of 'non-academic' subjects like art and crafts, physical education and domestic subjects. There are those who take the view that the B.Ed. course should be regarded fundamentally as a form of professional education; and that it need not be any less liberal and cultural because of this, if it is indeed seen as education and not just training. Others are planning B.Ed. courses which are similar in nature and function to university general degree courses. In this

Q

case the 'professional' element in the course would be excluded from the degree course and appear only in that part of the total course which would qualify for a professional certificate.

Discussion of this issue tends to be bedevilled by conceptions about 'pure' and 'applied' studies which, as Professor P. B. Medawar trenchantly points out in a recent article entitled 'Anglo-Saxon Attitudes' (*Encounter*, August, 1965), are mainly misconceptions, 'a by-product of the literary propaganda of the romantic revival.' In fact, what the study of a subject 'for its own sake' in a university course really means is that the subject is studied *as if* the students were going on to be university teachers or research workers in the subject. This does not mean that the study has no value for those who are not; but it does mean that the value has to be demonstrated in terms of qualities of mind, habits and attitudes which will transfer from the course of study to the later field of work and life. Now where this later field is the application of this subject in education, though at a different level from that in which it is learned, it should not be too difficult to make some provision for transfer without doing any violence to the nature of the subject at the advanced level. It is a similar problem to the one discussed earlier concerning the relation between the study and practice of education. It is by understanding the nature of the subject, what processes are involved in its study, what specific contribution it can make to the curriculum at different levels of education and how a transfer of the skills involved can be ensured from a context of learning to a context of application that the student will be best prepared for his future work.

Discussion of these issues is not, apparently, included in most university degree courses.* Many graduates, when they begin their year in the education department, find it very difficult to answer questions about the nature of and the processes involved in

* There are some common exceptions to this: philosophy and psychology, for obvious reasons; geography because of its nature as a field of study, contributed to by various forms of thought; and 'new' subjects which have had to justify themselves to get in to the curriculum.

the study of the subject which has occupied much of their attention for many years. Presumably both they and their teachers have taken it for granted. But surely such considerations should have a place in the study of any subject at the university level; and it may well be that the introduction through the B.Ed. courses of the study of education at the undergraduate level may promote a greater interest in the educative process in the university as a whole.

INDEX

This index should be used in conjunction with the bibliographies accompanying chapters four, five and six. References to authors listed there are not repeated here unless there is substantial treatment in the text.